Credit Derivatives

Mark J.P. Anson, Ph.D., J.D., CFA, CPA

Published by Frank J. Fabozzi Associates

332.632
A62c

This book is dedicated to my wife, Mary Hayes,
for her patience and indulgence.

Cover design by Scott C. Riether

© 1999 By Frank J. Fabozzi Associates
New Hope, Pennsylvania

ALL RIGHTS RESERVED. No part of this publication may be reproduced, stored in a retrieval system, or transmitted, in any form or by any means, electronic, mechanical, photocopying, recording, or otherwise without the prior written permission of the publisher and the copyright holder.

This publication is designed to provide accurate and authoritative information in regard to the subject matter covered. It is sold with the understanding that the publisher is not engaged in rendering legal, accounting, or other professional services.

ISBN: 1-883249-61-9

Printed in the United States of America

Table of Contents

University Libraries
Carnegie Mellon University
Pittsburgh PA 15213-3890

About the Author

Mark J.P. Anson, Ph.D. is the Portfolio Manager for the OppenheimerFunds Real Asset Fund. Prior to joining OppenheimerFunds, he was a Registered Options Principal in Equity Derivatives for Salomon Brothers Inc., and a practicing attorney specializing in the futures and derivatives markets. Dr. Anson earned his law degree from the Northwestern University School of Law and his Ph.D and Masters in Finance from the Columbia Graduate School of Business. He has also earned the Chartered Financial Analyst, Certified Public Accountant, and Certified Management Accountant degrees. Dr. Anson is a frequent contributor to academic and professional publications on the topics of risk management, derivatives, and portfolio management.

Chapter 1

Why Credit Risk Is Important

INTRODUCTION

C redit derivatives are financial instruments that are designed to transfer the credit exposure of an underlying asset or issuer between two or more parties. They are individually negotiated financial contracts that may take the form of options, swaps, forwards, credit linked notes, and other structures where the payoffs are linked to, or derived from, the credit characteristics of a referenced asset or issuer. With credit derivatives, a financial manager can either acquire or hedge credit risk.

Many asset managers have portfolios that are very sensitive to changes in the spread between riskless and risky assets and credit derivatives are an efficient way to hedge this exposure. Conversely, other asset managers may use credit derivatives to target specific exposures as a way to enhance portfolio returns. In each case, the ability to transfer credit risk and return provides a new tool for portfolio mangers to improve performance.

There are three important types of credit risk: default risk, downgrade risk, and credit spread risk. *Default risk* is the risk that the issuer of a bond or the debtor on a loan will not repay the outstanding debt in full. Default risk can be complete in that no amount of the bond or loan will be repaid, or it can be partial in that some portion of the original debt will be recovered. *Downgrade risk* is the risk that a nationally recognized statistical rating organization will lower its credit rating for an issuer based on perceived earning capacity. Lastly, *credit spread risk* is the risk that the spread over a reference rate will increase for an outstanding debt obligation. Credit spread risk and downgrade risk differ in that the latter pertains to a specific, formal credit review by an independent agency, while the former is the financial markets' reaction to perceived credit deterioration.

However, before we can discuss credit derivatives we must first review the underlying risk which these new financial instruments transfer and hedge. This chapter provides a short discussion on the importance of credit risk. In particular, we provide a review of the credit risks inherent in three important financial markets: high yield bonds, highly leveraged bank loans, and sovereign debt. Each of these markets is especially attuned to the nature and amount of credit risk undertaken with each investment. Indeed, most of the discussion and examples provided in the remaining chapters will focus on these three investment markets.

CREDIT RISK AND THE HIGH YIELD BOND MARKET

A fixed income debt instrument represents a basket of risks. There is the risk from changes in interest rates (duration and convexity risk), the risk that the issuer will refinance the debt issue (call risk), and the risk of defaults, downgrades, and widening credit spreads (credit risk). The total return from a fixed income investment such as a corporate bond is the compensation for assuming all of these risks. Depending upon the rating on the underlying debt instrument, the return from credit risk can be a significant part of a bond's total return.

However, the default rate on credit risky bonds can be quite high. Estimates of the average default rates for high-yield bonds range from 3.17% to 6.25%.[1] In fact, default rates have been as high as 11% for high yield bonds in any one year.[2] Three factors have been demonstrated to influence default rates in the high yield market. First, because defaults are most likely to occur three years after bond issuance, the length of time that high yield bonds have been outstanding will influence the default rate. This factor is known as the aging affect. Second, the state of the economy affects the high yield default rate. A recession reduces the economic prospects of corporations. As profits decline, companies have less cash to pay

---

[1] See Edward Altman, "Measuring Corporate Bond Mortality and Performance," *The Journal of Finance* (June 1991), pp. 909-922; and Gabriella Petrucci, "High-Yield Review — First-Half 1997," Salomon Brothers Corporate Bond Research (August 1997).

[2] See Jean Helwege and Paul Kleiman, "Understanding the Aggregate Default Rates of High-Yield Bonds," *The Journal of Fixed Income* (June 1997), pp. 55-61.

their bondholders. Finally, changes in credit quality affects default rates. Recent research has demonstrated that credit quality is the most important determinant of default rates, followed by macroeconomic conditions. The aging factor plays only a small role in determining default rates.[3]

Credit derivatives, therefore, appeal to financial managers who invest in high yield or junk bonds, real estate, or other credit dependent assets. The possibility of default is a significant risk for asset managers, and one that can be effectively hedged by shifting the credit exposure.

In addition to default risk for junk investments, there is the risk of downgrades for investment grade bonds and the risk of increased credit spreads. Downgrade risk occurs when a nationally recognized statistical rating organization such Standard & Poors, Moody's Investors Services, Duff & Phelps Credit Rating Company, or Fitch IBCA reduces its outstanding credit rating for an issuer based on an evaluation of that issuer's current earning power versus its capacity to pay its fixed income obligations as they become due. For instance, through the first six months of 1997, 83 corporate bond issues representing $14.7 billion were downgraded at least one rating category.[4]

Credit spread risk is the risk that the interest rate spread for a risky bond over a riskless bond will increase after the risky bond has been purchased. For instance, in the United States, corporate bonds are typically priced at a spread to comparable U.S. Treasury bonds. Should this spread widen after purchase of the corporate bond, the portfolio manager would suffer a diminution of value in his portfolio. Credit spreads can widen based on macroeconomic events such as volatility in the financial markets.

As an example, in October of 1997, a rapid decline in Asian stock markets spilled over into the U.S. stock markets, causing a significant decline in financial stocks.[5] The turbulence in the finan-

---

[3] Helwege and Kleiman, "Understanding the Aggregate Default Rates of High-Yield Bonds," p. 57.

[4] See Peter Acciavatti and Robert Manowitz, *1997 High Yield Semi-Annual Review* (New York: Chase Securities Inc., 1997), p. A-83.

[5] For instance, the Dow Jones Industrial Average suffered a one day decline of value of 554 points on October 27, 1997.

cial markets, both domestically and worldwide, resulted in a flight to safety of investment capital. In other words, investors sought safer havens of investment to avoid further losses and volatility. This flight to safety resulted in a significant increase in credit spreads of corporate bonds to U.S. Treasuries.

For instance, at June 30, 1997, corporate bonds rated BB by Standard & Poor's were trading at an average spread over U.S. Treasuries of 215 basis points.[6] However, by October 31, 1997, this spread had increased to 319 basis points. For a $1000 market value BB-rated corporate bond with a duration of 5 years, this resulted in a loss of value of about $52.50 per bond.

In their simplest form, credit derivatives may be nothing more than the purchase of credit protection. The ability to isolate credit risk and manage it independently of underlying bond positions is the key benefit of credit derivatives. Prior to the introduction of credit derivatives, the only way to manage credit exposure was to buy and sell the underlying assets. Because of transaction costs and tax issues, this was an inefficient way to hedge or gain exposure.

Credit derivatives, therefore, represent a natural extension of the financial markets to unbundle the risk and return buckets associated with a particular financial asset, such as credit risk. They offer an important method for investment managers to hedge their exposure to credit risk because they permit the transfer of the exposure from one party to another. Credit derivatives allow for an efficient exchange of credit exposure in return for credit protection.

However, credit risk is not all one-sided. There are a number of reasons why a seller of credit protection may be willing to assume the credit risk of an underlying financial asset or issuer. For instance, in 1997 there were more credit rating upgrades than downgrades. Through the first half of 1997, a total $23.2 billion of corporate bonds were upgraded compared to a total of $14.7 billion that were downgraded.[7] One reason for the net credit rating upgrades was a strong stock market which encouraged public offerings of stock by credit risky companies. A large portion of these equity

[6] See Chase Securities Inc., "High-Yield Research Weekly Update," *Chase High-Yield Research* (November 4, 1997), p. 43.
[7] See Acciavatti and Manowitz, *1997 High Yield Semi-Annual Review*, pp. A-79 to A-83.

financings were used to reduce outstanding costly debt, resulting in improved balance sheets and credit ratings for the issuers. A second reason for the net upgrades was a strong economy which contributed to superior operating results for domestic corporations. Consequently, asset managers had ample opportunity in 1997 to target specific credit risks which benefited from a ratings upgrade.

In addition to credit upgrades, there are other credit events which have a positive effect on credit risky bonds. Mergers and acquisitions, for instance, are a frequent occurrence in the high yield market. Even though a credit risky issuer may have a low debt rating, it may have valuable technology worth acquiring. High yield issuers tend to be small to mid-cap companies with viable products but nascent cash flows. Consequently, they make attractive takeover candidates for financially mature companies.

Lastly, with a strong economy, banks have been willing to provide term loans to high yield companies at more attractive rates than the bond markets. Consequently, it has been advantageous for credit risky companies to redeem their high yield bonds and replace the bonds with a lower cost term loan. The resulting premium for redemption of high yield bonds is a positive credit event which enhances portfolio returns.

CREDIT RISK AND THE BANK LOAN MARKET

Similar to a high yield bond, a commercial loan investment represents a basket of risks. There is the risk from changes in interest rates (duration and convexity risk), the risk that the borrower will refinance or pay down the loan balance (call risk), and the risk of defaults, downgrades, and widening credit spreads (credit risk). The total return from a commercial loan is the compensation for assuming all of these risks. Once again, the credit rating of the borrower is a key determinant in the pricing of the bank loan.

The corporate bank loan market typically consists of syndicated loans to large and mid-sized corporations. They are floating-rate instruments, often priced in relation to LIBOR. Corporate loans may be either revolving credits (known as *revolvers*) that are legally committed lines of credit, or term loans that are fully funded commitments with fixed amortization schedules. Term loans tend to be concentrated in the lower credit rated corporations because revolvers usually serve as backstops for commercial paper programs of fiscally sound companies. Therefore, we will primarily focus on the application of credit derivatives to term bank loans.

Term bank loans are repriced periodically. Because of their floating interest rate nature, they have reduced market risk resulting from fluctuating interest rates. Consequently, credit risk takes on greater importance in determining a commercial loan's total return.

Over the past several years, the bank loan market and the high yield bond market have begun to converge. This is due partly to the relaxing of commercial banking regulations which has allowed many banks to increase their product offerings, including high yield bonds. Contemporaneously, investment banks and brokerage firms have established loan trading and syndication desks. The credit implications from this "one-stop" shopping is twofold.

First, the debt capital markets have become less segmented as commercial banks and investment firms compete in the bank loan, junk bond, and private placement debt markets. This has led to more flexible, less stringent bank loan constraints. For instance, the average cash flow sweep for bank loans has declined from 68% in 1994 to 64% in 1996. Additionally, over the same time period, the average prepayment requirement from equity issuance has declined from 82% to 74%.[8] Finally, in 1996, the average debt to cash flow multiple climbed to 5.5, its highest level in the 1990s.[9] Bottom line, the increased competition for business in the commercial loan market has resulted in more favorable terms for debtors and less credit protection for investors.

Second, hybrid debt instruments with both bank loan and junk bond characteristics are now available in the capital markets. These hybrid commercial loans typically have a higher prepayment penalty than standard commercial loans, but only a second lien (or no lien) on assets instead of the traditional first claim. Additionally, several com-

---

[8] See Keith Barnish, Steve Miller and Michael Rushmore, "The New Leveraged Loan Syndication Market," *The Journal of Applied Corporate Finance* (Spring 1997), pp. 79-88.

[9] See Loan Pricing Corporation, *Gold Sheets 1997 Annual*, Vol. III, No. 1 (1997), p. 38.

mercial loan tranches may now be offered as part of a financing package where the first tranche of the bank loan is fully collateralized and has a regular amortization schedule, but the last tranche has no security interest and only a final bullet payment at maturity. These new commercial loans have the structure of high yield bonds, but have the floating rate requirement of a bank loan. Consequently, the very structure of these hybrid bank loans make them more susceptible to credit risk.

Just like the junk bond market, bank loans are also susceptible to the risk of credit downgrades and the risk of increased credit spreads. Downgrade risk occurs when a nationally recognized statistical rating organization reduces its outstanding credit rating for a borrower. Credit spread risk is the risk that the interest rate spread for a risky commercial loan will increase after the loan has been purchased due to not only changes in credit rating — a microeconomic analysis — but also based on macroeconomic events such as recession or expansion.

For instance, during the U.S. economic recession of 1990-1991, the credit spread for B rated bank loans increased on average from 250 basis points over LIBOR to 325 basis points, as default rates climbed to 10%.[10] Not surprisingly, over this time period the total return to B rated bank loans underperformed the total return to BBB and BB rated bank loans by 6.41% and 8.64%, respectively. Conversely, during the economic expansion years of 1993-1994, the total return to B rated bank loans outperformed the total return to BBB and BB rated bank loans by 3.43% and 1.15% as the default rate for B rated loans declined in 1993 and 1994 to 1.1% and 1.45%, respectively.[11]

In the event of a default, commercial bank loans generally have a higher recovery rate than that for defaulted high yield bonds due to a combination of collateral protection and senior capital structure. Nonetheless, estimates of lost value given a commercial bank loan default are about 35% of the loan value.[12] Even for asset-backed loans, which

---

[10] See Elliot Asarnow, "Corporate Loans as an Asset Class," *The Journal of Portfolio Management* (Summer 1996), pp. 92-103; and Edward Altman and Joseph Bencivenga, "A Yield Premium Model for the High-Yield Debt Market," *Financial Analysts Journal* (September-October 1995), pp. 49-56.

[11] See Asarnow, "Corporate Loans as an Asset Class," p. 96, and Altman and Bencivenga, "A Yield Premium Model for the High-Yield Debt Market," p. 51.

[12] See Asarnow, "Corporate Loans as an Asset Class," p. 94, and Barnish, Miller and Rushmore, "The New Leveraged Loan Syndication Market," p. 85.

are highly collateralized and tightly monitored commercial loans where the bank controls the cash receipts against the collateralized assets, the average loss of value in the event of default is about 13%.[13]

The loss in value due to a default can have a significant impact on the total return of a bank loan. For a commercial bank loan the total return comes from two sources: the spread over the referenced rate (LIBOR+) and the return from price appreciation/ depreciation. As might be expected, B rated bank loans are priced on average at higher rates than BBB rated bank loans — an average 250-300 basis points over LIBOR compared to 50 basis points over LIBOR for BBB rated loans. Yet, over the time period 1988-1994, the cumulative return to B rated bank loans was 10 percentage points less than that for BBB rated loans.[14] The lower total return to B rated loans was due to a negative price return of −10.26%. Simply put, changes in credit quality reduced the total return to lower rated bank loans despite their higher coupon rates.

Credit risk, however, can also provide opportunities for gain. Over the same time period, the cumulative total return to BB rated bank loans exceeded that of BBB bank loans by 11.6%.[15] Part of this higher return was due to higher interest payments offered to induce investors to purchase the lower rated BB bank loans, but a significant portion, over 5%, was due to enhanced credit quality. Consequently, over this time period, portfolio managers had ample opportunity to target specific credit risks and improve portfolio returns.

Similar to the junk bond market, the ability to isolate credit risk and manage it independently of underlying investment positions is the key benefit of credit derivatives. Prior to the introduction of credit derivatives, the only way to manage credit exposure was to buy and sell bank loans or restrict lending policies. Because of transaction costs, tax issues, and client relationships this was an inefficient way to hedge or gain exposure.

Furthermore, credit derivatives offer an attractive method for hedging credit risk in lieu of liquidating the underlying collateral in a bank loan. Despite the security interest of a fully collateralized

---

[13] See Asarnow, "Corporate Loans as an Asset Class," p. 95.
[14] See Asarnow, "Corporate Loans as an Asset Class," p. 95.
[15] See Asarnow, "Corporate Loans as an Asset Class," p. 95.

bank loan, there may be several reasons why a bank manager or portfolio manager may be reluctant to liquidate the collateral.

From a bank manager's perspective, the decision to liquidate the collateral will undoubtedly sour the customer relationship. Most banks consider loans as part of a broader client relationship that includes other non-credit business. Preserving the broader relationship may make a bank reluctant to foreclose.

Conversely, institutional investors focus on commercial loans as stand-alone investments and consider the economic risks and benefits of foreclosure. From their perspective, seizure of collateral may provoke a litigation defense by the debtor. The attempt to foreclose on collateral may result in dragging the investor into protracted litigation on issues and in forums which the institutional investor may wish to avoid. Additionally, foreclosure by one creditor/investor may trigger similar responses from other investors leading to a feeding frenzy on the debtor's assets. The debtor may have no choice but to seek the protection of the bankruptcy laws which would effectively stop all seizures of collateral and extend the time for collateral liquidation. Lastly, there may be possible collateral deficiencies such as unperfected security interests which could make collateral liquidation problematic.[16]

The seizure, holding, and liquidation of collateral is also an expensive course of action. The most obvious costs are the legal fees incurred in seizing and liquidating the collateral. Additional costs include storage costs, appraisal fees, brokerage or auction costs, insurance, and property taxes. Hidden costs include the time spent by the investor and its personnel in managing and monitoring the liquidation process.

In sum, there are many reasons why the seizure and liquidation of collateral may not be a feasible solution for bank loan credit protection. Credit derivatives can solve these problems through the efficient exchange of credit risk. Furthermore, credit derivatives avoid the inevitable disruption of client relationships.

---

[16] A security interest is effective between a lender and a borrower without any perfection. Perfection is the legal term for properly identifying an asset as collateral for a bank loan such that other lenders and creditors will not attach their security interests to the identified collateral except in a subordinated role.

CREDIT RISK IN THE SOVEREIGN DEBT MARKET

Credit risk is not unique to the domestic U.S. financial markets. When investing in the sovereign debt of a foreign country, an investor must consider two crucial risks. One is political risk — the risk that even though the central government of the foreign country has the financial ability to pay its debts as they come due, for political reasons (e.g. revolution, new government regime, trade sanctions), the sovereign entity decides to forfeit (default) payment.[17] The second type of risk is credit risk — the same old inability to pay one's debts as they become due.

A sovereign government relies on two forms of cash flows to finance its government programs and to pay its debts: taxes and revenues from state owned enterprises. Taxes can come from personal income taxes, corporate taxes, import duties, and other excise taxes. State owned enterprises can be oil companies, telephone companies, national airlines and railroads, and other manufacturing enterprises.

In times of economic turmoil such as a recession, cash flows from state owned enterprises decline along with the general malaise of the economy. Additionally, tax revenues decline as corporations earn less money, as unemployment rises, and as personal incomes decline. Lastly, with a declining foreign currency value, imports decline, reducing revenue from import taxes.

The extreme vicissitudes of the sovereign debt market are no more apparent than in the emerging market arena. Here, the "Asian Tigers" — Hong Kong, Taiwan, Korea, and Singapore enjoyed a real average growth rate over the 1986-1996 period of about 8% per year. During this period, investors could have earned an average of 14% by investing in the public (or quasi-public) debt of these countries.

However, as the "Asian Contagion" demonstrated, the fortunes of the emerging markets countries can deteriorate rapidly. Exhibit 1 presents the monthly price chart for J.P. Morgan's Emerging Bond Index (EMBI) for the year from December 31, 1996 to July 31, 1998. EMBI is a weighted average of the returns to sovereign bonds for 15 emerging market countries from Latin America, Eastern Europe, and Asia.

---

[17] This raises the interesting idea of whether such a construct as a political derivative could be developed. While this may currently seem farfetched, it is no less implausible than credit derivatives once appeared.

Exhibit 1: J.P. Morgan EMBI Index

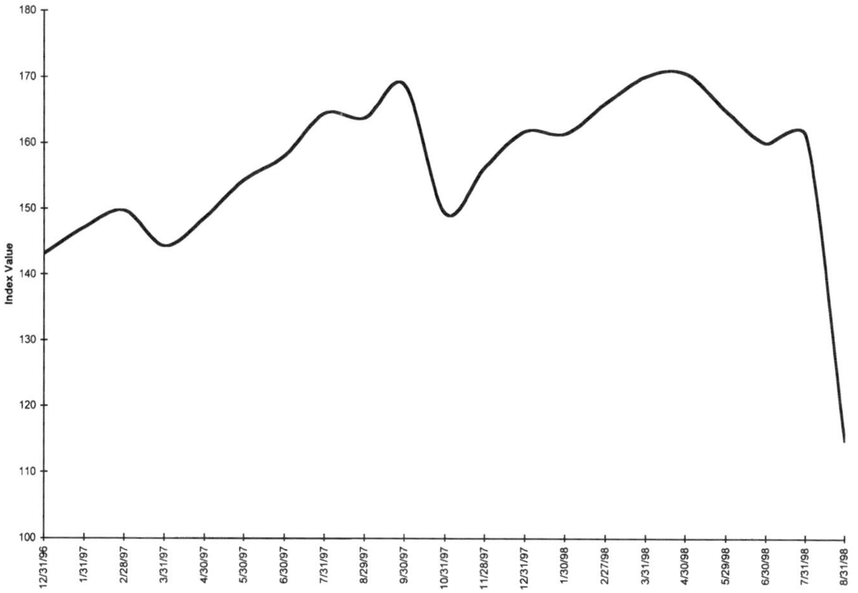

As Exhibit 1 demonstrates, the performance of the EMBI index was generally positive for most of 1997, with a total return of more than 18% for the first three quarters of 1997. However, this good performance soured dramatically in the month of October. From a high of almost 172 points on October 7, the index tumbled to 144 by November 10, a decline of over 16%. In the space of about one month, the declining fortunes of a broad sample of emerging market sovereigns wiped out most of the gains which had been earned over the 9 previous months.

Once again, we point out that credit risk is not all one sided. Even though there was a rapid decline in the credit quality of emerging market sovereign debt in 1997, such a steep retreat presented opportunities for credit quality improvement. For instance, from its low point of 144 in November 1997, the EMBI index rebounded to a value of 172 by the end of March 1998, a gain of over 19%. Those investors who chose to include emerging market debt in their portfolios in the first quarter of 1998 earned excellent returns. In fact, the returns to EMBI for the first quarter of 1998 outperformed U.S. Treasury bonds.

Even so, this recovery was short lived. In the second quarter of 1998, emerging market debt resumed its downward slide. In fact, in August 1998, emerging markets, as measured by the EMBI index, suffered a 29% decline.

For example, consider the Russian 10% government bond due in 2007. In July 1997 when this bond was issued, its credit spread over a comparable U.S. Treasury bond was 3.50%. As of July 1998, this credit spread had increased to 9.25%, an increase of 5.75%. In fact, the change in credit spread was so large, it was even greater than the current effective yield of a 30-year U.S. Treasury bond in July 1998!

The Russian bond was sold with a coupon of 10% in July 1997. If we assume that in July 1998, when the credit spread was 9.25%, the Russian bond had 9 remaining annual coupon payments and a final balloon payment of $1,000 at maturity, and that the rate on a 9-year U.S Treasury bond was 5.8%, then the current value of the bond in 1998 would be $759.46, a decline of $240.53, or 24% of its face value in one year's time.

If the reader thinks that the above example may be extreme, consider that in August 1998 the Russian economy suffered a total collapse and the credit spread for Russian debt increased to 53% over comparable U.S. Treasury bonds! This tremendous widening of credit spreads led to billions of dollars of losses by banks, brokerage houses, and hedge funds, as Russian investments were written down to 10 cents on the dollar.[18]

CONCLUSION

In the lower credit quality investment markets, credit risk is of paramount importance. High yield bonds, leveraged commercial loans, and emerging market sovereign debt are three examples where credit risk and return can provide yield enhancement as well detrimental returns. As the returns to the EMBI index show, the rapidly changing credit quality of an issuer can lead to a roller coaster of

---

[18] See "Financial Firms Lose $8 Billion So Far," *The Wall Street Journal* (September 3, 1998), p. A2.

returns. These steep drops in value followed by rapid recoveries provide ample opportunities to both hedge credit risk as well as embrace it.

These opportunities for credit risk management have led to tremendous growth over the past few years. From virtually nothing in the early 1990s, a current estimate of credit derivative activity is $100 billion notional value for 1998, up from $65 billion in 1997.[19] Credit risk is the biggest unmanaged risk investors take when they invest in the capital markets, and this is most apparent in the fixed income market. The level of credit derivative activity is expected to grow as portfolio managers, lenders, and borrowers become more sophisticated about shifting this important risk factor.

Traditionally, investment managers have sought to achieve their ideal risk and return profile by trading in the underlying securities. However, credit derivatives allow portfolio managers to more efficiently control their portfolios in two ways. First credit derivatives can avoid the tax consequences with the sale of an underlying asset. Second, credit derivatives allow portfolio managers to pinpoint the exact risks which they wish to include in their portfolio. In sum, credit derivatives are more flexible and efficient than trading in the underlying securities.

---

[19] See Margaret Elliot, "Waking Up to Credit Risk," *Derivatives Strategy* (April 1998), pp. 33-38.

Chapter 2

Credit Options

INTRODUCTION

C redit options are one of the basic building blocks of credit derivatives. They operate in the same way as equity or fixed-income options. The portfolio manager purchases the right, but not the obligation, to buy (a call option) or sell (a put option) the specified credit risk at the strike price until expiration of the option. As long as the portfolio manager is purchasing the option, she only risks losing the cost of the option (called the option premium).

This chapter is divided into three parts to demonstrate the use of credit options in the high yield, bank loan, and emerging market debt markets.

CREDIT OPTIONS IN THE HIGH YIELD MARKET

Credit options are different from standard debt options because while the latter is designed to protect against market risk (i.e., interest rate risk), credit options are constructed to protect against credit risk. Thus, the purpose of credit options is to price credit risk independently of market risk. Credit options may be written on an underlying asset or on a spread over a referenced riskless asset. These two types of options — one triggered by a decline in the value of an asset and one triggered by the change in the asset's spread over a comparable risk-free rate — have different payout structures.[1]

---

[1] Note that credit options are different from options on credit risky assets. In the latter case, these options are on the outright asset, but the asset is subject to credit risk, i.e., the issuer may default on the security. Conversely, credit options recognize the possibility of default and construct the payoff on the option to be a function of the decline in asset value due to default. For a thorough analysis of options on credit risky assets, see Robert Jarrow and Stuart Turnbull, "Pricing Derivatives on Financial Assets Subject to Credit Risk," *The Journal of Finance* (March 1995), pp. 53-85.

Credit Options Written on an Underlying Asset

In its simplest form, a credit option can be a *binary option*. With a *binary credit option*, the option seller will pay out a fixed sum if and when a default event occurs with respect to a referenced credit (e.g., the underlying issuer is unable to pay its obligations as they become due). Therefore, a binary option represents two states of the world: default or no default. It is the clearest example of credit protection. At maturity of the option, if the referenced credit has defaulted, the option holder receives a predetermined payout. If there is no default at maturity of the option, the option buyer receives nothing and forgoes the option premium. A binary credit option could also be triggered by a rating downgrade.

A *European binary credit option* pays out a fixed sum only at maturity if the referenced credit is in default. An *American binary credit option* can be exercised at any time during its life. Consequently, if an American binary credit option is in the money (a default event has occurred), it will be exercised immediately because delaying exercise will reduce the present value of the fixed payment.

Exhibit 1 presents a binary credit put option, where the payout is dependent upon whether the referenced credit is in default. Actual default is not necessary. Instead, the strike price of the option can be set to a minimum net worth of the underlying issuer below which default is probable. For instance, if the firm value of the referenced credit (assets minus liabilities) falls to $100 million, then the option will pay a specified amount. In practice, high yield bonds trade considerably below their face value and the recovery rate on senior secured defaulted bonds is about 58 cents on the dollar.[2] Consequently, the payout to the credit option does not need to cover the full face value of the bond to protect the portfolio manager, it can be set to 42 cents or $420 for every $1,000 of face value.

Mathematically, the payoff to a binary credit put option is stated as:

$$P[V(t);\$100,000,000] = \begin{array}{l} \$420 \text{ if } V(t) \leq \$100,000,000 \\ 0 \text{ if } V(t) > \$100,000,000 \end{array} \quad (1)$$

---

[2] See Edward Altman and Vellore Kishore, "Almost Everything You Wanted to Know about Recoveries on Defaulted Bonds," *Financial Analysts Journal* (November/December 1996), pp. 57-64.

Exhibit 1: Binary Credit Put Option

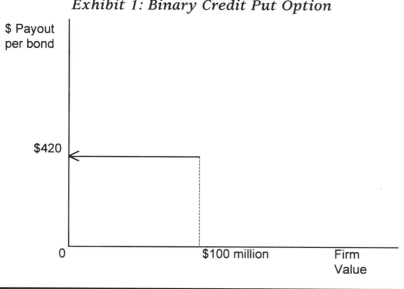

where:

$100,000,000 = the strike price set equal to a minimum firm value

$V(t)$ = the value of the firm at maturity t of the option

$420 = a fixed payment if a default has occurred

Equation (1) demonstrates the payoff for a put option. The option pays a fixed sum of $420 per bond if the value of the referenced credit declines below a minimum value ($100 million), and nothing if the value of the referenced credit at maturity of the option is above the strike price.

An alternative to binary options is an option where the option writer agrees to compensate the option buyer for a decline in the value of a financial asset below a specified strike price. This type of option is also a put option that is in-the-money only when the value of the underlying asset declines below the strike price. In practice, these types of credit options are usually specified in terms of the acceptable default spread of the bond in question. That is, upon exercise of the credit option, the payoff is determined by subtracting the market price of the bond from the strike price, where the strike price is determined by taking the present value of the bond's cash flows discounted at the risk-free rate plus the strike credit spread over the remaining life of the outstanding bond.

Mathematically, this is determined by the following formula:

$$P[D(t); K] = \text{Max } [0, K - D(t)] \tag{2}$$

where:

K	=	$F[\exp-(r + \text{spread})(T - t)]$
$D(t)$	=	the market value of a financial asset at time t, the maturity of the option
F	=	the face value of a zero-coupon debt instrument
r	=	the riskless rate
spread	=	the specified (strike) credit spread over the riskless rate
T	=	the maturity of the bond
t	=	the time to maturity of the option
exp	=	the exponential power of e

Recall from Chapter 1 that the credit spread on BB rated bonds was 215 basis points in June 1997, the lowest spread in several years. It would not be unreasonable for an investor to expect the credit spread to widen back to an historical average in excess of 300 basis points, resulting in a decline in value of BB rated bonds. To protect against this anticipated decline in value, a portfolio manager could purchase a credit put option.

Assume that in June 1997 the portfolio manager purchases a $1,000 face value 5-year zero-coupon BB bond, at a credit spread which is 215 basis points to comparable U.S. Treasury bonds. However, to protect against a widening of the credit spread with respect to these bonds, the portfolio manager also purchases a 1-year credit option for $50 whose strike is established at a credit spread of 225 basis points. In June 1997, comparable U.S. Treasury bonds were trading at a rate of 6.25%. Using equation (2), the strike of the credit option (K) is then set equal to $1,000[\exp-(6.25\% + 2.25\%)(5 - 1)] = $712. If the high yield bond trades below this value, then the portfolio manager receives the difference between $712 and the market value of the bond. This example is demonstrated in Exhibit 2.

Exhibit 2: Credit Put Option on BB Rated Debt Issue

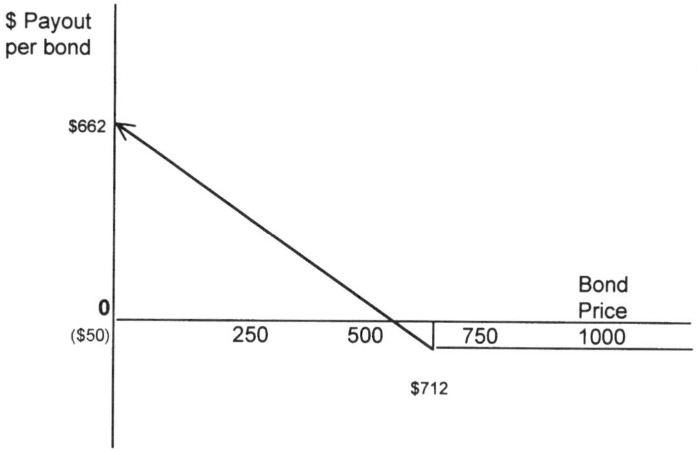

Valuing credit options in the form of equation (2) implicitly assumes constant market risk, i.e., that interest rate volatility is not essential. For short-dated options this assumption is not critical. However, constant instant rates become problematic if the option tenor is long. We discuss this point in more detail in Chapter 5.

Equation (2) expresses the strike price of a credit option on a zero-coupon bond. However, most corporate bonds pay a coupon. A simple solution for credit options on a coupon-paying bond is to adjust the strike price of the credit option based on all cash flows paid over the life of the bond. Thus, the strike price K must be the sum of a series of the type expressed in equation (2) where F, the face value of the bond, is replaced by the future cash flow (either a coupon payment or maturity value of the bond) and time T is the payment date of the bond cash flow.

Credit derivatives may be used to exploit inefficiencies in the market when there is imperfect correlation between stock prices and interest rates. For instance, when interest rates and stock prices are negatively correlated, corporate debt values may be higher than when the correlation is positive. Credit spreads in the market may not correctly reflect the correlations between stocks and the term structure of interest rates. As a result, investors may hold a portfolio of corporate bonds and credit derivatives, which may cost less than equivalent riskless debt yet offer the same risk and return characteristics.

Credit options may also be used in conjunction with other derivative transactions. For instance, with respect to over-the-counter derivatives such as swaps and off-exchange options, downgrade provisions in the derivative documentation can protect a derivative buyer from credit risk. However, the buyer must be able to establish a downgrade trigger at some point before the counterparty is in the throes of financial distress. Additionally, the downgrade trigger provision terminates the transaction; a credit option hedges the credit exposure but does not automatically truncate the transaction cash flows.

Credit Spread Options

The second type of credit option is a call option on the level of the credit spread over a referenced benchmark such as U.S. Treasury securities. If the credit spread widens, the referenced asset will decline in value. This type of credit option is structured so that the option is in-the-money when the credit spread exceeds the specified spread level. The payoff is determined by taking the difference in the credit spreads multiplied by a specified notional amount and by a risk factor. In a mathematical format, the payoff at maturity of the option may be specified as:

$$C[\text{spread}(t); K] = (\text{spread} - K) \times \text{notional amount} \times \text{risk factor} \quad (3)$$

where:

$\text{spread}(t)$ = the spread for the financial asset over the riskless rate at the maturity of the option at time t

K = the specified strike spread for the financial asset over the riskless rate

The notional amount is a contractually specified dollar amount established at the outset of the option.

The risk factor is determined by the sensitivity of the underlying financial asset to changes in interest rates. This sensitivity is measured by the calculations for duration and convexity. For example, consider the BB rated, 7.75 Niagra Mohawk Power bond due in 2008. In September 1998, this bond was trading at a price of $104.77 with a yield to maturity around 7.08%. Using standard formulas, the duration and convexity for this bond were 6.96 and 62.427, respectively.[3]

At the time that this bond was offering a yield of 7.08%, the 10-year Treasury bond was yielding about 5.3% for a credit spread of 178 basis points. This was a very narrow spread considering Niagra Mohawk Power's BB credit rating. Perhaps the market was implying that the credit risk of Niagra Mohawk was closer to BBB than BB. Alternatively, it could be that the bond was overvalued by the market.

---

[3] Modified duration may be calculated as:

$$\frac{C/y^2 \times [1 - 1/(1+y)^n] + n \times (100 - C/y)/(1+y)^{n+1}}{P}$$

where

C = the semiannual coupon
y = the yield to maturity divided by 2
n = the number of semiannual periods
P = the current price of the bond

See Frank J. Fabozzi, *Bond Markets, Analysis and Strategies, second edition* (Englewood Cliffs, NJ: Prentice Hall, 1993).

Plugging in values from our example above, we get:

$$\frac{3.875/(0.0354)^2 \times [1 - 1/(1.0354)^{20}] + 20 \times (100 - 3.875/0.0354)/(1.0354)^{21}}{104.77}$$

$$= 13.925$$

Converting this number to an annual basis requires dividing by 2 (the number of coupon payments per year) to yield 6.96.

Convexity may be calculated as:

$$2C/y^3 \times [1 - 1/(1+y)^n] - 2Cn/y^2(1+y)^{n+1} + [n(n+1) \times (100 - C/y)]/(1+y)^{n+2}$$

Plugging in the proper numbers yields:

$$2 \times 3.875/(0.0354^3 \times [1 - 1/(1.0354)^{20}] - 2 \times 3.875 \times 20/(0.0354)^2(1.0354)^{21} + [20 \times 21 \times (100 - 3.875/0.0354)]/(1.0354)^{22} = 26{,}162.77$$

On an annualized basis per \$100 of par bond, convexity equals $26{,}162.77/(2^2 \times 104.77) = 62.427$.

For a 1% increase in interest rates, the approximate percentage change in the price of the bond could be expected to be:

$$-(6.96) \times (0.01) + \tfrac{1}{2} \times (62.427) \times (0.01)^2 = 6.65\%$$

Therefore, an approximate risk factor for this bond with respect to an increase in the credit spread is 6.65.

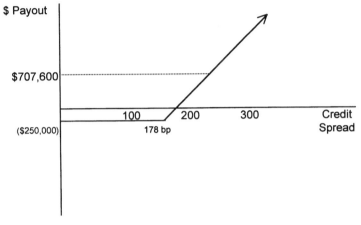

Exhibit 3: Credit Call Option
Credit Spread Option Struck at 178 Basis Points

If the portfolio manager believed that the bond was overvalued, she could purchase a credit spread option struck at 178 basis points. This is the same as the portfolio manager expressing a view that the price of the referenced asset is inflated at the current market spread, and she expects the credit spread to widen out to more normal levels.

Suppose that the portfolio manager believes that the credit spread for this bond will increase to 250 basis points during the course of the next year. She can purchase a $20 million notional at-the-money call option on the credit spread between the debt of Niagra Mohawk Power and U.S. Treasuries. The tenor of the option is one year, the premium costs 125 basis points, and the risk factor is 6.65. At maturity of the option, the portfolio manager will receive:

(change in credit spread) × (notional amount) × (risk factor)

If the credit spread does indeed widen to 250 basis points at maturity of the option, the portfolio manager will earn:

$$(0.0072 \times \$20,000,000 \times 6.65) - \$250,000 = \$707,600$$

This payout is demonstrated in Exhibit 3.

Credit spreads can be viewed from either a macroeconomic or microeconomic analysis. Under a macroeconomic view, a slowdown in the economy can lead to a flight of capital to more secure investments such as U.S. Treasury securities, resulting in wider credit spreads across all securities. This type of analysis was realized during July and August 1998 as financial turmoil around the world resulted in a flight to U.S. Treasury bonds and wider credit spreads in the high yield market. Under a microeconomic analysis, a buyer of a credit option can express the view that the credit quality of the underlying referenced issuer will decline due to poor operating performance. In either scenario, the price of the referenced asset "cheapens" relative to U.S. Treasury securities.

Alternatively, credit spread options may be used as income enhancement tools. The portfolio manager may believe that the credit spread for Company A will not exceed 300 basis points. To monetize this view, she can sell a put option on the credit spread with the strike set at 300 basis points. Additionally, the portfolio manager can agree to physically settle the option. In effect, the portfolio manager has agreed to buy the debt of Company A at a spread to U.S. Treasuries of 300 basis points — her targeted purchase price — and she can use the premium received from the sale of the credit option to finance the purchase price should the put be exercised.

Credit spread options are relative value options. Their value is not derived from the absolute price change of the underlying referenced asset, but rather from the price change of the referenced asset relative to U.S. Treasury securities. By purchasing a call option on the credit spread between the referenced asset and U.S. Treasuries, the option is in the money only if the price of the referenced asset declines more than the prices of U.S. Treasury securities (i.e. the credit spread widens).

Credit spread options are, therefore, underperformance options. Similar to outperformance options where the payoff is contingent on the relative outperformance of one referenced asset over a second referenced asset, the payoff of a credit spread call option is contingent upon the relative underperformance of a referenced asset compared to U.S. Treasury securities.

Credit spread options are not designed to protect against market risk such as interest rate spikes where both the Treasury security and the referenced asset decline in value at the same time. Instead, credit options are another form of insurance against a credit decline in the referenced asset or issuer. This strategy can be used to protect the value of an existing portfolio position should its spread relative to U.S. Treasuries increase. However, this type of option will not protect against an absolute decline in value of the referenced asset if the value of U.S. Treasury securities also decline.

Credit spread options may also be used by corporate treasurers to hedge the credit risk embedded in future borrowing requirements. Typically, the spread paid by corporations based on different rating levels compared to U.S. Treasury securities tends to widen during periods of economic downturns. Credit call options on the spread over U.S. Treasuries can protect against an overall rise in the risk premiums for different rating levels. The payoff from the option can be used to offset the increased funding costs.

CREDIT OPTIONS IN BANK LOAN MANAGEMENT

Traditionally, the term loan market was strictly the domain of banks. Banks bought and sold loans among themselves with little participation from institutional investors such as pension funds, investment companies, and hedge funds. However, over the past few years, the bank loan market has developed into a liquid market for high yield investors. This development, in turn, has spawned the need for, and use of, credit derivatives to embrace or tame the bank loan market. The examples below demonstrate that credit options are as applicable for bank loan management as they are for high yield bonds.

Credit Options Written on an Underlying Bank Loan

Similar to our discussion of high yield bonds, we begin our discussion of credit options on bank loans with an example of a binary credit option. Exhibit 4 presents an option where the payout is dependent upon whether the referenced credit is in default. As previously discussed in Chapter 1, the expected loss on a defaulted commercial loan is about 35 cents on every dollar. Therefore, a binary credit option can be structured to pay $350 for every $1,000 of loan value in the event of default.

Exhibit 4: Binary Credit Default Option on a Bank Loan

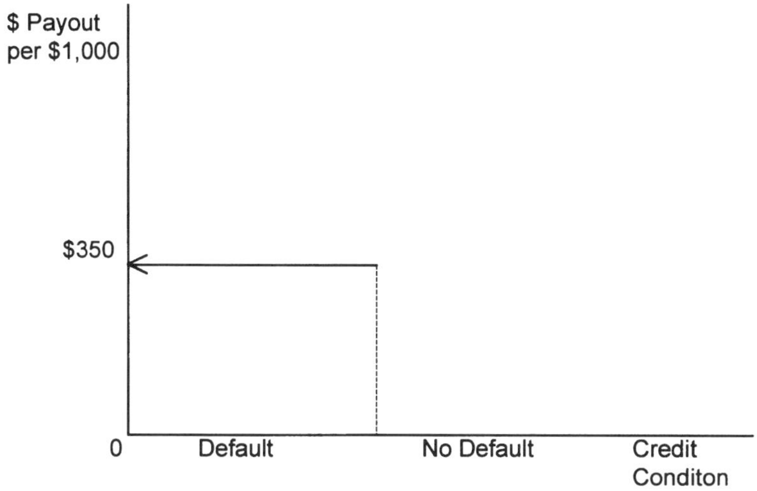

Mathematically, the payoff to a binary put option is stated as:

$$P[\text{Loan}(T);\$1,000] = \begin{array}{l} \$350 \text{ if default} \\ \$0 \text{ if no default} \end{array} \quad (4)$$

where

Loan(T) = the value of the commercial loan at maturity of the option

$350 = a fixed payment per $1,000 of loan value if a default has occurred

Equation (4) demonstrates the payoff for a put option. The option pays a fixed sum of $350 per $1,000 of loan value if the borrower defaults, and nothing if the borrower remains solvent. Note that this type of option does not have to depend on the borrower defaulting on a specific loan; it can be established such that any default on any fixed obligation of the borrower triggers the option value.

An alternative to binary options is an option where the option writer agrees to compensate the option buyer for a decline in the value of a financial asset below a specified strike price. This type of credit option has two advantages over the binary option discussed above. First, the expected loss of 35 cents for every $1 is an average loss rate. Depending on the remaining credit strength of the borrower, the default loss may be more or less than 35 cents. Second, a credit option with a specified strike price does not have to wait for a default event to be in the money.

Credit options written on a commercial loan work differently than a credit option written on a traditional fixed income asset such as a high yield bond. The reason is the amortization of loan principal. Most bank loans typically have an amortization schedule, established at the outset of the loan, which determines how much interest and principal is paid each period. Instead of a bullet payment at maturity, the principal is paid back over time according to the amortization schedule.

The amortization of principal over time reduces the default risk to the investor. With the passage of time, as more and more of the principal is repaid, the potential loss to the investor is reduced. This is in contrast to a bond where the repayment of principal is deferred until maturity. The declining principal at risk of a commercial loan has important implications for determining the strike price for a credit option.

We consider two cases, one where the investor is concerned about a credit deterioration, and one where the investor is concerned about default. In the first case, a credit deterioration can come about as a result of general financial market turmoil leading to a widening of credit spreads after the loan is issued (a macroeconomic event), or it can result from a credit rating downgrade due to the weakening of the financial status of the underlying borrower (a microeconomic event). The borrower continues to make its scheduled payments, but now its credit spread has increased, reducing the value of the amortizing cash flows. In the second case, the borrower defaults on the commercial loan, essentially canceling further payments. Both situations will reduce the value of a commercial loan, with a credit deterioration being the less severe example.

Taking the example of a credit deterioration option, assume an institutional investor has purchased a $1,000, 5-year BB rated bank loan priced at 150 basis points over LIBOR. With 5-year LIBOR at about 6%, and with annual amortization, each yearly payment of principal and interest would be $247 ($172 principal and $75 interest for the first year). At the end of the first year, the amortized value of the bank loan would be $1,000 − $172 = $828.

Exhibit 5: Credit Deterioration Put Option on
BB Rated Bank Loan

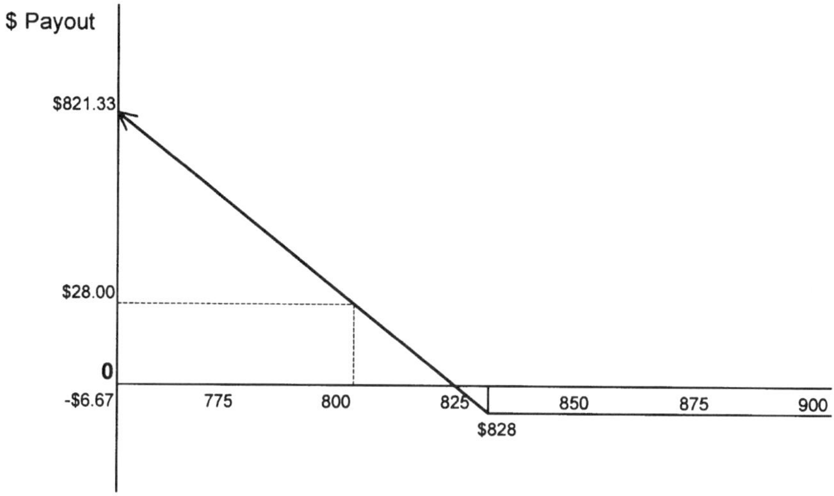

If the investor wishes to protect himself from credit deterioration by the end of the first year, he should purchase a 1-year credit put option struck at $828. This is demonstrated in Exhibit 5. Assume that the borrower is, in fact, downgraded to single B by the end of the first year of the bank loan. The value of the bank loan would decline from $828 to $800. The market price of $800 is determined by taking the remaining four amortization payments of $247 and discounting them at LIBOR + 300, the average rate for single B bank loans. Mathematically, the strike price for the credit put option at the end of the first year is determined as:

$$K_1 = \$1000 - (A - I_1) \tag{5}$$

where

K_1 = the strike price for the option at the end of the first year of the bank loan

A = the periodic (annual) amortization payment

I_1 = the accrued interest payable at the end of the first year

What equation (5) and the simple example above demonstrate is that the strike price for a credit put option on a commercial

loan is *time dependent*.[4] Over time, as the borrower pays its obligations and the loan is amortized, the amount that can be lost by the
investor declines. Consequently, the strike price for the credit put
option must be adjusted over time to reflect the amortization of the
principal balance of the loan; the strike price declines with the passage of time.

More generally, to protect against credit deterioration for any
time t, the strike price on a credit put option for an amortizing commercial loan is determined by:

$$K_t = P_{t-1} - (A - I_t) \tag{6}$$

where

$$
\begin{array}{lll}
K_t & = & \text{the strike price at time t} \\
P_{t-1} & = & \$1{,}000 - \Sigma(A - I_j) \\
A & = & \text{the constant amortization amount} \\
I_j & = & \text{the interest payments over the time interval 1 to } t-1 \\
\Sigma & = & \text{the summation sign over the time period } j = 1 \text{ to} \\
& & j = t-1 \\
I_t & = & \text{the interest payment for period } t \\
\$1{,}000 & = & \text{the principal borrowed by the debtor}
\end{array}
$$

Additionally, based on our definition of P_{t-1} in equation (6),
the above formulation of the strike price may be reduced to:

$$K_t = \$1{,}000 - \Sigma(A - I_j) \tag{7}$$

where the other terms are as defined as before and Σ is the summation over the time period $j = 1$ to $j = t$.

How will the credit deterioration put option be priced? While
a full blown discussion of credit option pricing models is deferred
until Chapter 5, a simple example should help. The essential question to answer is what is the probability of a credit downgrade for
the borrower from BB to B?

---

[4] The time dependency of the strike price for credit options has been noted with respect to cou-
pon-paying bonds with a bullet payment at maturity. See Yiannos A. Pierides, "Valuation of
Credit Risk Derivatives," Chapter 13 in Frank J. Fabozzi (ed.), *The Handbook of Fixed Income
Options* (Burr Ridge, IL: Irwin Professional Publishing, 1996).

This probability can be determined through the formation of transition credit matrices which use historical data to determine the statistical likelihood of credit downgrades and upgrades.[5] By using these transition matrices, and the term structure of credit spreads for different credit rating levels, a distribution of returns can be derived for the underlying bank loan.[6] From this distribution, the probability of a downgrade to a single B rating can be determined. Denoting this probability A, the investor can then use a simple 1-period binomial pricing tree to determine the current price of the option.

Assume that A is 0.25. That is, with a 25% probability, the investor expects the credit rating of the borrower to be downgraded from BB to B, and with a $1 - A = 75\%$ probability, the borrower's credit rating will remain at BB or better. If we assume a 1-year risk neutral rate of 5%, a strike price of $828, and that the value of the bank loan declines to $800 if the borrower is downgraded to single B, then the price of a credit deterioration put option on the BB bank loan is $6.67:

$$P[\text{Loan}(T); \$828] = [(0.25) \times (\$828 - \$800) + (0.75) \times (\$0)]$$
$$\div (1 + 0.05) = \$6.67$$

This binomial pricing is demonstrated in Exhibit 6.

The above credit option assumes that there is a risk of widening credit spreads or a credit downgrade, but no default. That is, the borrower continues to meet its amortization payments, but the value of the loan has decreased because either credit spreads have generally increased (a macroeconomic event) or the borrower's credit situation has deteriorated (a microeconomic event).

If the investor considers the possibility of default, the determination of the strike price is different. Unlike zero-coupon bonds, default on a commercial loan can occur prior to maturity at any

---

[5] For a demonstration of a transition credit matrix, see Gailen Hite and Arthur Warga, "The Effect of Bond-Rating Changes on Bond Price Performance," *Financial Analysts Journal* (May/June 1997), pp. 35-51.

[6] If the investor assumes a normal distribution, then all that is needed to derive the distribution is the expected return on the bank loan and its variance. In practice, normal distributions are not observed for bank loans and other investment securities. Consequently, simulation techniques such as Monte Carlo simulation are used to model the hypothetical distribution of returns.

scheduled payment date. Default occurs on a payment date if the borrower fails to meet its amortization payment. In the event of default, the ex-amortization price of the loan (market price of the loan after an amortization payment) is not defined on the payment date because the borrower has effectively canceled all future payments. Consequently, the strike price for a credit default option must be based on the loan value plus its scheduled amortization payment.[7]

Stated another way, it is to the advantage of the borrower to default right before the scheduled date of an amortization payment. Consider the same $1,000, 5-year, BB rated term loan with annual amortization payments of $247. At the end of the first year, the borrower is scheduled to pay $247, with four remaining payments of $247 for each of the next four years. If, in fact, the borrower defaults just before the first payment date, the present value of the investor's loss at the time of the first amortization payment is:

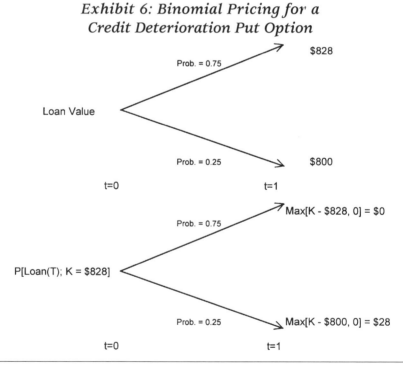

Exhibit 6: Binomial Pricing for a Credit Deterioration Put Option

---

[7] This point has been noted by Pierides, "Valuation of Credit Risk Derivatives," with respect to coupon-paying bonds.

$$\$247 + \$247/(1.075) + \$247/(1.075)^2 + \$247/(1.075)$$
$$+ \$247/(1.075)^4 = \$1,075$$

To fully protect against default risk at the end of the first year, the strike price for a credit option must be set at $1,075. As indicated above, the strike price is equal to the loan value at the end of year 1 ($828) plus the scheduled amortization payment ($247). It may seem odd that the strike price at the end of the first year is higher than the initial market value of the loan ($1,000), but this is because the time value of the amortization payments has increased by the time the investor gets to the end of the first year. (Note, for example, that the first amortization payment is no longer discounted because it is currently due and payable.)

If we assume a probability of default of 10%, a decline in loan value by 35 cents on the dollar right after default, a 1-year risk neutral rate of 5%, and a strike price of $1,075, then the price of the option may be determined using the simple binomial model discussed above. The credit option value may be determined by:

$P[\text{Loan}(T); K=\$1,075]$
$\quad = [(0.10) \times (\$1,075 - \{0.65\} \times \{\$1,075\}) + (0.90) \times (\$0)]$
$\quad \div (1.05) = \$35.83$

This credit default option is demonstrated in Exhibit 7.

As in the case of credit deterioration, the strike price for a credit default option is time dependent. Over time, the strike price will decline as more and more of the outstanding principal is paid back by the borrower. Two points should be noted with respect to the difference in strike prices at time $t = 1$ between the credit deterioration option ($K_1 = \$828$) and the credit default option ($K_1 = \$1,075$).

First, it makes intuitive sense that the strike price for the credit default option is higher than that for the credit deterioration option because in the former case the investor is concerned with loss of principal, while in the latter case the investor is concerned not with loss of principal but with earning an appropriate credit spread given the borrower's current credit situation. Therefore, the level of credit protection is higher for the default case and a higher exercise price must be established to protect against default risk. Second, because of its higher exercise price, the cost of the credit default option will be greater than that for the credit deterioration option. Once again, this makes common sense; the greater the credit protection, the more expensive the credit option.

Similar to the junk bond market, credit derivatives may be used to exploit inefficiencies in the market when there is imperfect correlation between stock prices and interest rates. If interest rates and stock prices are negatively correlated, commercial loan values may be higher than when the correlation is positive. Credit spreads in the market may not correctly reflect the correlations between stocks and the term structure for bank loans. Therefore, investors may hold a portfolio of commercial loans and credit derivatives, which may cost less than equivalent riskless debt yet offer the same risk and return characteristics.

Credit Spread Options on Bank Loans

The second type of credit option is a call option on the level of the credit spread over a referenced benchmark such as LIBOR. If the credit spread widens, the referenced asset will decline in value. This type of credit option is structured so that the option is in the money when the credit spread exceeds the specified strike level.

Exhibit 7: Credit Default Put Option on BB Rated Bank Loan

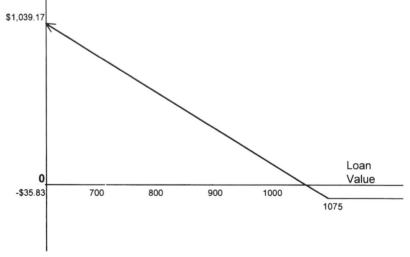

As an example we will continue with our $1,000 5-year, BB rated term loan with annual amortization payments of $247. At the initiation of the loan, its fair value is determined by:

$$\text{Loan}(t0) = \$247/(1+L+s) + \$247/(1+L+s)^2$$
$$+ \$247/(1+L+s)^3 + \$247/(1+L+s)^4$$
$$+ \$247/(1+L+s)^5 = \$1,000 \qquad (8)$$

where

L = the 5-year LIBOR rate

s = the market credit spread for BB rated loans

Plugging in the 5-year LIBOR rate of 6% for L, we can solve for the value of the credit spread (s) which will equate the present value of the amortization payments to the value of the Loan at $t=0$ of $1,000. From our discussion above, we already know that this value is 1.5%. What equation (8) illustrates is that the value of the loan is dependent on the credit spread. As the credit spread increases, the value of the loan decreases. Therefore, a call option struck on the credit spread qualifies as a credit derivative because its value increases as the credit quality of the borrower decreases. Consequently, a call option on the credit spread can offer the same credit protection as a credit put option on the loan's market value.

The payoff on a credit spread option is determined by taking the difference in the credit spreads multiplied by a specified notional amount and by a risk factor. In a mathematical format, the payoff at maturity of the option may be specified as:

$$C[\text{spread}(T); K]$$
$$= (\text{spread}(T) - K) \times \text{notional amount} \times \text{risk factor} \qquad (9)$$

where

spread(T) = the spread for the financial asset over the riskless rate at the maturity of the option

K = the specified strike spread over LIBOR for the loan

Exhibit 8: Credit Call Option
Credit Spread Option Struck at 150 Basis Points

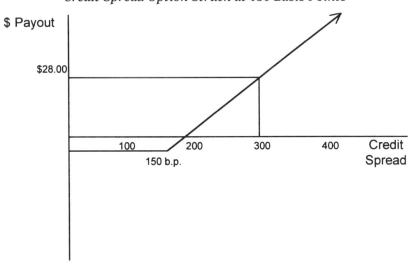

The notional amount is a contractually specified dollar amount equal to the amount of the outstanding loan and the risk factor is based on measures of duration and convexity (see our prior example for high yield bonds).

Assume the portfolio manager purchases a $1,000 notional call option with a strike price equal to the current credit spread over LIBOR for a BB rated bank loan. The tenor of the option is one year and the risk factor for the bank loan is 1.867. At maturity, the portfolio manager will receive the following payout:

(change in credit spread) × (notional amount) × (risk factor)

If the borrower is downgraded to single B and the credit spread widens to 300 basis points, at maturity of the option the portfolio manager will earn:

$$[(3\% - 1.5\%) \times \$1000 \times 1.867] = \$28$$

Note that this credit spread option compensates the portfolio manager for the decline in amortized loan value from $828 to $800. This is demonstrated in Exhibit 8.

Macroeconomic and microeconomic analysis applies to credit spread options on bank loans just as it does to high yield bonds. Under a macroeconomic view, a slowdown in the economy can lead to declining corporate revenues and shrinking profit margins. Consequently, credit spreads will widen across industry sectors. Alternatively, under a microeconomic view, the economic prospects of a debtor corporation may decline despite a booming economy. In each case, a buyer of a credit spread option can express the view that the credit quality of the underlying referenced issuer will decline and that the price of the referenced asset will "cheapen" relative to a benchmark interest rate.

Once again, we note that credit spread options are relative value options. Their value is not derived from the absolute price change of the underlying referenced asset, but rather from the price change of the referenced asset relative to LIBOR. By purchasing a call option on the credit spread between the referenced loan and LIBOR, the option is in the money only if the price of the referenced asset declines more than would be warranted by an increase in LIBOR (i.e., the credit spread widens).

CREDIT OPTIONS IN EMERGING MARKETS

Nowhere has credit risk been more apparent in 1997-1998 than in the emerging market arena. The severe recession throughout southeast Asia, the virtual collapse of the Russian economy, and the near meltdown of Latin America demonstrated in the extreme the need to hedge credit risk. Although credit derivatives should not be considered solely for credit protection, this was clearly a time to batten down the hatches. The following examples reflect this defensive position.

Options On an Underlying Foreign Bond

Credit options in the emerging market debt market operate much the same as credit options on high yield bonds. The key difference is that with high yield bonds, the underlying issuer is a corporation, while in the emerging markets, the underlying issuer is the sovereign government. Therefore, the same types of credit spread options apply as well as credit put options on the underlying sovereign debt. A couple of examples should help.

In January 1998, bondholders forced the International Finance Corporation of Thailand (IFCT, a government sponsored bank) to buy back $500 million in bonds several years before their maturity. The bond issue contained a put provision that allowed investors to put the bonds back to the issuer at face value if the sovereign credit rating of Thailand fell below investment grade.

In addition to the put option, investors also receive 50 basis points in additional coupon income should the bonds fall two rungs in credit rating, and an additional 25 basis points for each additional rating downgrade until the below investment grade threshold was reached. The bonds became putable when Moody's Investor Services cut the sovereign rating of Thailand to Ba1.

The investors who purchased these IFCT bonds bought a cash instrument plus a basket of credit options. First, the ability to put the bonds back to the issuer should the government of Thailand lose its investment credit rating was a credit put option, where the strike price was set equal to the face value of the bonds. This option was in the money and exercisable only if the credit rating of Thailand declined to below investment grade. Otherwise, it paid nothing. Mathematically, this put option looked like:

$$P[V(t); \$500,000,000]$$
$$= \begin{array}{l} \$500,000,000 - V(t) \text{ if credit rating} \\ \text{remains below investment grade} \\ \$0 \text{ if credit rating remains investment grade} \end{array} \qquad (10)$$

where

$\$500,000,000$ = the face value of the IFCT bonds
$V(t)$ = the market value of the IFCT bonds at time t

Equation (10) looks very similar to equation (1), with one important difference. In equation (1), the payout to the binary put option was specified in advance. In other words, if the value of the corporation fell below the threshold value, the option holder knew exactly the payoff she would receive from the put option. In contrast, in equation (10) the option holder receives a payment only if the credit rating declines below investment grade, but she does not know in advance what value the IFCT bonds will trade if the sovereign risk of Thailand declines below investment grade. Therefore, equation (10) demonstrates a *contingent credit put option*. To provide adequate protection, the bondholders received a binary put option whose value was measured as the difference between the face value of the bonds of $500,000,000 and the market value of the bonds at the time Thailand's credit rating declined below investment grade. Exhibit 9 demonstrates this contingent credit put option.

Second, the ability to earn additional yield as the credit rating of Thailand deteriorated is the same as a series of binary call options, each triggered by a ratings downgrade. To see this, just remember that a call option is the right to receive a payoff if the option is in the money at the time of exercise. In this case, at the time of Thailand's ratings downgrades, the bondholders had the right to call for additional coupon income equal to 50 basis points initially (for the first two credit downgrades) and then 25 basis points thereafter. Mathematically, the first binary credit call option can be represented as:

$$C[CR(t);ICR]$$
$$= \frac{\text{\$2,500,000 if } CRt \text{ is two grades below } ICR}{\text{\$0 if } CRt \text{ is not two grades below } ICR} \tag{11}$$

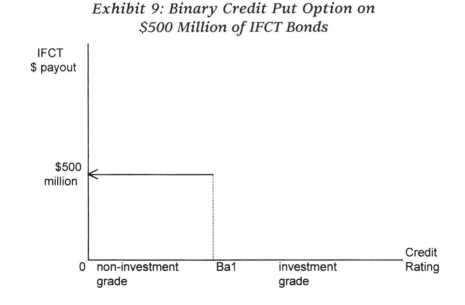

Exhibit 9: Binary Credit Put Option on $500 Million of IFCT Bonds

Exhibit 10: Credit Call Options on the IFCT Credit Rating

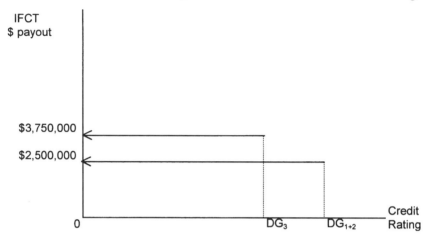

DG$_{1+2}$ indicates the first two credit downgrades
DG$_3$ indicates the third downgrade

where

$CR(t)$ = the credit rating of Thailand at time t

ICR = the initial credit rating of Thailand at the time of bond issuance

$\$2,500,000 = 0.005 \times \$500,000,000$

After the first binary credit call option has been exercised and paid, each remaining binary credit call option would pay $1,250,000 with each additional ratings downgrade up to the point of the exercise of the binary credit put option for the face value amount of the bonds. These series of binary credit spread options provide a payoff stream that resembles the step function in Exhibit 10.

Why would the IFCT issue bonds with a basket of credit options attached, and why would investors want to purchase them? For the IFCT, the reason was one of cost. By selling a basket of binary credit options attached to its bonds, it was able to reduce its initial funding costs by over 75 basis points, or $3,750,000 per year. Even though it subsequently had to pay out on the options, initially, its funding costs were lower. From an investor standpoint, the reason was protection. Investors were willing to accept a lower coupon payment up front in return for credit protection against downgrades. Given the meltdown in the Asian financial markets in 1997 and 1998, it is a safe conclusion that investors made the better deal.[8]

Credit Spread Options on a Foreign Bond

Just as credit spread options can be written and purchased on a high yield bond, similar options can be constructed for foreign bonds. Although not as well developed as credit options on an underlying bond, this type of credit option is growing in emerging markets. Given the recent volatility in the emerging markets in 1997 and 1998, this type of option is a natural progression.

Exhibit 11 presents a sample of sovereign credit spreads over a 1-year period from July 1997 to July 1998. These spreads are measured against a comparable U.S. Treasury bond (in most cases, the 10-year bond). As can be seen from the exhibit, the credit spreads for emerging market debt increased dramatically over the 1-year period. In fact in some cases, the credit spread experienced a more than fourfold increase.

Exhibit 11: One Year Change in Emerging Market Credit Spreads
(In basis points to a referenced U.S. Treasury security)

Bond Issue	July 1, 1997 Spread	July 1, 1998 Spread
Indonesia 7.75% '06	118	782
Korean Development Bank 7.25% '06	84	526
Phillipines 8.75% '16	196	382
Hungary National Bank 5.75% '03	81	85
Poland 7.125% '04	72	142
Russia 10% '07	351	925
Argentina 11% '06	259	437
Brazil C	428	675
Columbia 7.625% '07	148	380
Mexico 9.875% '07	244	361
Venezuela 9.125% '07	250	478

[8] The IFCT bond had a relatively short life. It was issued in July 1997 and redeemed in January 1998. The coupon was increased from 7⅛% to 7⅝% in October 1997 and from 7⅝% to 7⅞% in November 1997 due to rating downgrades.

Using Exhibit 11, let's take the example of a credit spread put option on the Venezuela 9.125% 2007 bonds. Although Venezuela is far from the more extreme examples of emerging market credit deterioration (see, for instance, the change in the credit spread for Russia, Indonesia, or Korea), it does provide a good example of what an emerging market recession can do to credit spreads.

Venezuela receives significant foreign exchange revenues from the sale of oil. Venezuela is the third largest oil producing nation in OPEC; its economy is dependent upon the price of oil in world commodity markets. However, an economic slowdown throughout Asia in 1997 and 1998 coupled with an increase in global oil production led to a collapse of crude oil prices during this time period.[9] This, in turn, led to shrinking oil revenues for Venezuela and a declining credit rating.

When offered at par in 1997, the spread for these bonds was 250 basis points over a comparable U.S. Treasury bond. In March 1998, a brokerage house offered to sell a European credit put option on these bonds at a strike price to be calculated using a credit spread of 400 basis points over a comparable U.S. Treasury bond. The option tenor was 3 months and the price was 60 basis points of the notional amount being hedged. If the credit spread on the Venezuela bonds increased above 400 basis points, the option would be in the money and the bondholder could collect a cash payment from the broker-dealer. Mathematically, the value of the option at maturity can be described as:

$$P[V(t);K] = K - V(t) \tag{12}$$

where

K = the strike price determined by discounting the cash flows of the Venezuelan bond at a credit spread of 400 basis points over U.S. Treasuries

$V(t)$ = market price of the Venezuelan bonds at maturity determined at the current credit spread

---

[9] Crude oil prices declined from a price of about $21.00 per barrel in October 1997 to as low as $12.00 per barrel in June 1998.

Suppose this option was purchased on April 1, 1998 with a maturity date three months later on July 1, 1998. At that time of purchase, the credit spread for these bonds was 329 basis points. Assume that the notional value of the option was $10 million of face value Venezuelan bonds, and that on July 1 the value of the Venezuela bonds will be determined by taking the present value of the 9 remaining annual coupons of $912,500 plus the present value of the final $10 million balloon payment plus the current coupon due and payable of $912,500.

The strike price was set on April 1 using a credit spread of 400 basis points over a referenced U.S Treasury rate of 5.9%. At a discount rate of 9.9%, the strike price of the credit put option was $10,211,657 (the strike price is greater than the $10 million face value because on April 1, 1998, 75% of the first coupon payment of $912,500 had been amortized).

As Exhibit 11 indicates, three months later the credit spread had increased to 478 basis points, while the U.S Treasury market had remained relatively stable. Using the same reference Treasury rate of 5.9% and a credit spread of 478 basis points, the price of the Venezuelan bonds on July 1, 1998 was $10,040,673. At maturity the credit spread put option was in the money by $170,984. The cost of the option was 60 basis points, or $60,000, so that the net profit was $120,984.

As 1997 and 1998 demonstrated, the emerging market debt market is an uncertain and volatile place. Credit spreads can change dramatically in a very short period of time. Not only did the credit spread put option provide an economic gain, it also reduced uncertainty. If there had been a dramatic collapse of Venezuela's credit quality, the put option would have provided even more insurance. As it was, the option could have provided peace of mind for an emerging markets portfolio manager, as well as providing her with some additional portfolio income.

CONCLUSION

Credit options can come in all shapes, sizes, and flavors. The examples in this chapter demonstrated that credit options can be constructed on a credit spread referenced to another interest rate, or they may be constructed on an underlying asset. No matter what construction is applied, the common characteristic to each is that the payoff at maturity is dependent upon the underlying credit quality of the referenced asset or issuer.

Credit options can be used either to protect against deteriorating credit quality or to enhance income. The choice is up to portfolio managers: do they wish to hedge credit risk or target it? The key point is that before the advent of credit options, portfolio managers had neither a convenient nor efficient format by which they could identify, embrace, and control credit risk.

Chapter 3

Credit Swaps

INTRODUCTION

S waps are another essential building block in the derivatives universe. They typically arise from the asset side of the balance sheet, and are designed to change one or more attributes of the cash flows arising from an underlying asset. The most common form of a swap is an interest rate swap where one party agrees to exchange or swap the fixed payments received from an asset on its balance sheet for the floating payments from an asset on the counterparty's balance sheet.

As might be expected, swaps are customized transactions. Similar to credit options, they are privately negotiated trades where each party must depend on the performance of his counterparty. Swaps are usually documented under a standard set of forms published by the International Swap and Derivatives Association (ISDA). These forms will be discussed more fully in Chapter 7.

Credit swaps come in two flavors: credit default swaps and total return swaps. Credit default swaps are used to shift credit exposure to a credit protection seller. They have a similar economic effect to credit options discussed in Chapter 2. Total return credit swaps are a way to increase an investor's exposure to credit risk and the returns commensurate with that risk.

CREDIT DEFAULT SWAPS

A *credit default swap* is similar to a credit option in that its primary purpose is to hedge the credit exposure to a referenced asset or issuer. In this sense, credit default swaps operate much like a standby letter of credit. A credit default swap is the simplest form of credit risk transference among all credit derivatives.

Exhibit 1: Credit Default Swap with a Cash Payment Upon Default

There are two types of credit default swaps. In the first type, the swap buyer pays a fee in return for credit insurance. In the second type, the swap buyer gives up the returns to a credit risky asset in exchange for a fixed payment. We review both types of credit protection in the following examples.

Credit Default Swaps as Credit Insurance

In the first type of credit default swap, the credit protection buyer pays a fee to the credit protection seller in return for the right to receive a payment conditional upon the default of a referenced credit. The referenced credit can be a single asset, such as a commercial loan, or a basket of assets, such as a junk bond portfolio. The credit protection buyer continues to receive the total return on the referenced asset. However, should this total return be negative, i.e., the referenced basket of assets has declined in value (either through defaults or downgrades), the total return receiver will receive a payment from the credit protection seller. This type of swap is presented in Exhibit 1.

This type of swap may be properly classified as credit insurance, and the swap premium paid by the investor may be classified as an insurance premium. The dealer has literally "insured" the investor against any credit losses on the referenced asset.

Credit events for default protection can be defined to be a missed coupon payment, a bankruptcy, a debt rescheduling, a foreclosure, a downgrade, a credit event upon a merger, or any other credit event that the credit protection buyer chooses to hedge. By swapping premium payments for contingent credit event payments, swap participants can create synthetic loans or securities that separate credit risk from market risk.

Exhibit 2: Credit Default Swap for a Manufacturing Company

| CUSTOMER | ← Sale of Goods — Accounts Rec → | MANUFACTURER | ← Cash Payment if Default — Swap Premium → | BANK |

Because there are so many different types of credit events to protect against, credit default swaps are tailor-made for the credit protection buyer. The reference asset can be a high yield bond, a bank loan, an emerging market debt security or any other basket of assets. Additionally, the tenor, or length of time of the swap, can be set equal to the maturity of the referenced asset or be constructed for a shorter time period to match an investment horizon. Credit default swaps are usually cash settled, i.e., through a netting of payment obligations, but they can also be settled through physical delivery of the underlying instrument.

Furthermore, the cash payment by the credit protection seller in the event of default may be a predetermined fixed amount or it may be determined by the decline in value of the referenced asset. If it is the latter case, the amount of asset value deterioration is typically determined by a poll of several swap dealers. If no credit event has occurred by the maturity of the swap, both sides terminate the swap agreement and no further obligations are incurred.

Credit default swaps do not need to be limited to the investment world. Consider a manufacturer that depends on one customer (or a small "basket" of customers) for the majority of its revenues. By selling its manufacturing goods in return for an accounts receivable, the manufacturing company has extended credit to its customer. Therefore, the manufacturing firm can purchase the same type of credit protection to protect against the default of its large customer.

Exhibit 2 demonstrates this type of credit default swap. Note the similarity of this structure to that of the credit default swap presented in Exhibit 1. Instead of making an investment in a cash asset, the manufacturing firm has made an investment in its customer because by extending purchasing credit to its customer, the manufacturing firm has provided working capital to that customer.

The methods used to determine the amount of the payment obligated of the credit protection seller under the swap agreement can vary greatly. For instance, a credit default swap can specify at the contract date the exact amount of payment that will be made by the swap seller should the referenced credit party default. Conversely, the default swap can be structured so that the amount of the swap payment by the seller is determined after the default event. Under these circumstances, the amount payable by the swap seller is determined based upon the observed prices of similar debt obligations of the borrower in the bond market. Finally, the swap can be documented much like a credit put option where the amount to be paid by the credit protection seller is an established strike price less the current market value of the referenced asset.

Mechanically, the contractual documentation for a 1-period credit default swap will identify the referenced asset, its initial value (V_0), the time to maturity of the swap (T), and a referenced payment rate (R). The payment R may be a single bullet payment or can be a floating rate benchmarked to LIBOR. At maturity, if the value of the asset has declined, the credit protection buyer receives a payment of $V_0 - V_T$ from the credit protection seller and pays the referenced payment rate R. If the referenced asset has increased in value, the credit protection buyer receives the value $V_T - V_0$ from the underlying asset and pays R. In this simple one period example, the credit default swap acts very much like a credit put option described in Chapter 2. However, for multi-period transactions, there are two differences between a credit default swap and a put option.

First, the credit protection buyer can pay for the protection premium over several settlement dates, t_1 through time T, instead of paying an option premium up front. Second, the credit protection buyer can receive payments $V_{t_2} - V_{t_1}$ at intermediate settlement dates where $t_2 \leq T$ and $0 \leq t_1 < t_2$. Therefore, if the value of the referenced asset continues to deteriorate, the credit protection buyer may receive several payments. Alternatively, the swap terms can state that upon occurrence of a default event, a payment is made by the credit protection seller, and then the swap automatically terminates.

Credit Insurance for Emerging Markets

The considerable credit risk associated with emerging market debt makes it a fertile ground for credit insurance. Consider the following example with respect to Latin American debt.

In November 1997 a dealer offered to sell a credit default swap to managers of international bond funds. The swap terms contained both a referenced issuer, the Republic of Argentina, and a referenced security, Argentina Global 10.95% bond due 11/1/99. The swap contained a referenced issuer so as to objectively determine an event of default, while the referenced security was used to measure the lost value in the event of a default.

In this swap, default could occur several ways. These included:

1. any event which would constitute a Cross Default under ISDA terminology. (While we will discuss swap contractual terminology in more detail in Chapter 7, for now consider a Cross Default event as a default by the Argentina government on any of its outstanding debt obligations.)
2. if the Argentina government declared bankruptcy on all of its debt obligations.
3. any waiver, deferral, rescheduling or other adjustment on any specified indebtedness (e.g., any outstanding government bonds, bank loans or other obligations) which is on terms unfavorable to the relevant creditors.
4. if any specified indebtedness became the subject of a distressed exchange or was repudiated by the Argentina government.
5. any dissolution, insolvency, receivership, bankruptcy, or any other analogous events with respect the Republic of Argentina under any relevant laws.

In sum these provisions provided for a credit event if the Republic of Argentina defaulted, reorganized, or rescheduled any outstanding debt obligation, or if the Republic declared bankruptcy, or if, under local or international law, its creditors began insolvency proceedings. Generally, swap contracts attempt to include any type of credit event which could adversely affect the underlying issuer's credit standing in the financial markets.

The tenor of the swap was two years (set equal to the maturity of the referenced security), and the notional value of the swap was $10 million. The buyer of the default swap was required to pay 2.25% annually ($225,000) for the credit protection. In return, the seller of the credit swap promised to pay a default payment amount equal to:

notional amount $\times$ [100% – recovery rate of referenced security]

Therefore, the dealer/credit protection seller promised to pay the fund manager the full amount of the Argentina Global 10.95% bond less any recovery rate. The recovery rate on a referenced asset is simply the amount of face value (expressed in percentage terms) that a bondholder could recover on the asset if the bondholder sold the asset in the open market. For instance, if a credit event did occur and a bondholder of the Global 10.95% bond could sell it in the market for 70 cents on the dollar, the recovery rate would be 70%. The dealer would then pay the mutual fund manager the

notional amount $\times$ [100% – 70%] = $3,000,000

Under the terms of the swap, the recovery rate for the referenced security was determined by taking the post-default market value (exclusive of any accrued but unpaid interest), expressed as a percentage. The post-default market value was to be determined by taking the arithmetic mean of the bid prices from three dealers for the referenced security divided by its face value. The solicitation of outside bids from other dealers is a standard ISDA contractual technique to ensure an objective market price.

Note that this type of credit swap did not protect a fund manager from a general deterioration in the credit rating of the Republic of Argentina. As long as Argentina continued to pay its required interest payments as they became due, did not restructure any of its outstanding debts, and did not repudiate any of its outstanding obligations, no credit event would occur. However, the credit protection buyer would still be required to make two annual payments of $225,000.

Credit Default Swap as an Exchange of Payments

Instead of contracting to receive a payment upon default, the credit protection buyer can pay the total return on a referenced asset to the credit protection seller in return for receiving a floating payment. The credit protection buyer keeps the referenced asset on its balance sheet but receives a known payment on the scheduled payment dates for the referenced asset. In return, it pays to the credit protection seller on each cash flow date the total return from the referenced asset. This credit default swap is presented in Exhibit 3.

Note that the credit protection buyer is obligated to pay the total return to the credit protection seller, whether this amount is positive or negative. But how does the credit protection buyer pay a negative return if the referenced asset declines in value? The answer is that she doesn't.

If the total return is negative, then the credit protection buyer receives a payment from the credit protection seller equal to the amount of the negative return earned on the referenced asset. This amount is in addition to the floating payment that the credit protection seller must pay under the swap agreement. Therefore, not only is the investor reimbursed for her lost asset value, but she also receives a swap premium on top of it. Considered in this light, it is easy to see the popularity of these instruments.

Default swaps usually contain a minimum threshold or materiality clause requiring that the decline in the referenced credit be significant and confirmed by an objective source.[1] This can be as simple as a credit downgrade by a nationally recognized statistical rating organization or a percentage decline in market value of the asset. Additionally, the payment by the credit protection seller can be set to incorporate a recovery rate on the referenced asset. This value may be determined by the market price of the defaulted asset several months after the actual default.

Large banks are the natural dealers for credit default swaps because it is consistent with their letter of credit business. On the one hand, banks may sell credit default swaps as a natural extension of their credit protection business. Alternatively, a bank may use a credit default swap to hedge its exposure to a referenced creditor who is a customer of the bank. In this way the bank can limit its exposure to the client without physically transferring the client's loans off its balance sheet. Therefore, the bank can protect its exposure without disturbing its relationship with its client.

Exhibit 3: Credit Default Swap with a Periodic Payment

[1] These contractual details will be discussed more thoroughly in Chapter 7.

Exhibit 4: Bilateral Credit Default Swap

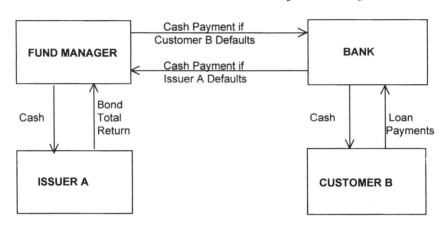

A variation on the exchange of payments is an exchange of credit risk. In other words, credit default swaps do not need to be unilateral, they can also be bilateral; the parties to the swap can agree to exchange default protection. An investor can swap the default risk of one referenced asset or credit for the default risk of another asset or credit. Consider a fund manager who has an overexposure to the junk bonds of Issuer A, while a bank has reached its credit limits with respect to Customer B. The fund manager and the bank can agree to swap the default risk of Issuer A for Customer B. From the fund manager's perspective, she gets a more diversified portfolio credit exposure. Conversely, the bank manager will free up credit lending potential for Customer B. The bank can now acquire more of the debt of Customer B, keeping its client relationship intact. At the same time, both the fund manager and the bank receive credit protection for part of their investment portfolio. This mutual exchange of default risk is demonstrated in Exhibit 4.

Another advantage of this bilateral credit default swap is that no cash flows are required to be exchanged unless a default occurs. Therefore, if the fund manager likes the credit profile of Customer B but is less sanguine about Issuer A, it is her expectation that she will not make any payments under the swap agreement. From her perspective, she gets his credit protection without cost.

TOTAL RETURN CREDIT SWAP

A *total return credit swap* is different from a credit default swap in that the latter is used to hedge a credit exposure while the former is used to increase credit exposure. A total return credit swap transfers all of the economic exposure of a reference asset or a referenced basket of assets to the credit swap purchaser. As the examples below demonstrate, total return credit swaps allow the investor to pinpoint the exact type and amount of credit exposure she wishes to receive.

The General Framework

A total return credit swap includes all cash flows that flow from the referenced assets as well as the capital appreciation or depreciation of those assets. In return for receiving this exposure to an underlying asset, the credit swap purchaser pays a floating rate plus any depreciation of the referenced asset to the credit swap seller.

The underlying asset basket may be composed of any type of referenced credit to which the total return receiver wishes to become exposed. This may include loan participation interests, junk bonds, accounts receivables, or other high-yielding debt. It is usually the case that the total return receiver chooses the exact credit risks to be incorporated into the referenced asset basket.

If the total return payer owns the underlying referenced assets, it has transferred its economic exposure to the total return receiver. Effectively then, the total return payer has a neutral position which typically will earn LIBOR plus a spread. However, the total return payer has only transferred the economic exposure to the total return receiver; it has not transferred the actual assets. The total return payer must continue to fund the underlying assets at its marginal cost of borrowing or at the opportunity cost of investing elsewhere the capital tied up by the referenced assets.

The total return payer may not initially own the referenced assets before the swap is transacted. Instead, after the swap is negotiated, the total return payer will purchase the referenced assets to hedge its obligations to pay the total return to the total return receiver. In order to purchase the referenced assets, the total return payer must borrow capital. This borrowing cost is factored into the floating rate that the total return receiver must pay to the swap seller. Exhibit 5 diagrams how a total return credit swap works.

In Exhibit 5 the dealer raises cash from the capital markets at a funding cost of straight LIBOR. The cash that flows into the dealer from the capital markets flows right out again to purchase the referenced asset. The asset provides both interest income and capital gain or loss depending on its price fluctuation. This total return is passed through in its entirety to the investor according to the terms of the swap. The investor, in turn, pays the dealer LIBOR plus a spread to fulfill its obligations under the swap.

From the dealer's perspective, all of the cash flows in Exhibit 5 net out to the spread over LIBOR that the dealer receives from the investor. Therefore, the dealer's profit is the spread times the notional value of the credit swap. Furthermore, the dealer is perfectly hedged. It has no risk position except for the counterparty risk of the investor. Effectively, the dealer receives a spread on a riskless position.

In fact, if the dealer already owns the referenced asset on its balance sheet, the total return swap may be viewed as a form of credit protection that offers more risk reduction than a default swap. To see this, consider the example of the default swap discussed above. This instrument has only one purpose: to protect the investor against default risk. If the underlying issuer defaults, the default swap provides a payment. However, if the underlying asset declines in value but no default occurs, the credit protection buyer receives no payment. In contrast, under a total return credit swap, the dealer's assets are protected from declines in value. In effect, the investor acts as a "first loss" position for the dealer because any decline in value of the referenced assets must be reimbursed by the investor.

Exhibit 5: Total Return Credit Swaps

The investor, on the other hand, receives the total return on a desired asset in a convenient format. Furthermore, the investor does not have to worry about financing costs or balance sheet disclosure. Lastly, the investor can take advantage of the dealer's "best execution" in acquiring the underlying asset.

Total Return Swaps in the Bank Loan Market

To provide a specific example of Exhibit 5, let's consider the details of a 3-year swap on a term bank loan.[2] A large AA insurance company recently purchased a 3-year total return swap on a $10 million piece of Riverwood International's Term Loan B. Term Loan B was actually a tranche of size $250 million, but the insurance company only wanted credit exposure to a portion of the term loan.

This demonstrates one of the advantages of a credit swap: customization. An investor may like the credit risk of a particular bank loan tranche, but may not have sufficient appetite for the whole loan. A total return credit swap allows the investor to choose a big or small piece of credit exposure depending on her appetite for the credit risk. Furthermore, the term loan had a maturity in 10 years while the holding period horizon of the insurance company was three years. Therefore, the credit swap can accommodate the insurance company's investment horizon while the term loan does not.

The seller of the swap was a large institutional bank. In order for the insurance company to purchase the credit swap, the bank effectively loaned the insurance company the $10 million notional amount of the swap. The bank in fact did not disburse $10 million to the insurance company, but instead charged the insurance company interest on $10 million dollars as if the bank had loaned the full amount. In this transaction, the bank charged the insurance company LIBOR + 75 basis points. Since the insurance company's normal borrowing rate was 12.5 basis points over LIBOR, the bank effectively charged the insurance company a swap processing fee of 62.5 basis points, equivalent to $62,500 on an annual basis.

---

[2] This example is an expanded discussion of a bank loan swap presented by Keith Barnish, Steve Miller, and Michael Rushmore, "The New Leveraged Loan Syndication Market," *The Journal of Applied Corporate Finance* (Spring 1997), pp. 79-88.

In addition to the annual fee, the insurance company was required to put up $1 million of collateral as security for the effective loan. This $1 million was invested in U.S. Treasury securities.

In return for paying this fee, the insurance company received the total return on the Riverwood International term loan. The total return included the floating interest on the term loan of LIBOR + 300 basis points plus any gain or loss in market value of the loan. In sum, the bank passed through the swap to the insurance company all of the interest payments and price risk as if the insurance company had the term loan on the asset side of its balance sheet.

The benefit to the insurance company was the net interest income earned on the swap. The insurance company agreed to pay LIBOR + 75 basis points to the bank in return for LIBOR + 300 received from the Riverwood International term loan. The annual net interest income from the credit swap paid to the insurance company was:

$$\$10,000,000 \times [(\text{LIBOR} + 300 \text{ bp}) - (\text{LIBOR} + 75 \text{ bp})]$$
$$= \$10,000,000 \times 2.25\% = \$225,000$$

Provided that Riverwood International did not default on any portion of the term loan, the insurance company also received the interest income on the Treasury securities.

Why would the bank want to enter into this transaction? Perhaps, the bank bit off more than it wanted to chew when it purchased the full tranche from Riverwood International. The total return credit swap with the insurance company allowed the bank to reduce its credit exposure and collect a fee. In effect, the bank got paid to reduce its credit risk.

And what about the insurance company? Was this a good deal for it? The answer is yes if we consider the alternative to the credit swap. Assume, that instead of the credit swap, the insurance company could have purchased a $10 million portion of the Riverwood International term loan at its normal financing cost of LIBOR + 12.5 basis points, held the term loan on its balance sheet for three years, and then sold it at the end of its holding period. The question we need to answer is which alternative provided a greater return: the total return credit swap, or the outright purchase of the term loan?

Exhibit 6 details the holding period returns to the two alternatives. In the first case, the insurance company borrows $1 million at its normal financing rate to purchase the Treasury security collateral and receives three annual net payments of $225,000 from the bank as well as interest income on the Treasury securities. Additionally, in year 3, the insurance company receives back the $1 million of collateral. These cash flows are discounted at the insurance company's cost of capital of 3-year LIBOR + 12.5 basis points.

In the second case, the insurance company receives the full payment of LIBOR + 300 on the term loan, but must finance the full $10 million for three years. It receives an annual cash flow of $950,000, and sells its investment at the end of three years for $10 million.

Exhibit 6: Investment Returns for a Total Return Bank Loan Credit Swap

Assumptions

Asset	$10,000,000 Bank Term Loan
Maturity	Three years
1 Year LIBOR	5.78125% (constant)
3 Year Treasury	6.00%
Discount Rate	5.90625%

Term Loan value remains constant

	Investment Alternatives	
	Credit Swap	Purchase Term Loan
Initial Investment	($1,000,000)	($10,000,000)
Annual Cash Flows (loan value remains constant)		
Year 1	$285,000	$950,000
Year 2	285,000	950,000
Year 3	1,285,000	10,950,000
Present Value of annual cash flows	$1,604,983	$10,961,833
Net Present Value	$604,983	$961,833
IRR	29%	9%
Initial Investment	($1,000,000)	($10,000,000)
Annual Cash Flows (loan value declines by $1,000,000)		
Year 1	$285,000	$950,000
Year 2	285,000	950,000
Year 3	285,000	9,950,000
Present Value of annual cash flows	$763,132	$10,120,431
Net Present Value	($236,868)	$120,431
IRR	–7%	6%

To keep the analysis simple, assume that the insurance company bought a 3-year U.S. Treasury note as collateral with a maturity equal to the tenor of the swap and with an annual coupon of 6.00%, that 1-year LIBOR remains constant at 5.78125%, and that there is no change in value of the Riverwood International term loan. The discount rate for present value purposes is 5.90625% (LIBOR + 12.5 basis points).

Under the credit swap, the insurance company will receive each year a cash flow of $225,000 from the bank and $60,000 from the Treasury note. In addition, in year 3, the insurance company will receive back its $1 million collateral contribution. Under the outright purchase of the term loan, the insurance company will receive each year a cash flow of $950,000. At the end of three years the insurance company sells the term loan in the market for its original investment of $10 million. Exhibit 6 details these assumptions as well as a comparison of the cash flows for each alternative.

As can be seen from the exhibit, the outright purchase of the term loan results in a higher net present value than the credit swap. The net present value for the term loan is $961,833 and for the credit swap it is $604,983, a difference of $356,850. However, the credit swap requires a much smaller capital requirement than the outright purchase of the term loan. Even though the credit swap results in lower total cash flows, it provides an internal rate of return (IRR) which is three times greater than that of the term loan purchase.

This example demonstrates the use of leverage in a swap. The smaller capital commitment of the credit swap allows the insurance company to earn a higher rate of return on its investment than the outright purchase of the term loan. In fact, the leverage implicit in the swap is 10:1. Economically, the credit swap is more efficient because it allows the insurance company to access the returns of the bank loan market with a smaller required investment.

However, what if the value of the term loan had declined at the end of three years? Assume that over the 3-year holding period, the value of the Riverwood International bank loan declined in value to $9 million. Under the credit swap investment, the $1 million loss in value would wipe out the posted collateral value. At the end of year three, the insurance company would receive only the cash flow from the interest income, $225,000 from the swap, and $60,000 in interest from the posted collateral.

Under the purchase scenario, the insurance company would receive back $9 million of its committed capital. Additionally, in each year the insurance company would receive the $950,000 interest income from the term loan. Exhibit 6 also compares the two investment choices under the assumption of a $1 million decline in loan value.

Under the total return credit swap, the net present value of the investment is now a negative $236,868. Conversely, a decline in loan value of $1 million still leaves the purchase scenario with a positive net present value of $120,431. Comparing the IRR on the two investments, we now see that the credit swap yields a negative IRR of −7%, while the purchase of the term loan yields a positive IRR of 6% — slightly more than the insurance company's cost of borrowed funds. Exhibit 6 demonstrates that the embedded leverage in the credit swap can be a double-edged sword. It can lead to large returns on capital, but can also result in rapid losses.

Total Return Swaps in the High Yield Bond Market

Total return credit swaps need not be limited to bank loans. For example, consider an investor who believes that the fortunes of Company A (currently rated BB) will improve over the next year, and that the company's credit spread relative to U.S. Treasury securities will decline. The investor can express the view that the corporate credit spread for Company A will tighten over the next year by paying a rate equal to the 1-year Treasury note plus 30 basis points and receiving the total return on Company A's high yield bond.

In Exhibit 7, the investor receives the coupon on Company A's high yield bond plus any price appreciation or depreciation on the asset. In return, the investor must pay to the dealer the 1-year Treasury rate plus 30 basis points. Assume that at the time of the swap, Company A has issued a high yield bond at par with a 5-year maturity, and a credit spread of 300 basis points over the 5-year Treasury note. The current 5-year Treasury rate is 6.25% and the 1-year Treasury rate is 5.7%.

Exhibit 7: Total Return Credit Swap on a High Yield Bond

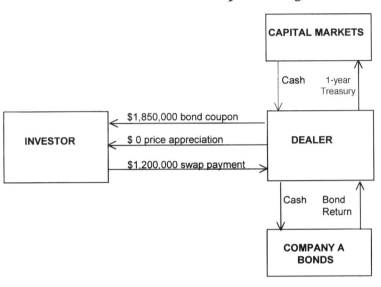

In one year, the swap will mature. The investor will receive an annual coupon of 9.25%, will pay a swap rate of 6% to the dealer, and will receive any price appreciation or depreciation on Company A's junk bonds. Assume that the notional value of the swap is $20 million and that after one year the credit spread on Company A's bonds has in fact decreased to 275 basis points, but that the Treasury yield curve has shifted upward and the 4-year Treasury rate has increased to 6.5%.

At the maturity of the swap, the investor will pay $1,200,000 to the dealer (6% × $20 million) and will receive a coupon payment of $1,850,000. What about the price appreciation of the junk bond? Unfortunately, there is none. Even though the investor guessed right on the declining credit spread for Company A, a general rise in interest rates offset this credit gain. At the end of one year, the appropriate discount rate for the Company A's bond is 9.25% — exactly equal to the bond's stated coupon. Consequently the market value of the bond has not changed, it is still priced at par.

This subtle point highlights one of the disadvantages of a total return swap: the return to the investor is dependent on both credit risk (declining or increasing credit spreads) and market risk (declining or increasing market rates). Two types of market interest rate risk can affect the price of a fixed income asset.[3] *Credit independent market risk* is the risk that the general level of interest rates will change over the term of the swap. This type of risk has nothing to do with the credit deterioration of the underlying issuer or asset. *Credit dependent market interest rate risk* is the risk that the discount rate applied to the value of an asset will changed based on either perceived or actual default risk.

In the example above, the underlying asset was adversely affected by market interest rate risk, but positively rewarded for accepting credit dependent market interest rate risk. To remedy this problem, we remind the reader that swaps are custom-tailored transactions. The investor could negotiate to receive the coupon income on Company A's debt plus any change in value due to changes in the credit spread. Now the investor has expressed a view exclusively of credit risk; credit independent market risk does not affect the swap value.

In this case, in addition to the coupon income, the investor will receive the difference between the present value of Company A's bond at a current spread of 275 basis points and the present value of Company A's bond at a credit spread of 300 basis points. We already know from the discussion above, that at a credit spread of 275 basis points the bonds are worth their par value of $20 million. However, if we use a discount rate of 9.5% (6.5% 4-year U.S. Treasury rate plus 300 basis points), the market value of the bonds would be $19,839,776. The difference of $160,224 is the change in value due to declining credit spreads. Exhibit 8 presents these cash flows.

CONCLUSION

As demonstrated above, the market for credit swaps is as varied and flavorful as credit options. Credit swaps are privately negotiated contracts, and therefore, can be custom tailored to meet an investor's particular needs. The reference asset can be almost any bond, bank loan, or other fixed income asset. Furthermore, the tenor of the swap can

---

[3] For a more thorough discussion on this topic, see Christopher L. Culp and Andrea M.P. Neves, "Credit and Interest Rate Risk in the Business of Banking," *Derivatives Quarterly* (Summer 1998), pp. 19-35.

be set to match the maturity of the underlying asset, or it can be set for a shorter time horizon than that of the referenced asset. This flexibility is one of the hallmarks that makes swap contracts so popular.

Credit swaps may be used either as defensive investment tools to hedge or eliminate credit exposure, or as offensive weapons to embrace credit risk. As a defensive measure, credit default swaps provide an effective risk management tool. There may be tax, accounting or regulatory reasons why the outright sale of an asset is not an efficient manner for hedging credit risk. Credit default swaps can hedge credit risk without raising these other issues.

With respect to embracing credit risk, total return credit swaps may provide several benefits over purchasing the referenced assets themselves. First, the total return receiver does not have to finance the purchase of the referenced assets. Instead, it pays a fee to the total return payer in return for receiving the total return on the referenced assets. In effect, the total return receiver has rented the balance sheet of the total return payer: the referenced assets remain on the balance sheet of the total return payer, but the total return receiver receives the economic exposure to the referenced assets as if they were on its balance sheet.

Exhibit 8: Credit Spread Swap on a High Yield Bond

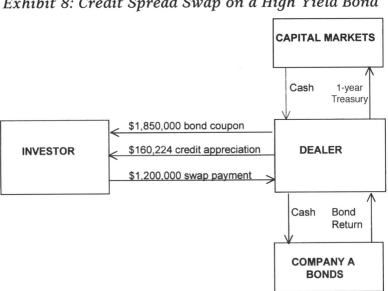

Second, the total return receiver can achieve the same economic exposure in one swap transaction that would otherwise take several cash market transactions to achieve. In this way a total return swap is much more efficient than the cash market. For example, if a total return receiver wanted to gain exposure to the commercial loan market, it could purchase loan participation interests through various loan syndications. However, it would take several syndication transactions to achieve the same economic exposure that a total return credit swap can offer in one transaction. Furthermore, a total return credit swap can offer a diversified basket of referenced assets.

Third, the total return receiver can take advantage of the natural expertise of the total return payer. Large money-center banks are natural dealers in the total return credit swaps. Their core business is the credit analysis of customers and the lending of money. To the extent the total return receiver is not as experienced in credit analysis as a large money-center bank, it can rely on the bank's expertise to choose appropriate credit risks for the underlying basket of referenced assets.

Fourth, a total return swap can incorporate leverage. Leverage is the ability to achieve a greater economic exposure than capital invested. Exhibit 6 demonstrated how an insurance company achieved a leverage factor of 10 to 1 in a bank loan credit swap. The ability to use leverage through a credit swap as compared to the outright purchase of the bank loan increased the internal rate of return on the investment from 9% to 29%. However, Exhibit 6 also demonstrates that the leverage embedded in a swap is a double-edged sword. On the one hand, it can significantly boost the return to invested capital. On the other hand, if the referenced asset declines in value, the losses can pile up quickly.

Chapter 4

Credit Forwards, Credit Linked Notes, and Other Credit Derivative Structures

INTRODUCTION

This chapter includes a collage of other credit derivative structures. While the creativity of financial engineers to design new structures should not be underestimated, these new structures tend to be built with the same essential building blocks that were discussed in Chapters 2 and 3.

Included in this chapter is a discussion of credit-linked notes which contain either an embedded credit option, a credit swap, or a combination of these derivatives. Since a credit linked note is a cash investment listed on the balance sheet, it may be more palatable to certain investors who either do not have the ability to enter swap transactions or do not like the off-balance sheet nature of swap agreements. Additionally, this chapter discusses special legal structures that are designed as passthrough vehicles for credit exposure. Again, these corporate structures may be more acceptable to certain investors who would otherwise shun the derivatives market.

We begin this chapter with a discussion of credit forwards. These instruments are similar in economic exposure to a one period credit swap. In fact, a several period credit swap may be viewed as a series on one period credit forwards incorporated under one credit swap agreement. Therefore, the type of credit exposure they provide should be familiar to the reader in light of the discussion of credit swaps in Chapter 3.

CREDIT FORWARDS

Credit forward contracts, like credit options and credit swaps, may be contracted either on asset values or on credit spreads. They can be used by corporations that wish to lock in their funding costs, or by portfolio managers who wish to purchase credit exposure. In particular, corporations can purchase credit forward contracts referenced to their own debt to hedge their cost of capital.

Consider the example of a corporate treasurer who, in June 1997, intends to seek a 5-year commercial loan within the next six months, but is concerned that over this time period his firm's credit rating may decline from BB to B. Macroeconomic events such as the turmoil that occurred in the worldwide financial markets in 1997-1998 could result in credit downgrades. Alternatively, the treasurer may expect poor future operating performance for his firm, which may increase the company's credit spread to that of a single B credit risk.

To hedge this risk, the treasurer can purchase a 6-month credit spread forward contract at the company's current commercial loan spread of 150 basis points. If the credit spread for the company's debt widens above 150 basis points, the treasurer will receive a positive payment. However, if the credit spread declines below 150 basis points, the treasurer must make a payment to the credit forward seller.

The payment amount at maturity of the credit forward is determined by the following equation:

$$[\text{credit spread at maturity} - \text{contracted credit spread}] \times \text{risk factor} \times \text{notional value} \tag{1}$$

where the credit spread at maturity is the observable market spread at maturity of the credit forward; the contracted credit spread is the spread established at the outset of the forward agreement; the risk factor of the referenced credit asset is determined as described in Chapter 2; and, the notional value is the dollar amount of economic exposure.

Assume that, in fact, the credit rating of the borrower declines to single B by December 1997 and its commercial loan rate rises to 300 basis points over LIBOR. Additionally, assume that the risk factor on the commercial loan is about 2.5 and the amount to be financed is $100 million. At maturity of the credit forward contract, the treasurer will receive:

$$[3\% - 1.5\%] \times 2.5 \times \$100,000,000 = \$3,750,000$$

However, if the credit spread declined to 50 basis points at maturity of the credit forward, the treasurer must pay:

$$[0.5\% - 1.5\%] \times 2.5 \times \$100,000,000 = -\$2,500,000$$

Exhibit 1 demonstrates the payout for a credit forward.

This example of credit forwards highlights an essential difference between all forward and option contracts. The purchaser of a forward contract receives the upside appreciation of the underlying asset, but also shares in its depreciation. In the example above, the treasurer is required to make a payment to the credit forward seller if the credit spread declines in value. In the unlikely event that the credit spread narrowed to zero, the maximum the treasurer would have to pay is $3,750,000.

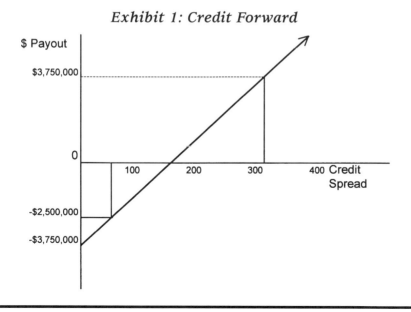

Exhibit 1: Credit Forward

In contrast, the credit spread options discussed in Chapter 2 allow the treasurer to profit from any increase in the credit spread while limiting her downside to the option premium paid. Therefore, there is a tradeoff between credit options and credit forwards. Credit options limit the treasurer's downside but only at the cost of an upfront option premium. Conversely, credit forwards require no upfront payment but do not limit the treasurer's downside.

How effective is this credit forward protection? Consider the commercial financing case of $100 million dollars over 5 years at a BB spread of 1.5% over LIBOR. If we assume 5-year LIBOR equals 6%, then the annual amortization payments for the commercial loan will be $24,716,417. Now suppose that by the time the corporate treasurer comes to the capital markets, her company's credit rating has declined to single B and the appropriate credit spread is 3% over LIBOR. The 5-year annual amortization payments of $24,716,417 discounted at 9% would equal $96,138,242. In other words, at a credit spread of 3% over LIBOR, and with 5 annual payments of $24,716,417, investors would be willing to lend only $96,138,242 to the corporate treasurer instead of $100 million. In sum, the treasurer would have a financing shortfall of $3,861,758. However, if the corporate treasure had purchased the credit forward at a credit spread price of 1.5%, she would have recovered $3,750,000 of the financing shortfall and effectively hedged her company's credit exposure.

In addition to hedging financing costs, credit forwards are a useful tool to forecast future default premiums. By constructing zero-coupon yield curves for commercial loans and Treasury securities and subtracting these curves to obtain their difference, it is possible to derive a zero-credit spread curve. From the zero credit curve it is then a simple matter to derive forward credit spreads.[1]

Deriving forward credit spreads has two important implications. First, these derived spreads represent the market's unbiased expectation regarding future credit spreads. Consequently, they reflect the credit market's best guess as to future default probabilities. Second, implied forward credit spreads can be compared to current market spreads for possible arbitrage opportunities. In fact,

---

[1] For a discussion of this process, see Charles Smithson and Hal Holappa, "Credit Derivatives," *Risk* (December 1995), pp. 38-39.

existing credit spreads should be priced close to the implied forward credit spreads to limit such arbitrage opportunities. A large discrepancy between implied and existing spreads would reflect a fundamental mispricing of credit risk, and offer an opportunity to profit from credit exposure. We provide a demonstration of this process in the appendix to this chapter.

CREDIT LINKED NOTES

Credit linked notes are hybrid instruments which combine the elements of a debt instrument with either an embedded credit option or credit swap. They are cash market instruments, but represent a synthetic high-yield bond, loan participation interest or credit investment. Credit linked notes may have a maturity of anywhere from three months to several years, with 1 to 3 years being the most likely term of credit exposure. These notes are often issued as 144A private securities. Like credit options, forwards and swaps, credit linked notes allow an investor to take a tailored view towards credit risk.

Credit linked notes may contain embedded options, embedded forward contracts, or both. Credit linked notes with embedded options can affect a credit view of the investor with respect to declining or improving credit spreads of an underlying borrower. For example, an investor may be willing to sell a put option on the commercial loan borrowing rate of a corporate debtor in return for a higher coupon payment on the credit linked note. Suppose that under normal market conditions, an investor might expect to receive a coupon of 7% on a "plain vanilla" medium term note. However, if the investor believes that the commercial lending rate for a referenced borrower is priced fairly, she can monetize this view by selling a binary put option against the lending rate and receiving the put premium in the form of a higher coupon paid on the note.

This is demonstrated in Exhibit 2 where the investor buys a note and simultaneously sells to the issuer of the note a binary put option on the credit rating of a chosen BBB borrower and receives 25 basis points of premium. The notional amount of the option is the same as the face value of the note ($10 million), and the binary payout is set at 100 basis points — the difference between the average BBB and BB commercial lending rates.[2] If the option expires out of the money, the option premium provides incremental coupon income up to 7.25%. However, if the credit rating on the referenced creditor declines to BB, then the short put will expire in the money and the note buyer will receive a lower coupon payment of 6%.

Credit linked notes with an embedded call option have the advantage of principal protection. At maturity of the note, the note-holder is promised at least a return of his principal, or face value, of the note with a chance for additional appreciation if the credit option matures in the money. Credit linked notes with embedded forwards, however, do not have the advantage of principal protection. Depending on the ending value of the embedded credit forward, the noteholder may receive more or less than the face value of the credit note. Credit notes linked to forward contracts, therefore, entail greater risk to the noteholder than credit notes linked to option contracts. The tradeoff for the greater risk is usually in the form of a higher coupon payment.

Exhibit 2: Credit Linked Note with a Short Binary Put Option

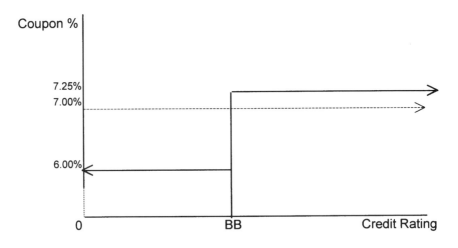

[2] This was the average difference between BBB and BB commercial lending rates over the time period 1988-1994. See Elliot Asarnow, "Corporate Loans as an Asset Class," *The Journal of Portfolio Management* (Summer 1996), pp. 92-103.

In practice, the cost of a credit linked note to the investor (in terms of lower coupon payments) can be quite high. Unlike the more common equity linked note, for example, where there is a large options and futures market for equity indices, there is no exchange traded market for credit options. Without a deep, liquid market for credit options, the issuer of the credit linked note may not be able to effectively hedge the credit exposure embedded in the note. The only way for the issuer to accurately hedge its short credit exposure is to buy the underlying asset at its financing cost. This financing cost, in turn, is passed on to the investor in terms of a lower coupon payment.

Just like total return swaps, credit linked notes may contain leverage which can enhance return, but only at the increased risk of loss of principal to the noteholders. For instance, a credit linked note with a leverage factor of 2 will increase in value by 2 basis points for every 1 basis point decline in value of the referenced credit spread. However, if the referenced credit spread increased by 1 basis point by the maturity of the note, the credit investor would receive back only 99.98 of its invested principal.

Credit linked notes can become quite complicated, combining both embedded options and embedded forwards. Consider the credit linked note in Exhibit 3. This note is short a call option on a referenced loan spread struck at 300 basis points, long a put option on the loan spread struck at 100 basis points, and long a credit spread forward contract priced at a current loan spread of 200 basis points. If the loan spread remains at 200 basis, the investor will receive the par value of the note at maturity. If the loan spread widens, the credit investor will receive at maturity a payment in excess of the par value. However, the appreciation of the note is capped at a loan spread of 300 basis points by the short credit call option. Conversely, if the loan spread narrows, the principal value of the note returned at maturity will decline. The depreciation of the note is stopped by the long credit put option struck at a loan spread of 100 basis points.

In Exhibit 3, the long protective credit put option can be financed by the sale of the credit call option. Some upside potential is sacrificed to pay for downside protection. Between the loan spread range of 100 and 300 basis points, the principal value of the note is allowed to fluctuate.

Exhibit 3: Credit Linked Note with an Embedded Forward, an Embedded Short Credit Call, and an Embedded Long Credit Put

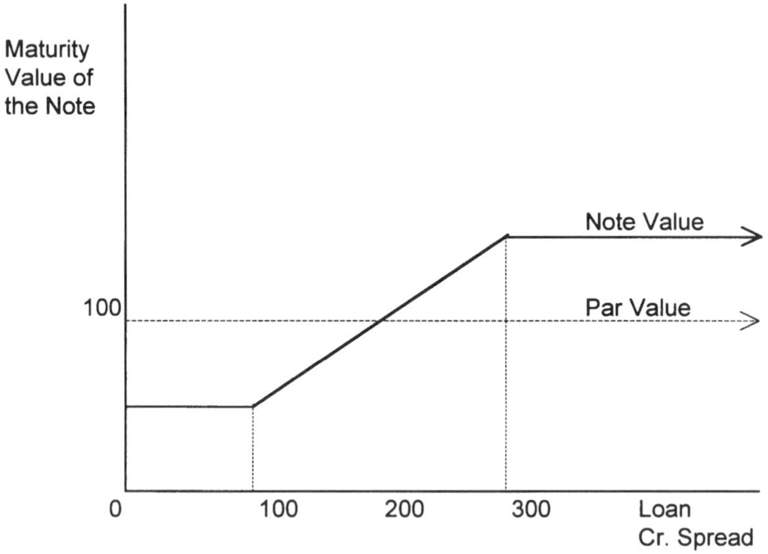

SPECIAL PURPOSE VEHICLES

Within the last three years, new credit derivatives have sprung up targeted at pension, mutual and endowment fund managers. These credit derivatives offer a conduit through which credit exposure may pass in the convenient form of a security.

There may be many reasons why a fund manager may be reluctant to enter into a swap agreement. First, swap contracts may not be an approved investment vehicle with the fund's directors. Second, fund managers as well as risk managers may be uncomfortable with the off balance sheet nature of swap agreements. Third, a mutual fund's prospectus may limit the fund's ability to invest in swap agreements. Lastly, there are disclosure and liability issues. A fund's prospectus may not have sufficient disclosure regarding the nature and amount of swap agreements that the fund may enter into, ripe material for investor lawsuits.

For these reasons, several Wall Street houses have developed what are known as *Special Purpose Vehicles* (SPVs). These SPVs are typically set up as trusts or special purpose corporations that issue securities to investors, the returns of which are tied to the credit characteristics of an underlying pool of junk bonds, bank loans, or emerging market debt securities. These structures are known by various names: Chase Manhattan's *Secured Loan Trust Notes*, Barclay de Zoette Wedd's *Asset-Linked Trust Securities* (ALTS), or J.P. Morgan & Co.'s *BISTRO* products. Each of these products works in the same fashion. They are designed to provide the efficiencies of financial engineering without the problematic issues of entering into a derivative transaction.

A special purpose vehicle, typically a trust, is set up for each transaction. Fund managers purchase a trust certificate that the trust records on its balance sheet as an outstanding debt obligation, and the manager records on its balance sheet as a privately issue 144A security.[3] The proceeds from the sale of the trust certificates are used to purchase U.S. Treasury notes, which the trust holds on the asset side of its balance sheet.

So far, so good. The investment fund has purchased a cash security, the trust has recorded an outstanding bond, and the trust has used the proceeds from its debt issuance to purchase Treasury notes. The interest earned on the Treasury notes is passed through to the investment fund as part of the coupon payments on the trust certificates.

Next, the trust enters into a total return swap with an outside dealer, the same dealer that established the trust in the first place. The dealer pools together a basket of credit risky assets such as bank loans and enters into a total return credit swap with the trust whereby the dealer will pay the total return on the basket of referenced loans to the trust, and the trust will pay to the dealer LIBOR plus a spread. The trust, in turn, passes through to its certificate holders the return on the basket of loans that it receives from the dealer.

Notice how this structure insulates the investment fund from the derivative transaction. The trust acts as a middleman or buffer

---

[3] These private securities are typically in the form of Securities and Exchange Commission (SEC) Rule 144A securities which are not required to be registered with the SEC, but which may be sold only to Qualified Institutional Buyers. See SEC Release No. 33-6862, CCH par. 84,523, April 30, 1990, amended in SEC Release No. 33-6963, CCH par. 85,052, effective October 28, 1992.

between the investment fund and the dealer so that the investment fund does not need to enter into a swap agreement. Let's put some numbers on a typical transaction.

Assume that the investment fund purchases $20 million of certificates from the trust.[4] The maturity of the certificates is in two years. The trust uses the $20 million to purchase a 2-year U.S. Treasury note yielding 6%. The trust also enters into a 2-year swap agreement with the dealer, whereby the dealer will pay to the trust the total return on a $100 million basket of bank loans.

Note that the notional value of the swap transaction does not have to equal the amount of trust certificates sold. Under the swap agreement, the trust agrees to pay the dealer LIBOR +100 basis points on a notional value of $100 million, while the dealer agrees to pay the trust the average interest income on the $100 million basket of bank loans of LIBOR + 250 plus any price appreciation or depreciation of the bank loans. Exhibit 4 demonstrates one of the clever facets of this structure: it allows the investment fund to receive leveraged returns even though its own investment in the trust is not leveraged.

Notice that for the dealer, all of the cash flows net out to a single annual fee of 100 basis points. The dealer receives a $100 million cash inflow from the capital markets, and uses this amount to purchase the basket of term loans. The dealer pays for this funding at straight LIBOR. From the term loans, the dealer receives LIBOR + 250 in coupon income plus any change in price of the loans (together, the coupon income and the price change equal the total return on the loans) which the dealer simultaneously agrees under the swap agreement to pass on to the trust. The trust agrees to pay the dealer LIBOR + 100 which covers the dealer's funding costs at LIBOR plus adds 100 basis points. All of these inflows and outflows cancel out and what is left is an annual inflow to the dealer of 100 basis points times the notional value of $100 million, or an annual cash flow of $1 million.

---

[4] In practice the trust will also sell a small portion of equity certificates to another investor such as a hedge fund, a high net worth individual, or an estate. The purpose of this equity sale is so that the trust's assets will be consolidated on the balance sheet of the equity investor and not the investment fund. Otherwise the investment fund would have to consolidate the trust's assets and contractual obligations on its balance sheet, including the total return credit swap.

Exhibit 4: Special Purpose Vehicle with a Leveraged Credit Swap

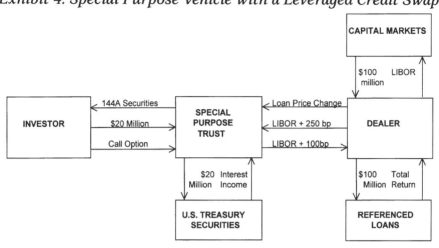

From the investment fund's perspective, it receives the return on all of the trust's assets and contractual obligations. This includes the net income on the swap of 150 basis points plus any increase or decrease in value of the bank loans plus the interest income earned on the collateral. Assume that over the term of the trust certificates and swap agreement, there is no change in value of the bank loans. Then what the investment fund earns is the 2-year Treasury rate plus 150 basis points on the notional value of $100 million.

This highlights the power of leverage in these special purpose vehicles. Remember that the investment fund only committed $20 million of capital but received 150 basis points of income on $100 million of bank loan exposure. This is economically equivalent to earning 750 basis points on $20 million. *Plus* the investor receives the income from the 2-year Treasury note. Therefore, what the investment fund earns on its investment in the SPV is a rate of return that is 7.5% greater than a comparable Treasury note. The ability to add 750 basis points of credit spread return in the investment fund's portfolio far exceeds the credit spread the fund could receive if it purchased the term loans outright from the issuer.

The $20 million of U.S. Treasuries serves as collateral for the trust's side of the swap. If the basket of referenced bank loans declines in value, this collateral will pay for the decline. For this reason, the trust's position is typically referred to as the "first loss position." This means that the first $20 million of loss on the basket of bank loans comes at the expense of the trust and the trust's certificate holders. If the bank loan basket declines by $20 million, the dealer gets to liquidate the Treasury note collateral and terminate the swap. The trust pays out any accrued interest earned on the collateral to the certificate holders (the fund) and the trust certificates are then rendered worthless. The remaining $80 million "second loss position" is retained by the dealer because it still owns the basket of bank loans.

This structure can be designed so that the investment fund can either let the dealer construct the pool of bank loans or it can choose the basket of bank loans to be referenced in the swap. Furthermore, if any one loan in the basket defaults, the investment fund may have the choice of having the dealer sell the loan in the open market for its recovery value, or purchasing the loan itself. This option allows the investment fund to purchase the defaulted loan if it believes that the market has underestimated the loan's recovery value.

One of the downsides of this type of transaction is that the documentation tends to be intense. To conduct a credit swap through a special purpose vehicle such as a trust, the following documentation will need to be negotiated:

- the trust document
- the master swap agreement and supplementary schedule
- swap confirmations
- a note indenture
- a private placement memorandum

Negotiating these documents is time consuming as well as legally intensive, and considerable expenses may be incurred by inside and outside legal counsel.

As a final example of how special purpose vehicles can be used in the credit derivative market, consider the example of a principal protected high yield note. In this example, investors purchase $50 million in trust certificates from a SPV which mature in four years. The SPV uses this money to buy a $40 million zero-coupon Treasury strip which compounds annually at 6% and matures in four years with a face value of $50 million. The Treasury strip provides the principal protection for the certificate holders if the certificates are held to maturity.

Exhibit 5: Special Purpose Vehicle for a Principal Protected High Yield Note

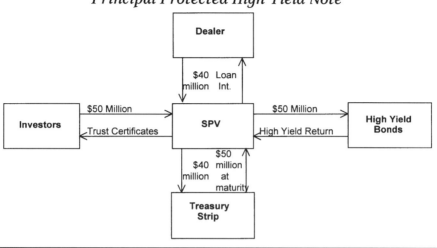

The SPV then borrows $40 million from a dealer or bank and combines this amount with the remaining $10 million received from the investors to purchase a pool of high yield bonds. The SPV then passes through to the investors the returns from the high yield bonds less interest expense from the borrowing and the fees to establish the SPV.

The result is that investors receive high yield returns but with an investment grade credit rating. The fact that the trust certificates are principal protected by the Treasury strip facilitates a favorable credit rating for the SPV. The SPV can afford to lose up to $10 million on its pool of high yield investments. Up to this point, the investors will receive at least their principal back. This structure is demonstrated in Exhibit 5.

COLLATERALIZED BOND AND LOAN OBLIGATIONS

Another recent development in the credit markets has been *collateralized bond obligations* (CBOs) and *collateralized loan obligations* (CLOs). Similar to the mortgage market, these securities are a form of bond or loan securitization. For a CBO, pools of high yield bonds are formed and securities are issued against the returns from the bond pool. In a similar fashion, banks form pools of commercial and industrial loans and issue securities against the loan pool.

Exhibit 6: Collateralized Loan Obligations

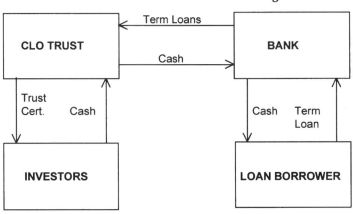

In each case, these pools are a convenient way for a bank to remove high yield bonds or highly leveraged loans from its balance sheet. Simultaneously, the bank can reduce its credit risk and free up credit limits for valued customers. Exhibit 6 shows how a simple CLO structure is formed.

CBOs first came into existence in the late 1980s, while CLOs did not make their appearance in the credit markets until the early 1990s. This market is small, but growing. Over $35 billion was estimated to be securitized through CBO and CLO programs in 1997.[5]

The security tranches issued on a CLO program are divided by credit rating. In the first tranche, debt with the highest priority is issued against the highest credit quality loans in the pool. This senior debt tends to have a lower return and volatility than that of the composite loan pool's return and volatility. Credit enhancements such as a letter of credit may be added to the senior tranche to give the CLO security an investment grade rating. The second or mezzanine tranche is usually securitized with the average loan in the pool. Here, the credit rating of the second tranche may not be any greater than that of the average loan in the pool, but this tranche still has the advantage of a diversified pool of loans and the seniority to the last CLO tranche. The final tranche, subordinated to the two other CLO tranches, is securitized with the

---

[5] See Omri Ben-Amos, "Collateralized Issuance Zooming to New Heights," *American Banker* (August 18, 1997).

lowest credit quality loans in the loan pool. For this tranche, the risk is the highest, but the loans securitizing it are also the highest yielding.

Exhibit 7 provides a more detailed example of a CLO trust. Consider a bank that has four term loans on its books. The credit ratings of the underlying issuers are B and BB. The term loans all have a 3-year maturity, an average coupon of 9%, a face value of $800 million, and a current market value of $750 million. The bank sells these loans to the trust for a fee of 40 basis points ($3 million). Additionally, the bank sells to the trust a $100 million 3-year U.S. Treasury note with an annual coupon of 6%. Lastly, the trust purchases a credit default option from an AA insurance company. The option covers the first to default $75 million of any of the four term loans.

The CLO trust then issues three tranches of collateralized securities. The first tranche has a $100 million face value, a coupon of 7.5%, and is rated AAA. This tranche gets the highest credit rating because it is principal protected. The 3-year Treasury note will mature at the same time that the Tranche 1 securities become due and payable, and the proceeds from the Treasury note will be used to pay the Tranche 1 investors. However, the Tranche 1 investors receive a higher coupon than U.S Treasuries because they have a claim on a portion of the passthrough income from the term loans.

Exhibit 7: Constructing a CLO Trust

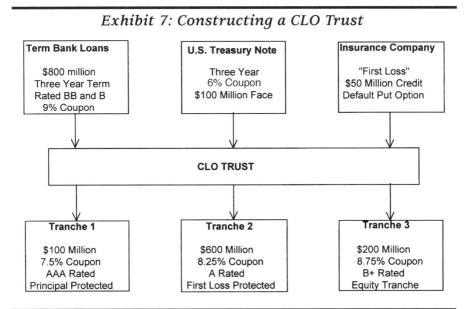

Exhibit 8: CLO Trust Annual Cash Flows

Inflows	
Income from bank loans, 9% on $800 million	$72,000,000
Income from Treasury note, 6% on $100 million	6,000,000
Total	$78,000,000
Outflows	
Coupon on Tranche 1, 7.5% on $100 million	$7,500,000
Coupon on Tranche 2, 8.25% on $600 million	49,500,000
Coupon on Tranche 3, 8.75% on $200 million	17,500,000
Total	$74,500,000
Net Annual Trust Income	$3,500,000

The second tranche has a face value of $600 million, a stated coupon of 8.25%, and is rated single A. This tranche has a higher rating than the underlying loans because it has first loss protection through the default put option purchased from the insurance company. However, the first loss protection only covers $75 million worth of loans. Therefore, this tranche does not have the same principal protection as Tranche 1, and consequently receives a lower credit rating.

The last tranche is the equity tranche. It does not get paid until Tranches 1 and 2 receive their payments. Consequently, this tranche bears all of the residual risk of the CLO trust, just as stockholders bear all of the residual risk in a corporation. This tranche has a face value of $200 million, a stated coupon of 8.75%, and is rated B+ (the average credit rating of the term loan pool).

Where does the trust get the money to pay for the bank's fee of $3 million or the credit default option? It receives the money from the spread. Note that the stated coupon on each tranche is less than the average interest coupon on the four term loans. The difference between the interest income earned on the term loans and that paid to the CLO security holders is spread income to the CLO trust. The trust uses this spread income to pay the bank fee and the insurance company for the credit default put option.

The excess income is demonstrated in Exhibit 8. Together, the Treasury note and the bank loans generate $78 million in annual income. The three CLO tranches, however, only require $74.5 million of annual cash outflows. The difference of $3.5 million is the residual income to the trust. Typically, the organizers of the trust are also the residual equity holders in Tranche 3. Therefore, this tranche receives the residual cash flows from the trust after deducting for the trust's expenses.

The underlying motivation for CLO structures is for a bank to diversify its risks by spreading them out in the capital markets. This is very similar to what banks do through a loan syndication. Instead of funding a term loan all by itself, a bank will sell pieces of it to other banks and financial institutions. The key difference with CLO securities is that they appeal to a broader range of investors than the concentrated bank loan market, and therefore, offer a bank an additional venue to market and sell credit risk.

CONCLUSION

Credit forwards are another basic tool for hedging and embracing credit exposure. The examples in this chapter demonstrate a key difference between a credit forward contract and a credit option. While credit forwards are rewarded for any upside appreciation, they also bear the risk if the trade turns against the buyer. This is in contrast to credit options discussed in Chapter 2 where the credit option buyer risks only the option premium. However, credit forward contracts appeal to many investors because, unlike credit options, they do not require an up front capital commitment.

As this chapter has demonstrated, financial engineers have been very creative in developing structures which allow investors and hedgers to isolate and trade credit risk. The newest generation of these structures is the special purpose vehicle that acts as an intermediary to consolidate, package, and distribute credit returns. The SPV is also a convenient format for those investors who may not be able to invest directly in the credit markets. Finally, SPVs can offer advantages not normally found in the high yield markets such as principal protection and leverage. In sum, the SPV is a flexible tool that can accommodate a wide spectrum of investment needs.

Lastly, collateralized loan and bond obligations are just another way to combine, package, and distribute credit risk to investors. The three main advantages to these structures are that they (1) can create a stream of returns from a pool of credit risks, thus offering convenient diversification, (2) can create different tranches of credit risk securities which allow investors to choose their favorite flavor, and (3) can transform less liquid investments, such as bank loans, into more liquid trust securities. Similar to SPVs, the flexibility of CBOs and CLOs caters to the demands of investors and the creativity of financial engineers.

APPENDIX: IMPLIED DEFAULT PROBABILITIES

In our discussion of credit forwards, we mentioned how implied default probabilities may be estimated from forward credit curves. In this appendix, we give a simple demonstration of how this can work. The distinguishing feature of every corporate bond, compared to U.S. Treasury securities, is default risk. The difference between yields on Treasury securities and corporate bonds may be thought of as the term structure of credit risk.

The credit spreads on corporate bonds relative to Treasury securities will vary with maturity. Litterman and Iben note that the term structure of credit risk generally reflects the fact that the financial markets imply a higher probability of default for corporate bonds each year into the future.[6] They suggest that the probability of default can be derived from the zero-coupon Treasury curve and the zero-coupon corporate curve. In other words, the forward credit spread curve must embody the market's forecast about future default probabilities. Litterman and Iben derive the following equation to determine the one-period probability of default:

$$\text{Probability[Default]} = 1 - \text{Probability [Solvency]} \qquad (1A)$$

where

$$\text{Probability[Solvency]} = \frac{\text{Price of a corporate zero bond}}{\text{Price of a Treasury zero bond}}$$

Corporate bonds contain credit risk. Therefore, the comparison of a corporate bond price to a Treasury bond price should reflect the market's estimate of default risk.

Smithson and Holappa expand this approach by considering recovery rates in the event of default.[7] Therefore, if an investor can estimate the magnitude of loss upon default, she can back out the implied forecasts of future default probabilities. In this format, the following equation is used to estimate the one-period probability of default:

---

[6] Robert Litterman and Thomas Iben, "Corporate Bond Valuation and the Term Structure of Credit Spreads," *Journal of Portfolio Management* (Spring 1991), pp. 52-64.
[7] See Smithson and Holappa, "Credit Derivatives."

$$1 - \text{Probability [Solvency]}$$
$$= \text{Probability [Default]} \times (1 - \text{Recovery rate}) \quad\quad (2A)$$
$$= 1 - \frac{\text{Price of a corporate zero bond}}{\text{Price of a Treasury zero bond}}$$

Once we have the zero-coupon curves and forward credit spread, we can extract either the forward probability of default or the expected recovery rate upon default. Since we have one equation and two unknowns, we must make an assumption about one of the unknown values and solve for the other.

Let's see how this works. Consider the BB issuer Niagra Mohawk Power Company that in July 1998 had the following term structure of interest rates:

Maturity	Bond	Market Yield	Zero-Coupon Yield
1 year	6.5% 99	6.49%	6.49%
2 years	7.0% 00	6.88%	6.90%
3 years	7.125% 01	7.01%	7.03%
4 years	7.25% 02	7.08%	7.10%

Similarly, for U.S Treasury securities, the yield curve in July 1998 was as follows:

Maturity	Bond	Market Yield	Zero-Coupon Yield
1 year	1 year Tbill	5.32%	5.32%
2 years	5.125 00	5.45%	5.453%
3 years	5.625 01	5.46%	5.463%
4 years	5.875 02	5.527%	5.535%

Zero-coupon yields can be derived by a method known as "bootstraping." To see how this works, note that the price of the 2-year Niagra Mohawk Power bond must be the same using the market yield as a discount rate and using the zero-coupon curve discount rates. For a 1-year period, the zero-coupon rate is just equal to the 1-year yield to maturity, or 6.49% (because there is only one cash flow left to discount, the final payment of $1,065 on the 1-year corporate bond).[8] However, for the 2-year corporate bond, we must solve the following equation to determine the 2-year zero-coupon corporate rate:

---

[8] For simplicity, we assume annual coupons.

$$\$70/1.0688 + \$1,070/(1.0688)^2$$
$$= \$70/1.0649 + \$1,070/(1 + x)^2 \qquad (3A)$$

The left side of equation (3A) is the standard market practice of discounting the remaining bond cash flows by the yield to maturity to derive the bond's current market price. The right side of equation (3A) discounts each cash flow not by a constant discount rate, but instead, by a zero-coupon discount rate which corresponds to the tenor or each cash flow. As mentioned above, we already know that the 1-year zero-coupon corporate rate is 6.49%. Therefore, for the equality in equation (3A) to hold, x must equal the 2-year zero-coupon corporate rate. Solving for x yields a rate of 6.90%.

In the same fashion we can derive zero-coupon rates for each tenor of Niagra Mohawk Power bonds as well as U.S. Treasury securities. These zero-coupon rates are presented in the tables above.

With these mechanics out of the way, we can now solve for implied future default probabilities. To solve equation (2A), we need the prices of zero-coupon corporate and Treasury bonds. These prices are easy to derive: they are just the inverse of the zero-coupon yields taken to the nth degree, where n equals the number of years to maturity.

Maturity	Zero Treasury Bond Price	Zero Corp. Bond Price
1	0.9490	0.9390
2	0.8990	0.8750
3	0.8525	0.8156
4	0.8060	0.7600

For Niagra Mohawk Power, we will assume a recovery rate of 50% upon default. We can now solve equation (2A) for the implied default probability for each year. For year 1, the solution is:

Probability [Default] $\times (1 - 0.5) = 1 - (0.939/0.949) = 0.0105$

Probability [Default] $= 0.0105/(1 - 0.5) = 0.021$

Therefore, the 1-year implied probability of default for Niagra Mohawk Power is 2.1%. We remind the reader that the actual probability of a default by Niagra Mohawk Power over the next year may be more or less than 2.1%. Furthermore, the investment manager may have a different estimate of the default probability over the 1-year horizon. Lastly, this implied default probability is dependent upon our assumption of the recovery rate for Niagra Mohawk bonds should a default occur. However, based upon our assumption of a 50% recovery rate and on the existing market term structure, this is our best forecast of default probability over the next year.

The Year 2 implied probability of default is a conditional probability. We must determine the implied probability of default in Year 2 given that Niagra Mohawk Power did not default in Year 1. This calculation is as follows:

$$\text{Conditional Probability[Default in Year 2]}$$
$$= \frac{1 - [(0.875/0.899) \times (0.949/0.939)]}{1 - 0.5} = 3.27\%$$

In a similar manner, we can calculate the conditional implied default probabilities for Year 3 (5.48%) and Year 4 (6.1%). The increasing default rates is consistent with the findings of Litterman and Iben that the term structure of default probabilities is generally upward sloping.

How can a manager implement a credit derivative trade with this information? Consider the binary credit default option discussed in Chapter 2. If the issuer defaults on its outstanding debt, the option holder receives a fixed payment. If there is no default, then the option holder receives no payment.

Expanding this binary option to our example, if Niagra Mohawk Power defaults, we assume a recovery of 50 cents on the dollar, or $500 for every $1,000 bond. If we consider the 2-year 7% bond, its market value is $1,002 and the expected loss in the event of default is $502. We also know that based on the zero-coupon credit curves (and our assumed recovery rate), the implied 1-year probability of default is 2.1%. Therefore, the expected cost of a 1-year binary default option on Niagra Mohawk Power bonds should be:

$$\text{Put[Default; Recovery Rate} = 50\%]$$
$$= \frac{[(0.021 \times \$502) + (0.979 \times \$0)]}{1 + 0.0532}$$
$$= \$10.00 \text{ per } \$1,000 \text{ bond}$$

The portfolio manager can compare this value to that quoted in the market. If the market price for a 1-year binary credit put option is priced above $10.00, she may decide to sell the option. Alternatively, if the default option is priced below $10.00, this would reflect good value for purchasing credit protection.

Chapter 5

Pricing Models for Credit Options

INTRODUCTION

C redit derivatives are relative newcomers to the derivatives markets. Given the youth of these instruments, price discovery remains one of the major issues associated with their use. In this chapter we review some of the current models for pricing credit derivatives. In some cases these models can become quite complicated, so parts of this chapter may be a bit more quantitative than the previous chapters. However, we will try to provide some intuition behind the mathematics of the models.

In general there are two types of credit option models. One model attempts to price credit options based on changes in firm value. These are the types of options discussed in Chapter 2 where the payoff to the credit option is dependent on the firm going into default or being downgraded. The second general type of credit model attempts to price credit options whose value is dependent upon changing credit spreads. The choice of the underlying economic model can lead to very different pricing functions.

We begin this chapter with a brief discussion on some of the basics of option pricing models. Next we discuss specific models developed to price credit derivatives. Lastly, we review some of the risks associated with using these pricing models.

A BRIEF REVIEW OF OPTION PRICING MECHANICS

Derivative instruments have become so ubiquitous in the financial markets, that we often forget their proper meaning: derivatives are instruments whose value is *derived* from the value of an underlying economic variable, such as a stock, bond, firm value or credit spread. Therefore, before we can begin to think about valuing a derivative instrument, we must first be able to describe the price movement of the underlying economic variable.

The price movement of an underlying economic variable can be thought of as a discrete process or a continuous process. In a discrete process, the underlying economic variable can only change in value at discrete points of time, e.g. once a day, week or month. However, in a continuous process, the economic variable can change in value at any time.

Fischer Black and Myron Scholes, in their seminal paper on option pricing published in 1973, first described a stochastic process for stock prices. In a discrete format the return to a stock investment may be described as:[1]

$$\Delta S/S = \mu \Delta t + \sigma \varepsilon \sqrt{\Delta t} \tag{1}$$

where

S = the stock price
ΔS = the change in stock price
μ = the expected return on the stock
σ = the stock price volatility
ε = a normally distributed random variable with a mean of 0, and a standard deviation of 1

In words, the return on a stock, $\Delta S/S$, is equal to its expected return over a time interval, $\mu \Delta t$, plus a random element represented by $\sigma \varepsilon \sqrt{\Delta t}$. The term $\sigma \varepsilon \sqrt{\Delta t}$ can be either positive or negative. Therefore, the actual return to the stock over time Δt can be more or less than its expected return, $\mu \Delta t$.

One of the nice properties of such a formulation is that the expected value of $\Delta S/S$ is equal to its expected return, $\mu \Delta t$, because the expected value of $\sigma \varepsilon \sqrt{\Delta t}$ is zero (the mean of ε is 0). However,

---

[1] See Fischer Black and Myron Scholes, "The Pricing of Options and Corporate Liabilities," *Journal of Political Economy* (May-June 1973), pp. 637-659.

at any given time, the random component $\sigma\varepsilon\sqrt{\Delta t}$ can add to or subtract from the expected return for the stock.[2]

In practice, the term $\varepsilon\sqrt{\Delta t}$ is expressed separately as Δz. This term is used to describe what is known as a Weiner process, or sometimes called Brownian motion. Under either name, its purpose is to describe random movements. The formulation for a Weiner process was originally developed to describe the random movement of small particles in physics. In economics and finance, Weiner processes are used to describe the random movements of economic variables such as stock prices, bond prices, or interest rates.

A Weiner process has some nice properties that lend themselves well to economics and finance. First, the expected value of Δz is 0. Therefore, over long periods of time, we would expect this random process to have no impact on stock returns because the random movements should cancel one another out. Second, its standard deviation is $\sqrt{\Delta t}$, and its variance is Δt. This a useful result because the variance of the stock in equation (1) over the time interval Δt is simply $\sigma^2 \Delta t$.

The purpose of this discussion on stochastic economic variables is to give the reader some idea how option pricing models are built. The models discussed below depend a great deal on the description of the underlying economic variable in terms similar to those presented above. More particularly, every option pricing model must begin with the specification of an underlying stochastic process.

Two other key concepts of derivatives pricing must be introduced. The first is "delta neutral hedging." The delta of a derivative security measures its change in value compared to the change in value of the underlying economic variable. This value is usually denoted by the Greek symbol Δ. For instance, the delta of a call option on a stock is measured by:

---

[2] The above formulation was presented in a discrete time format. If we assume that stocks can change at any given time, then the continuous time analog to equation (1) is:

$dS/S = \mu dt + \sigma dz$

where

dt is an infinitesimal change in time

dS is the change in the stock price over time interval dt

μ and σ are as defined above

$dz = \varepsilon\sqrt{dt}$

$$\Delta = \frac{\text{Change in call option price}}{\text{Change in stock price}} \quad (2)$$

where the change in the call option price is measured over very small changes in the stock price.

The reason why the concept of delta is so important is that it is possible to form riskless portfolios consisting of both the option and the stock. Such portfolios are referred to as "delta neutral" because no matter which way the stock price moves, the value of the options will change in such a way as to offset the change in stock value. In other words, options can be used as hedging tools to offset the change in value of a stock or some other asset value.

The use of options as hedging tools should not come as a surprise after the examples presented in Chapter 2, but the idea of forming riskless portfolios is new. To see how this works, assume that a call option on a stock has a delta with a value of 0.5. This means that for every $1.00 price move in the stock, the option will change in value by $0.50.

Consider a portfolio manager who forms a portfolio by purchasing one share of stock and selling two call options. Together, the two options will change in value by $1.00 ($0.50 × 2) for every $1.00 change in the stock price. However, because the portfolio manager sold the options, their value will move in the opposite direction of the stock price. Therefore, if the stock price increases by $1.00, the short option position will be worth minus $1.00, and vice versa.

Together, the short call options and the long stock form a portfolio whose overall Δ is zero:

$$\Delta \text{ of portfolio} = \frac{\text{Change in portfolio value}}{\text{Change in stock price}} \quad (3)$$

$$= \frac{\text{Change in options value} + \text{Change in stock value}}{\text{Change in stock price}}$$

$$= \frac{2 \times (-\$0.50) + 1 \times \$1.00}{\$1.00} = \frac{\$0.00}{\$1.00} = 0$$

This portfolio will not change in value if the stock price changes because the change in the stock price is exactly offset by the change in value of the two short call options. Therefore, this portfolio has a riskless or neutral position with respect to the underlying stock. No matter which way the stock price moves the two short options will offset it. This is what is meant by a "delta neutral" position.

As an aside, this is a good demonstration of why derivatives trading, and options trading in particular, is so popular. Using the example above, the portfolio manager sells call options to remove the stock risk from her fund. By selling the call options, the portfolio manager collects a fee. Therefore, the portfolio manager is *paid to reduce risk*. Considered in this light, it is easy to see the appeal of derivatives in portfolio management.

In practice, a portfolio will remain delta neutral only for a short period of time. Unfortunately, the delta of an option is not a static measure. Its value will change as the underlying stock price changes (which is why delta is measured only for very small changes in stock prices). Also the delta of an option will change with the passage of time.

Therefore, a delta neutral portfolio, once implemented, must be adjusted occasionally to maintain a riskless position. A portfolio manager who continually rebalances her portfolio to maintain a riskless/neutral position is said to be "dynamically hedging." Most of the "market neutral" hedge fund schemes use some form of dynamic hedging with cash securities and derivatives to maintain a riskless or neutral portfolio.

The last concept to be introduced with respect to derivative pricing models is risk neutral pricing. As we demonstrated above, it is possible to build a riskless/neutral portfolio using derivatives and the underlying economic asset. Since the hedged portfolio is neutral with respect to risk, we can argue that the return to such a portfolio should earn a risk neutral or risk-free rate of return over our holding period.

The ability to form riskless portfolios of stocks and options which earned a risk neutral rate of return allowed Black and Scholes to derive a mathematical (closed form) solution for options on stocks. Their solution did not involve any variables that were affected by an investor's risk preferences. Black and Scholes concluded that if risk preferences do not affect the pricing of the option, then any set of risk preferences may be used to solve for the value of the option. Specifically, the simplifying assumption that all investors are risk neutral may be used to determine the value of an option.

The importance of this conclusion is that in a risk neutral world, all assets, including stocks and options, must earn the same risk-free rate of return. The reason is that risk neutral investors are not concerned with risk, and therefore, do not need to be compensated for assuming it. The risk neutral value of a call option on a stock may be expressed as:

$$C(S, T, r) = \frac{1}{(1 + r)^T} E[\max\{S(T) - K, 0\}] \tag{4}$$

where

$C(S, T, r)$	= the value today of the call option that matures at time T
r	= the risk-free rate
T	= the time to the maturity of the option
$S(T)$	= the value of the stock at time T
$E[\max\{S(T) - K, 0\}]$	= the expectation of the option value at maturity

In words, at the maturity of the call option, the option holder expects to receive the greater of either the difference between the stock price and the strike price ($S(T) - K$), or 0. The term $E[\max\{S(T) - K, 0\}]$ is simply the mathematical expression to describe the expected value of the potential payout for the option at time T. Since this is the amount paid at time T in the future, it must be discounted back to the present by $1/(1 + r)^T$ to determine the value of the option today.

Although Black and Scholes developed risk neutral pricing for options on stocks, this principle is perfectly applicable for any derivative instrument that can hedge an underlying economic variable. Consequently, it may be applied to credit derivatives.

CREDIT OPTIONS ON DEBT SECURITIES

The value of high yield debt securities is dependent on the prospects of the underlying company. In fact, research has demonstrated that high yield debt securities are more sensitive to the value of the firm than they are to interest rates.[3] Therefore, any pricing model for options on credit risky debt must take into account the value of the underlying company.

This leads to the modeling of a credit put option on junk bonds as a *compound option*. A compound option is an option on an option. Although the pricing models for compound options can become quite complex, we provide a simple binomial example of how to determine the value of a compound credit option.

Credit Options as Compound Options on Firm Value

As discussed in Chapter 2, credit options may be constructed on the value of an outstanding bond issue. Recall that upon exercise of the credit option the payoff was determined by subtracting the market price of the bond from the strike price, where the strike price was determined by taking the present value of the bond's cash flows discounted at the risk-free rate plus the strike credit spread:

$$P[D(t); K] = \text{Max } [0, K - D(t)] \tag{5}$$

where

K	=	$F[\exp{-(r + \text{spread})(T - t)}]$
$D(t)$	=	the market value of a financial asset at time t, the maturity of the option
F	=	the face value of a zero-coupon debt instrument
r	=	the risk-free rate
spread	=	the specified (strike) credit spread over the riskless rate
T	=	the maturity of the bond
t	=	the time to maturity of the option
exp	=	the exponential power of e

In the simplest case presented above, there is only one cash flow associated with the bond (a zero-coupon bond). At maturity, the bond pays a face value, F, to the investor. However, equation (5) can be extended to coupon paying bonds. In this case the strike price is

---

[3] See B. Cornell and K. Green, "The Investment Performance of Low Grade Bond Funds," *Journal of Finance* (March 1991), pp. 29-48.

just the sum of the discounted cash flows associated with the bond where, for each cash flow, F is equal to the future payment. The future payment may be either the next coupon or the final maturity payment, and T is the payment date of the next cash flow. This is similar to the way we determined the strike price for bank loans in Chapter 2.

Within this framework, Das has derived a closed-form (mathematical) solution for credit put options on zero-coupon bonds based on firm value as the underlying stochastic process.[4] In his model, credit put options are dependent on the random movement of the value of the firm's assets and not that of interest rates. That is, the payoff to the option described by equation (5) is dependent upon the change in firm value. This is an interesting conclusion because no where in equation (5) is the value of the firm specified.

Das introduces firm value by noting that the value of a firm's outstanding debt may be thought of as the present value of risk-free debt minus a put option written on the firm's assets. Mathematically, this is expressed as:

$$D(t) = PV(F) - P(V, F, T, \sigma, r) \tag{6}$$

---

[4] See Sanjiv R. Das, "Credit Risk Derivatives," *The Journal of Derivatives* (Spring 1995), pp. 7-23. Das presents a closed form solution for credit put options of the form:

$P(V, \sigma, r, \text{spread}, T, t, F)$

$$= e^{-rt} \int_{-\infty}^{xV^*} (K - Ve^{(r - \sigma/2)t + x\sigma\sqrt{t}} + C(Ve^{(r - \sigma/2)t + x\sigma\sqrt{t}}, F, T - t, \sigma, r)\phi(x)dx$$

where
  V is the current value of the firm
  σ is the volatility of the returns on V
  r is the risk-free rate
  T is the maturity of the firm's debt
  t is the maturity of the option
  F is the face value of the outstanding debt
  K is the strike price for the credit put option
  V^* is the cutoff value of V above which the credit put option will not be exercised
  $x(V^*) = [\ln(V^*/V) - (r - \sigma^2/2)t] / \sigma\sqrt{t}$
  $\phi(\ )$ is the probability density function of the standard normal distribution
  C is the Black-Scholes call option value on firm value, V

We present a solution to the above equation in Appendix A that is consistent with the concept of a compound put option on a put option.

where

$$PV(F) \qquad\qquad = \text{ the present value of the firm's outstanding}$$
debt discounted at the risk-free rate

$$P(V, F, T, \sigma, r) = \text{ a put option written on the firm's assets with}$$
a strike price equal to the face value of the
outstanding debt, and a maturity of T

This may seem a bit confusing, but the debtholders of a firm may be viewed as simultaneously buying a riskless bond and selling a put option to the shareholders of the company.[5] If the firm approaches bankruptcy, the shareholders can vote to liquidate the company. This means that the shareholders can effectively "put" the company's assets back to the debtholders and walk away from the whole mess. The ability to walk away from a deal if it goes sour clearly has value, and this put value is subtracted from the value of a riskless bond (where default is not a potential outcome) to determine the value of a credit risky bond.[6]

As a result, a credit put option on credit risky debt may be thought of as a compound option on firm value. A compound option is a European option that, when exercised, gives the holder the right to purchase another option with a specified exercise price and maturity. Compound options may be written on the same asset or on a combination of assets.[7] In the example above, the credit put option is a compound option on a combination of assets — the credit risky bond and the underlying firm assets.

---

[5] See S. Esser, "High Yield Bond Analysis: The Equity Perspective," *Credit Analysis of Nontraditional Debt Securities*, Association of Investment Management and Research, 1995. This put option model derives from the original 1973 Black-Scholes paper that observed that corporate debt can be modeled by regarding equity as a call option on the assets of the firm. Default occurs when the firm's assets are no longer sufficient to make it rational for the firm's equity investors to provide the necessary funds to make the scheduled payment on the debt.

This analysis also follows from Merton who prices corporate debt within a contingent claims framework. See R.C. Merton, "On the Pricing of Corporate Debt: The Risk Structure of Interest Rates," *Journal of Finance* (1974), pp. 449-470.

[6] Much more will be made of this put option when we discuss credit risk management in Chapter 6.

[7] The solution for an option on a combination of equity assets is given by Robert Geske, "The Valuation of Compound Options," *Journal of Financial Economics* (1979), pp. 63-81. A compound option written on the same asset is usually known as a "split fee" option.

The nature of a compound option is easy to see if we substitute equation (6) into equation (5):

$$P[V; K, t] = \text{Max} [0, K - \{PV(F) - P(V, F, T, \sigma, r)\}] \qquad (7)$$

Equation (7) states that the payoff at maturity for a put option on credit risky debt (D) is equal to the strike price (K) minus the difference between the present value (discounted at the riskless rate) of the future bond payments (PV(F)) and a put option on the company's assets (P(V, F, T, σ, r)). Notice that in equation (7) the underlying economic variable of credit risky debt (D) has dropped out of the formula. It has been replaced by firm value (V).

Now that equation (7) identifies that the credit put option depends on firm value, a process must be formulated to describe the movement of this value. Das uses the following stochastic process to describe firm value:

$$\Delta V = (\alpha V - r_c F)\Delta t + \sigma V \Delta z \qquad (8)$$

where

ΔV = the change in firm value
α = $r - r_d$
r_d = the rate of continuous dividend payments
r_c = the rate of continuous coupon payments
r = the risk-free rate
F = the face value of firm debt
σ = the volatility of firm asset value
Δz = a standard Weiner process

This process indicates that over a time interval Δt, the value of the firm should increase by an amount equal to rV less the cost of dividends and coupon payments. Superimposed on this process is a random term represented by $\sigma V \Delta z$. The random term is used to introduce uncertainty into the model because if firm value could be determined with certainty, there would be no need for credit protection.

Note that the return to firm value in equation (8) is r, the risk-free rate. This term comes from our earlier discussion of risk neutral valuation. In the risk neutral world of options pricing, all assets earn the risk-free rate. The reason, once again, is that it is possible to form hedged portfolios using options and the underlying asset.

Since the credit put option can be combined with the credit risky debt to form a riskless portfolio, the concept of risk neutral pricing may be used to solve for the value of equation (7). The expected payoff may be expressed as:

$$P[V;K,t]$$
$$= \frac{1}{(1+r)^{\Delta t}} E\{\text{Max}[0, K - (PV(F) - P(V, F, T, \sigma, r))]\} \quad (9)$$

In Appendix A to this chapter, we take the aggressive reader through the mathematics of solving equation (9). Suffice for now to note that the option pricing solution to equation (9) requires a somewhat sophisticated knowledge of compound option pricing models. However, we can solve equation (9) using the general binomial pricing model first presented in Chapter 2.

A Binomial Approach for Valuing Compound Credit Options

The binomial option pricing model was first presented by John Cox, Stephen Ross, and Mark Rubinstein with respect to options on stocks.[8] In general, their model allows an asset to increase in value at a rate u with probability p, and to decrease at a rate d with probability $(1 - p)$. In general, the value of $u > 1$ and the value of $d < 1$. A condition that is typically imposed is that downward movements are the reciprocal of upward movements: $u = 1/d$.

If we review equation (9) above, we can see that the variables K and $PV(F)$ are constant in this equation. The only stochastic value to compute in equation (9) is the put option on firm value, $P(V, F, T, \sigma, r)$. Since this option is dependent on the movement of V, firm value, this is the variable that we must model through the binomial approach.

Under the binomial approach, over the period Δt, the value of the firm can either increase to uV with probability p, or decline to dV with probability $(1 - p)$. Therefore, the expected value of the

---

[8] See J. C. Cox, S. Ross and M. Rubinstein, "Option Pricing: A Simplified Approach," *Journal of Financial Economics* (October 1979), pp. 229-63. Their model was developed for non-dividend paying stocks which is consistent with our zero-coupon bond example.

firm in one period's time is $puV + (1 - p)dV$. The change in firm value over one period ($\Delta t = 1$) is demonstrated in Exhibit 1.

In our general discussion of option pricing above, we introduced the notion of risk neutral pricing. This principle states that the expected return from all traded securities is the risk-free rate, and that future cash flows can be valued by discounting at the risk-free rate. Therefore, over the time interval Δt, the value of the firm should increase to $Ve^{r\Delta t}$. This allows us to write the following equality:

$$Ve^{r\Delta t} = puV + (1 - p)dV \qquad (10)$$

Equation (10) states that the value of the firm in one period is equal to the probability of an upward move times uV plus the probability of a downward move times dV. This value is just the expected value of the firm in one period's time. Alternatively, we can state that the value of the firm today is equal to the discounted value of tomorrow's expected firm value:

$$V = e^{-r\Delta t} [puV + (1 - p)dV] \qquad (11)$$

The equality in equation (10) allows us to write:

$$e^{r\Delta t} = pu + (1 - p)d \qquad (12)$$

Exhibit 1: One-Period Change in Firm Value

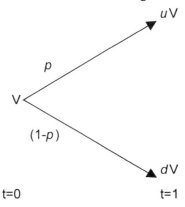

Expected Value of the Firm at t_1 = puV + $(1-p)d$V

Together, equations (10) and (12) and the condition that $u = 1/d$ allow us to solve for the values of p, u, and d. The solutions are:

$$p = (e^{r\Delta t} - d)/(u - d)$$

$$u = e^{\sigma\sqrt{\Delta t}}$$

$$d = e^{-\sigma\sqrt{\Delta t}}$$

where σ is the volatility of the firm's assets.

Let's put some numbers to this problem. Let V, the value of the firm equal $500, and F, the face value of outstanding debt, equal $300. The volatility of the firm's assets is 30%, the 1-year risk-free rate is 5%, and the 1-year risk-free rate one year from now is estimated at 6%. The strike price K is set to $300, the credit put option expires in one year, the debt matures in two years, and we use time intervals of 1 year ($\Delta t = 1$). Setting $\sigma = 0.30$ and $\Delta t = 1$, we get values of $u = 1.35$, $d = 0.74$, and $p = 0.51$.

In order to determine the value of the put option on firm value $P(V, F, T, \sigma, r)$, we must extend our binomial analysis to two periods because this option matures when the debt of the company matures, in two years. The first step is to construct a binomial tree of firm values going out two years. These values are shown in Exhibit 2.

From Exhibit 2, the value of the firm can take on three possible values at the end of two years, 911, 500, or 274. To obtain the value of the put option on firm value we must work backward in time through the tree. For example, starting with the end nodes at $t = 2$, only the node corresponding to d^2V (two downward movements of firm value) results in a positive value for the put option ($F - 274 = 26$). For the other two end nodes (udV and u^2V) the put option expires worthless because firm value exceeds the outstanding face value of debt ($F = 300$). This is demonstrated in Exhibit 3.

Working backwards in time, we next determine the value of the put option at time $t = 1$. At the node corresponding to $dV = 370$, the value of the put option is determined by:

$$\frac{0.51 \times 0 + 0.49 \times 26}{1.06} = \$12.01$$

Exhibit 2: Two-Period Binomial Tree for the Change in Firm Value

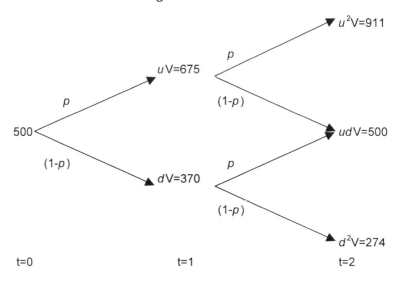

Exhibit 3: Binomial Valuation of a Put Option on Firm Value

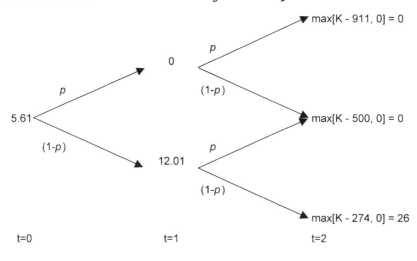

In other words, the value of the put at time $t = 1$ and corresponding to the node $dV = 370$ is equal to the expected value of the put at time $t = 2$ ($0.51 \times 0 + 0.49 \times 26$) discounted back to period one by the 1-year forward rate of 6%. Similarly, the value of the put at time $t = 1$ and corresponding to node $uV = 675$ is calculated as 0. Using the same procedure, we work backwards one more step to time $t = 0$, and find the value of the put option on firm value to be $5.61.

However, we need the value of this put option at time $t = 1$, the time when the credit put option on the firm's debt expires, not at time $t = 0$. How do we determine the expected value of this put option at time $t = 1$? Simple, we use the risk neutral principle of option pricing where all assets appreciate at the risk-free rate. Therefore, at time $t = 1$ the expected value of the put option on firm value is:

$$\$5.61 \times (1.05) = \$5.89$$

Now we have all of the pieces of the puzzle together to solve equation (9). The strike price K for the credit put option is 300, and the present value of the firm's outstanding debt at time $t = 1$ is $300/1.06 = 283$. From equation (9), the value of the credit put option at time $t = 0$ is:

$$P[V, K, t] = \frac{1}{1.05}[300 - 283 + 5.89] = \$21.80$$

At time $t = 0$ the value of the credit put option is equal to the expected value of the option at maturity ($300 - 283 + 5.89$) discounted back to the present ($1/1.05$). The value of the option is quite high because the strike price was set equal to the face value of the outstanding debt. The credit option strike was set at a high level to ensure no diminution in value from holding the credit risky debt securities. Although the cost of this credit option may seem expensive, its purpose is to prevent any loss from credit risk.

Implications and Extensions of Credit Options on Debt Securities

On a more general note, it can be observed that credit put options will be a decreasing function of firm value. As the value of the firm increases, the credit rating on the outstanding debt is also expected to increase and the value of the put option decreases. The idea that certain thresholds of firm value lead to higher credit ratings is a central concept of credit risk management discussed in the next chapter.

Credit put options, however, are increasing in the volatility of firm value for two reasons. First, as the volatility of the firm's assets increases, the value of outstanding bonds decreases because the source of cash flows necessary to repay the bonds has become less certain. This uncertainty increases the value of the put option. Second, an increase in volatility has the same value enhancing impact on the option pricing model as higher volatility has on the value of a put option on the firm's common stock.

Two potential issues may be raised with respect the credit option pricing presented in equations (5)-(9). The first is that this model assumes that interest rates are constant; only firm value is stochastic. In other words, the riskless rate, r, is assumed to remain fixed for the life of the option.

If the credit put option has a relatively short maturity, the simplifying assumption that interest rates are constant is not crucial to the valuation of the option. Furthermore, empirical evidence indicates that high yield investments such as junk bonds are less sensitive to interest rate changes than investment grade bonds, and are more sensitive to changes in firm value than investment grade bonds.[9] Nonetheless, for options with a long tenor, the assumption that interest rates remain constant may not be consistent with economic reality.

Equation (5) contains two components of risk: firm (credit) risk and interest rate risk associated with the random fluctuations of the risk-free rate. Initially, we assumed that the interest rate, r, was constant. Yet, to be completely effective, credit risk options need to be written on the credit risky portion of outstanding debt, separated from any effects attributed to the random fluctuation of interest rates. The only way to account for the fluctuation of the risk-free rate, r, in equation (5) is to also allow the strike price, K, to fluctuate.

Therefore, the incorporation of stochastic interest rates in equation (5) means that the strike price must also be stochastic. Simply put, as the general level of interest rates change, so must the strike price so that the option payout is dependent only on credit

---

[9] See Cornell and Green, "The Investment Performance of Low Grade Funds."

exposure. The tradeoff from stripping interest rate risk from the credit option strike price is complexity. The level of mathematical modeling required to add stochastic interest rates is extremely complex and we reserve this discussion for Appendix B to this chapter.

Because this type of credit put option contains both firm/credit risk and interest rate risk, sellers of this credit option must use two hedging instruments to eliminate the two sources of risk. One way to hedge this credit put option would be to buy a put option on the firm's stock and a risk-free bond which matches the duration of the junk bond upon which the credit put option is written. Hedging with stock put options and risk-free debt is consistent with the notion that credit risky debt may be considered as the difference between a risk-free bond and a put option written on the firm's assets.

A second limiting factor of the model discussed above is the assumption that firm value is an observable process. This means that the probability of default can be estimated with increasing confidence as the maturity of a bond draws near. As a result, default may not come as a random surprise. Default occurs only on a coupon date when the shareholders of the firm must decide whether to pay the debt liability or "put" the assets of the firm back to the bondholders. Presumably, by observing the stochastic process for firm value, the probability of default can be predicted with increasing precision as the time to coupon payment/maturity draws near.

However, Flesaker *et al* indicate that default may not be predicted with precision.[10] In fact, default comes as a surprise to investors. Consequently, bonds of all maturities will be subject to significant default risk.

In their model, they describe the possible default of a credit risky bond as a random process denoted Q_t that can take on only two values: 0 for the case of no default, and 1 for the case of default. At the time of purchase of the credit risky bond, $Q_0 = 0$. That is, the bond has not defaulted at the time of purchase.

During each time interval dt, the probability of Q_t changing from 0 to 1 is equal to λdt. The term λ may be considered the default rate for a particular bond or issuer, and λdt is the default probability over the

---

[10] See Bjorn Flesaker, Lane Hughston, Laurence Schreiber, and Lloyd Sprung, "Taking all the Credit," *Risk* (September 1994), pp. 104-108.

time interval *dt*. For instance, in Chapter 1 we noted that estimates of annual default rates for high yield bonds range from 3.17% to 6.25%. Therefore, if *dt* equals one year, λdt can range from 3.17% to 6.25%.

The fact that different studies on high yield bonds present different default rates, indicates that the default rate for credit risky bonds may not be constant. This is a key point of Flesaker *et al*, and they define the default rate λ as a stochastic process. The fact that λ is a random variable means that default will come as a surprise and cannot be predicted. Furthermore, as the time interval *dt* grows larger so does the probability of default, λdt. This makes sense because the longer the time period, the greater the opportunity for an issuer to default on a bond. Appendix C presents the basics of this model.

Instead of modeling default rates, Pierides suggests that a credit put option on a coupon-paying bond can be modeled as a barrier, or threshold, option.[11] That is, once the barrier is breached (in the case of a coupon-paying bond, default on a coupon payment date) the option will be immediately exercised. This type of barrier option is known as a "down-and-in" option. Down-and-in options become active only if a specified condition or barrier is crossed. This barrier condition is necessary because once a firm defaults on a bond, or goes bankrupt, the coupon dates and scheduled maturity may no longer apply and the payoffs to the option cannot be calculated. These circumstances require the credit put option to be a barrier option triggered by a default.

Barrier options, however, are path-dependent options — their value depends on the path taken of the underlying stochastic variable. There is no closed form (mathematical) solution. Instead, the path of the underlying stochastic variable (firm value) must be simulated many times to determine the payout of the credit option at maturity. Then the average of all of the simulated payouts must be calculated and discounted back to the present using risk neutral pricing.[12]

---

[11] See Yianos A. Pierides, "Valuation of Credit Risk Derivatives," Chapter 13 in Frank J. Fabozzi (ed.), *The Handbook of Fixed Income Options* (Chicago, IL: Probus Publishing, 1996), pp. 297-309.

[12] Path-dependent options are typically valued by Monte Carlo simulation. Monte Carlo simulation is appropriate for European-style derivatives; those that are exercisable only at maturity. For credit put options, the stochastic process of firm value as described in Das ("Credit Risk Derivatives") can be simulated to determine whether the option has attained the barrier at expiration.

OPTIONS ON A CREDIT SPREAD

Credit spread options were discussed in Chapter 2. As demonstrated there, these options are structured so that the option is in the money when the credit spread exceeds a specified (strike) spread level. Typically, the spread level is referenced to a benchmark interest rate such as U.S. Treasuries or LIBOR. Therefore, the stochastic variable that must be described with credit spread options is the underlying reference interest rate.

This section provides the theoretical background for pricing credit spread options. We also include an example of option pricing for credit spreads. Lastly, we discuss some of the practical applications of using these options in portfolio management.

Credit Spread Option Model

Recall from Chapter 2 that the payout at maturity to a call option on credit spread is:

$$C[S(T);K]$$
$$= \max[0, (S(T) - K) \times \text{Notional amount} \times \text{Risk factor}] \quad (13)$$

where $S(T)$ is the credit spread at maturity, K is the strike credit spread, and the notional amount and the risk factor are established at the outset of the option.

Longstaff and Schwartz examine an option pricing model for credit spreads.[13] First, they empirically examine credit spreads for a sample of investment grade bonds and find that credit spreads are mean reverting. In other words, credit spreads have a tendency over time to move back to some long-run average. If credit spreads are historically large, mean reversion predicts that these spreads will decline over time. Similarly, if credit spreads appear too low, they will revert upwards to the long-run mean.

The purpose of their empirical analysis is to demonstrate that credit spreads do not stay constant. In fact, they fluctuate just as interest rates do. Therefore, Longstaff and Schwartz propose that any option pricing model on credit spreads must take into account

---

[13] See Francis A. Longstaff and Eduardo S. Schwartz, "Valuing Credit Derivatives," *The Journal of Fixed Income* (June 1995), pp. 6-12.

the random movement of the reference interest rate as well as the credit spread itself. They provide two stochastic processes:

$$\Delta S = (a - bS)\Delta t + s\Delta Z_1 \qquad (14)$$

where

ΔS = the total change in natural logarithm of the credit spread

$a, b,$ and s = specified constants

ΔZ_1 = a standard Weiner process

This process indicates that the natural log of the credit spread (S) is pulled back to some long-run average at rate bS. Added to this mean reverting dynamic is a normally distributed stochastic term $s\Delta Z_1$.

Similarly for the reference interest rate, Longstaff and Schwartz define the following process:

$$\Delta r = (\alpha - \beta r)\Delta t + \sigma\Delta Z_2 \qquad (15)$$

where

Δr = the change in the reference interest rate

$\alpha, \beta,$ and σ = specified constants

ΔZ_2 = a second standard Weiner process which is correlated to ΔZ_1 with correlation coefficient ρ

Equations (14) and (15) look similar because they are based on the same type of mean reverting dynamics. In equation (15) the change in interest rates is pulled to its long-run average at rate βr. Superimposed on this process is the random element of $\sigma\Delta Z_2$. The credit spread and the reference interest rate are related through the random processes ΔZ_1 and ΔZ_2 with a correlation coefficient of ρ.

Using the risk neutral principles that we developed above, we can write the current value of the credit spread option at time of purchase as:

$$C[S(t);K] = \frac{1}{(1+r)^T} \times$$

$$E\{\max[0, (S(T) - K) \times \text{Notional amount} \times \text{Risk factor}]\} \qquad (16)$$

Recalling that in Longstaff and Schwartz' model $S(t)$ is the natural logarithm of the credit spread, then $\exp(S(t))$ equals the actual credit spread. With this conversion in mind, Longstaff and Schwartz find that the solution to equation (16) for a European option is:

$$C[S(t), r, T; K]$$
$$= 1/(1+r)^T [\exp(\mu + \eta^2/2) \times N(d1) - K \times N(d2)] \qquad (17)$$

where the natural logarithm of the credit spread, $S(T)$, is conditionally normally distributed with mean μ and variance η^2. The solutions for μ and η^2 are as follows:

$$\mu = \exp(-bT)S + 1/b[a - (\rho\sigma s/\beta)] \times [1 - \exp(-bT)]$$
$$+ (\rho\sigma s)/\beta(b + \beta) \times [1 - \exp(-(b + \beta) \times T)] \qquad (18)$$
$$\eta^2 = s^2 \times [1 - \exp(-2bT)]/2b \qquad (19)$$

Where all of the terms are as defined in equations (14) and (15). The function $N(d)$ is the cumulative standard normal distribution, and the values of $d1$ and $d2$ are:

$$d1 = [-\ln K + \mu + \eta^2]/\eta \quad \text{and} \quad d2 = d1 - \eta \qquad (20)$$

Let's put some numbers to these equations and see how they work. For equation (14), we set the parameter values: $a = -3.21$, $b = 0.8$, and $s = 0.5$. The value of a may seem a bit odd, but remember that equation (14) is expressed as the change in the natural logarithm of the credit spread, e.g. $\Delta\ln(S)$. Therefore, if we were to view a as some long range average value of $\ln(S)$, its value would be negative.

For equation (15), the parameters are set at: $\alpha = 0.06$, $\beta = 0.6$, and $\sigma = 0.05$. Because equation (15) applies to the mean reverting process for interest rates, as opposed to the mean reverting process for $\ln(S)$, the standard deviation, σ, can be expected to be lower than the value of s in equation (14).

To round out our example, assume that the current credit spread for a designated issuer is 200 basis points above the reference interest rate, r. Also, we assume that the correlation between the movement in interest rates and the movement in the credit spread, ρ, is 0.6, that the 1-year interest rate is 6%, and that the tenor of the credit spread option is 6 months ($T = 0.5$).

First, we determine the values of μ and η^2. From equations (18) and (19) their values may be determined as:

$$\begin{aligned}
\mu &= \exp(-0.8 \times 0.5)\ln(0.02) + (1/0.8) \\
&\quad \times (-3.21 - 0.6 \times 0.05 \times 0.5/0.6) \times (1 - \exp(-0.8 \times 0.5)) \\
&\quad + [(0.6 \times 0.05 \times 0.5)/0.6 \times (0.8 + 0.6)] \\
&\quad \times (1 - \exp(-(0.8 + 0.6) \times 0.5)) \\
&= -4.0267
\end{aligned}$$

$$\eta^2 = (0.5)^2 \times (1 - \exp(-2 \times 0.8 \times 0.5))/2 \times 0.8 = 0.055$$

The natural log of the credit spread is distributed with a mean of -4.0267 and a standard deviation of 0.23. If we take the value -4.0267 to the exponential power, we get: $\exp(\ln(S)) = 0.0178$. Therefore, the long-run mean of the credit spread is expected to be 178 basis points.

With this knowledge, we can now construct our credit spread option. Suppose the strike price of the option, K, is set equal to the current credit spread of 200 basis points. From equation (20), the values of $d1$ and $d2$ are -0.254 and -0.4886, respectively. We can now put all of this information into equation (17) to solve for the value of the option:

$$\begin{aligned}
C(S, K, T, r) &= (1/1.03)[\exp(-4.0267 + 0.055/2) \\
&\quad \times N(-0.254) - 0.02 \times N(-0.4886)] \\
&= 0.001
\end{aligned}$$

The cost of this option is 10 basis points. Recall from equation (16) that the payout for a credit spread option is the difference between the credit spread and the strike spread times a notional amount times a risk factor. Therefore, the 10 basis points must be multiplied by the same notional amount and risk factor to get the dollar cost of the option.

Assume that the credit spread option is written on a high yield bond with a current value of $10,000,000 and a risk factor of 5.[14] The cost of the option is:

$$(0.001) \times (\$10,000,000) \times (5) = \$50,000$$

---

[14] See Chapter 2 for a demonstration of how the risk factor is calculated.

Is this cost worth it? Consider that the current credit spread is 200 basis points and that the long-run average is 178 basis points, mean reversion would predict that the credit spread would decline (revert) back towards the mean. Therefore, with a strike spread of 200, our expectation is that this credit spread option will expire out of the money.

Yet, the purpose of the Longstaff and Schwartz model was to price an option on a stochastic credit spread. Even though our expectation is that the credit spread should decline to its long-run average, this result is not certain. Recall from equation (14) that a random element, $s\Delta Z$, was imposed on the mean reversion process for credit spreads. As a result, even though our expectation is that the credit spread will decline over time, the random factor could force the credit spread higher. The cost of $50,000 for this option hedges this random element.

Implications of Options on Credit Spreads

A reader who is familiar with option pricing models will note the similarity of equation (17) to the classic Black-Scholes option pricing formula for call options on stock. Just as in the Black-Scholes model, the value of the call option is increasing in the value of the underlying economic variable; in this case, the credit spread. However, the dynamics of the credit spread lead to some very different conclusions.

For instance, the value of the call option can be less than its intrinsic value. The reason for this result is the mean reverting nature of credit spreads. If the credit spread is currently above its long-run average, the intrinsic value of the option will be quite high. However, the current value of the put option will be less than the intrinsic value because the credit spread is expected to revert downward to the mean over the life of the option.

In the Black-Scholes model, there is no mean reversion. The stock price is expected to appreciate at the risk-free rate over the life of option. Consequently, the current value of the option must at least be equal to its intrinsic value.

A second important result is that the delta of the credit spread call option declines to zero as the time to maturity, T, gets larger. The reason for this result is once again mean reversion. As the time T increases, the opportunity for a credit spread to mean revert to its long-run average increases. Therefore, current changes in the credit spread are expected to have little effect on the final payout of the option; such changes should be canceled out by mean reversion by the maturity of the option.

The implication of this result is that long dated credit spread options will not provide useful hedging vehicles. Any changes in the current credit spread will have reverted by the time the option expires.

One drawback of the above model is that it does not explicitly incorporate the credit rating of the underlying issuer into the pricing of credit spread options. It is important to include credit rating information because credit derivatives are sensitive to an issuer's credit quality. Kijima and Komoribayashi propose a Markov chain model for valuing risky debt that incorporates credit ratings.[15]

---

[15] See Masaaki Kijima and Katsuya Komoribayashi, "A Markov Chain Model for Valuing Credit Risk Derivatives," *The Journal of Derivatives* (Fall 1998), pp. 97-108. In their model, they define the credit spread as:

$$S_j(t,T) = -1/(T-t) \times \ln[R + (1-R)P(t_j > T)]$$

where

S_j = the credit spread for a bond in credit class j
R = the recovery rate of a risky discount bond (with maturity value of \$1)
$P(t_j > T)$ = the probability that the bond does not default before its maturity
t_j = the default time for a credit risky bond
T = the maturity of the credit risky bond

And the payoff to a call option on the credit spread is the same as presented in equation (13): $\max[S(t,T) - K, 0]$. The key distinction in their model is the calculation of the survival probability for the credit risky bond, $P(t_j > T)$. This probability is defined as the probability of no default before time T for a Markov chain X starting from credit quality state j at time t:

$$P(t_j > T) = \Sigma q_{jk}(t,T) = 1 - q_{j,k+1}(t,T)$$

where

$$q_{j,k}(t, t+1) = P[X_{t+1} = k \mid X_t = j]$$

The term $q_{j,k}(t, t+1)$ represents the one step transition probability that an issuer currently rated credit quality j will change its credit quality to k over the next time period. The terms X are from a Markov chain $X = [X_t, t = 0,1,2...]$ on the state space $N = [1, 2, ...K, K+1]$, where state 1 represents the highest credit quality and state $K+1$ designates default.

Therefore, the survival probability $P(t_j > T)$ includes all of the transition probabilities which do not include the default state of $K+1$. This amount is represented by the summation, $\Sigma q_{jk}(t,T)$. The key point is that by incorporating the survival probability into the calculation for the credit spread, Kijima and Komoribayashi also incorporate credit rating changes because the survival probability is calculated using credit transition probabilities.

The individual credit transition probabilities are easily obtained from credit rating organizations such as Standard & Poor's which periodically produce credit transition matrices. An example of such a matrix is given in Exhibit 3 of Chapter 6.

The advantage of such a model is that it allows the credit spread to fluctuate based on the underlying issuer's credit rating.

As a final note, Flesaker *et al* indicate that by selling a put option on a credit spread an investor has sold a higher credit spread volatility than a sale of the yield volatility on the same bond. Higher spread volatility is the result of the less than perfect correlation between the subordinated debt of the high yield issuer and the comparable Treasury bond. Therefore, an investor can receive a higher put premium by selling richer spread volatility than a put on the underlying debt.

RISKS ASSOCIATED WITH PRICING MODELS

The models discussed above demonstrate the complicated nature of pricing credit derivatives. As the reader can see, these models are still evolving, and no single model exists to effectively price all credit derivatives. Consequently, several material risks must be considered with respect to credit derivatives trading.

Pricing Risk

Pricing risk is common to all derivative transactions. Pricing risk is closely tied with intellectual risk, discussed below. As the derivative markets have matured, the mathematical models used to price derivatives have become more complex. These models are increasingly dependent upon sophisticated assumptions regarding underlying economic parameters. Consequently, the prices of credit derivatives are very sensitive to the assumptions of the models.

For example, as discussed above, pricing of credit put options may involve compound option pricing, stochastic strike prices, and path-dependent barrier options. Which model to choose depends on the assumptions of the credit protection buyer and seller. If the term of the option is short and interest rates are assumed to be relatively constant, stochastic strike prices may not be necessary. Alternatively, if the referenced asset has a single coupon payment over the term of the option, path-dependent pricing may not be needed. Lastly, compound option pricing is only practical with European options — those exercisable at maturity.

Price risk is not unique to credit options. Consider the pricing of a credit default swap. The credit protection seller receives the total return on a referenced basket of assets in return for paying to the credit protection buyer a floating interest rate that is reset quarterly. To determine the present value of the credit swap, it is necessary to forecast the forward value of the quarterly credit payments, discount the individual forward values back to the present, and then take the summation of the present values. Therefore, a credit swap is a series of credit forward contracts with respect a referenced basket of assets.

The difficulty with this valuation is forecasting the future values of the credit payments. The large and infrequent nature of credit payments required under a credit swap makes it difficult to accurately forecast the future payment amounts. Furthermore, the credit payments are dependent on a credit downgrade or default, which are discrete events as opposed to a risk neutral appreciation of value under standard forward pricing models.

Given the relative immaturity of the credit derivative market, price discovery is one of the key issues facing credit derivatives. The complexity of the option models discussed above indicates that very sophisticated models must be used to properly value credit derivatives. However, until consistent valuation technology is developed, credit derivative purchasers must rely on the pricing of the credit dealer. The lack of uniform technology makes the pricing of credit derivatives less transparent and increases the pricing risk.

Intellectual Risk

Intellectual or model risk is a creature of the dealers in the financial markets who, over the last decade, have hired quantitative experts (so called "financial engineers") to build pricing models. As derivative instruments have grown in popularity and complexity, market participants have relied heavily on economic and mathematical models to determine their fair values. Given the complexity of some of the credit derivatives discussed above, it is economically feasible for only a relatively few individuals to understand these transactions. The concentrated knowledge of these instruments with only a few individuals within an organization can be risky if one or more of these experts leaves because the company's ability to manage its transaction risk will be compromised.

Additionally, the fair values produced by these mathematical models are dependent upon the assumptions and the choice of parameters that are inputs into the model. It is important not to accept these models as accurate black boxes, but rather, to understand the implications of the models if the underlying assumptions are wrong.

For example, the pricing of a call options on credit spreads requires an assumption about the correlation between the standard Weiner processes for a mean-reverting credit spread and that of mean-reverting interest rates. Absent explicit empirical data on the correlation coefficient between these two random processes, an assumption regarding their relation must be made. Yet this correlation coefficient is a key variable in determining the value of a credit call option. A change in the value of the correlation coefficient can lead to a large change in the value of the option.

For example, if we assume that there is no correlation between credit spreads and interest rates ($\rho = 0$) then, from equation (18), the long-run average credit spread becomes 193 basis points. The cost of the credit option from equation (13) is now 17.5 basis points. This translates into a dollar cost of $87,500 — a 75% increase over the original cost of the credit spread option.

Liquidity Risk

Currently, there are no exchange-traded credit derivatives. Instead, they are traded over-the-counter as customized transactions designed to hedge or expose a specific risk for the credit derivative buyer. The very nature of this customization makes credit derivatives illiquid. Credit derivatives will not suit all parties in the financial market and therefore a party to a tailored credit derivative contract may be unable to obtain a "fair value" should he wish to exit his position before maturity.

Furthermore, with a relatively new market for credit derivatives, the dealer market for transacting in these instruments is still developing. Consequently, participants in this market may find it difficult to price transactions and to hedge cash flow exposures in an efficient manner. As a result, credit derivative participants may find themselves more vulnerable to a higher volatility of cash flows than other more developed derivative instruments. This is all the more compounded by the lack of an exchange-traded product.

Lack of marketability, or liquidity risk, is hard to quantify. One way to manage this risk would be to take a "haircut" from the model or quoted price of the credit derivative. This haircutted price would incorporate the cost to the credit derivative seller to liquidate the credit derivative (or to repurchase it from the credit derivative buyer) before its maturity as well as the cost of unwinding the seller's hedge position for the derivative instrument. Consequently, a "fair exit price" may be a more accurate reflection of the true market value of the credit derivative rather than a theoretical or model value.

Counterparty Risk

Counterparty risk is related less to the pricing of credit options and more to the general use of credit derivatives. Although credit options may be used to reduce or eliminate the credit risk of an underlying asset, they introduce another form of credit risk: the risk that the counterparty will default on its contractual obligations. As noted above, credit derivatives are all traded over the counter. Over the counter derivatives depend on each side of the trade upholding their contractual bargain. If a credit protection seller does not fulfill its obligations, the credit protection buyer will become exposed to the credit risk of the underlying asset.

Therefore, for the credit protection buyer to suffer a loss two things must happen: there must be a deterioration of the credit quality of the underlying hedged asset, and the credit protection seller must default on the credit derivative contract. The joint probability of these two events occurring at the same time may be expected to be low. However, this probability may become nontrivial if the credit protection seller already has a large balance sheet exposure to the sector for which it sells credit insurance.

For instance, consider a portfolio manager who wishes to hedge her credit exposure to a high yield company in the mining sector. This manager should not purchase credit protection from a bank that lends heavily in the mining sector because the sale of the credit protection by the bank will only increase its already large credit exposure to this sector.

CONCLUSION

This chapter provided some of the details into the pricing of credit derivatives. As was noted, the models can vary significantly depending on whether the credit derivative is based on an underlying asset or a credit spread. Even then, there are considerable variations among the models. The lack of uniform pricing models was highlighted as one of the risks associated with the use of credit derivative pricing. Bottom line: this technology is still developing, and it may be some time before price transparency is achieved.

On a positive note, the rapid development of pricing models for credit derivatives does indicate the growing acceptance of these instruments in portfolio management. However, end users of credit derivatives are reminded that the market is still one of custom tailoring. The ability to tailor a credit derivative to meet a portfolio manager's specific needs is a two-edged sword. On the one hand, specific credit risks may be hedged or embraced. On the other hand, custom tailoring makes credit derivatives less liquid.

APPENDIX A

COMPOUND CREDIT PUT FORMULA

As described in equation (5) the payoff to a credit put option at maturity is:

$$P[D; K] = \text{Max } (0, K - D)$$

We can express the market value of debt as the difference between a riskless bond and a put option on firm value:[16]

$$D = e^{-r(T-t)}F - P(V, F, T, \sigma, r) \tag{1A}$$

where

$$
\begin{aligned}
P(V, F, T, \sigma, r) &= \text{a put option on firm value} \\
V &= \text{the value of the firm} \\
F &= \text{the face value of the firm's debt} \\
T &= \text{the maturity of the firm's debt} \\
\sigma &= \text{the volatility of returns on } V \\
r &= \text{the risk-free rate} \\
t &= \text{the current time}
\end{aligned}
$$

Substituting equation (1A) into equation (5) allows us to describe the payoff of the compound credit option as:

$$P[V;K] = \begin{array}{l} K - [e^{-r(T-t)}F - P(V, F, T, \sigma, r)]; \text{ if positive} \\ 0; \text{ otherwise} \end{array} \tag{2A}$$

From Black and Scholes[17] and Geske,[18] we may determine the value of the put option on firm value as:

$$P(V, F, T, \sigma, r) = e^{-r(T-t)}FN(-d2) - VN(-d1) \tag{3A}$$

where

$$d1 = [\ln(V/F) + (r + \sigma^2/2)(T - t)] \div \sigma\sqrt{T - t}$$

---

[16] See Esser, "High Yield Bond Analysis: The Equity Perspective."

[17] Black and Scholes, "The Pricing of Options and Corporate Liabilities."

[18] Geske, "The Valuation of Compound Options."

$$d2 = d1 - \sigma\sqrt{T-t}$$

In valuing a compound credit option, it is necessary to identify a critical value of the firm V^* such that below this value, the compound put option will be exercised. In other words, at V^* the intrinsic value of the compound option is 0. However, at any value below V^*, the option has value. To identify this value of the firm, we must use the put-call parity theorem of option pricing:

$$V + P = C + e^{-r(T-t)}F \tag{4A}$$

where V is the value of the firm's assets and C is a call option on the firm's assets. Equation (4A) implies that $P - e^{-r(T-t)}F = C - V$. Substituting this equality into equation (2A) we can define the critical firm value as:

$$0 = K + C(V^*, F, T, \sigma, r) - V^*$$

$$V^* = K + C(V^*, F, T, \sigma, r) \tag{5A}$$

If, at maturity of the credit put option (time t_1), $V(t_1) > V^*$ then the intrinsic value of this compound option, $K - V(t_1) + C$, is negative because $V(t_1) > K + C$. The reason is that the call option C does not increase in value one for one with the value of the firm (the delta of a call option is always ≤ 1). However, if $V(t_1) < V^*$, then $V(t_1) < K + C$, and the compound credit option has positive value.

At the maturity of the credit option, we can use the risk neutral discounted value approach to value the compound credit option:

$$P[V;K]$$

$$= e^{-r(t_1 - t)} \int_{-\infty}^{V^*} \left[K - e^{-r(T-t_1)}F + P(V, F, T, \sigma, r) \right] dV \tag{6A}$$

where the credit option will only be exercised below the critical firm value V^*. In other words, in a risk neutral world where all assets earn the same expected rate of return, the riskless rate, the current value of the compound credit option is the discounted expected value of the credit option at expiration. Substituting equation (3A) into equation (6A) yields:

$$P[V;K] = e^{-r(t_1-t)}$$

$$\int_{-\infty}^{V^*} \left[K - e^{-r(T-t_1)}F + e^{-r(T-t_1)}FN(-d_2) - V(t_1)N(d_1) \right](dV) \quad (7A)$$

If we set $V(t_1) = V(t)e^{r(t_1-t)}$, then equation (7A) may be rewritten as:[19]

$$P[V;K] = e^{-r(t_1-t)}$$

$$\int_{-\infty}^{V^*} \left[K - e^{-r(T-t_1)}F + e^{-r(T-t_1)}FN(-d_2) - e^{r(t_1-t)}V(t)N(d_1) \right](dV) \quad (8A)$$

The solution to this integral is:[20]

$$P[V;K] = e^{-r(t_1-t)}KN_1(a2) - e^{-r(T-t)}FN_1(a2)$$

$$+ e^{-r(T-t)}FN_2(a2, b2; -\rho) - VN_2(a1, b1; -\rho) \quad (9A)$$

where

$N_2(.,.;\rho)$	=	the bivariate standard normal density function with correlation ρ
$N_1(.)$	=	the univariate standard normal density function
ρ	=	$\sqrt{(t_1-t)/(T-t)}$
$a1$	=	$[\ln(V/V^*) + (r + \sigma^2/2)(t_1-t)] \div \sigma\sqrt{(t_1-t)}$
$a2$	=	$a1 - \sigma\sqrt{(t_1-t)}$
$b1$	=	$[\ln(V/F) + (r + \sigma^2/2)(T-t)] \div \sigma\sqrt{(T-t)}$
$b2$	=	$b1 - \sigma\sqrt{(T-t)}$

---

[19] This example follows from Steven B. Raymar and Aamir M. Sheikh, "The Valuation of Compound Options and American Calls on Dividend Paying Stocks with Time-Varying Volatility," *The Journal of Financial Engineering*, Vol. 5 (1997), pp. 243-266.

[20] See Raymar and Sheikh, "The Valuation of Compound Options and American Calls on Dividend Paying Stocks with Time-Varying Volatility."

APPENDIX B

STOCHASTIC STRIKE PRICES IN CREDIT PUT OPTIONS

The essentials of Das' stochastic interest rate model are below. For simplicity, Das assumes that the stochastic Weiner process that defines interest rates is independent of the stochastic Weiner process that defines firm value. Recall from equation (5) that:

$$K(T, t, Z, F, r^*) = F \times \exp[-\{1/(T-t) \times -\ln B(t) + r^*\} \times (T-t)]$$

where

F = the face value of the outstanding debt
r^* = credit spread
T = the maturity of the credit risky debt
t = the maturity of the credit option
$B(t)$ = $B(T, t, Z)$, the value at time t of a default free zero-coupon bond that matures at time T

By defining $B(t)$ as a function of T, t, and Z, Das introduces a stochastic process into the determination of interest rates. Even though $B(t)$ is free from default risk, it can change in value due to changes in interest rates. Since $B(t)$ is a discount bond, the negative of its natural logarithm reveals the current 1-period risk-free rate. Therefore, random changes in the value of $B(t)$ signal random changes in interest rates. The stochastic movement of $B(t)$ is captured by the following equation:

$$B(T, t, Z_2)$$
$$= B(0, T)/B(0, t) \times \exp[\sigma^2(T \times t)(T-t)/2 - \sigma(T-t)Z_2\sqrt{t}] \quad (1B)$$

where

σ = the volatility of discount bond prices
Z_2 = the outcome of a random variable drawn from a stochastic Weiner process

$B(0, T)$ = the current price for a default-free discount bond maturing at time T

$B(0, t)$ = the current price for a default-free discount bond maturing at time t

Therefore, $B(t)$ is stochastic, and is used to add a stochastic interest rate component to the determination of the strike price in equation (5). For each stochastic outcome of Z_2, the price of $B(t)$ is inverted to obtain the stochastic value of r which is then added to the credit spread $r*$ to determine the strike price.

Incorporating random strike prices into the Das model results in the following valuation formula for credit put options:

$$\text{Put}[\delta 1, \delta 2, \sigma, T, t, V(0), B(0), F, r_d, r*] =$$
$$\int_{Z1}\int_{Z2} \max[K(T, t, Z1, F, r*) - D(T, t), 0]\phi(Z1)\phi(Z2)dZ1dZ2 \quad (2B)$$

where

$dZ1$ = the Weiner process that is imposed on firm value

$dZ2$ = the Weiner process that is imposed on discount bond values

$\delta 1, \delta 2$ = coefficients that define the stochastic process of firm value as $dV = \mu Vdt + \delta 1 VdZ1 + \delta 2 VdZ2$

$dZ1$ and $dZ2$ are assumed to be independent of each other and the other terms are as defined as before.

As Das notes, solving the above equation is very difficult to compute as it requires integrating twice over the cumulative normal distribution function. However, Das presents a discrete time binomial model to provide approximate results to the equation above.

APPENDIX C

STOCHASTIC DEFAULT PROCESS

Similar to Jarrow and Turnbull,[21] Flesaker *et al*[22] establish a random process Q_t which can only assume two values: 0 if no default has occurred and 1 if there is a default. Once $Q_t = 1$ (default) it stays there; that is, there is no recovery from default. The probability of Q_t jumping from 0 to 1 is given by $\lambda_t\, dt$ and the probability that Q_t stays at 0 is $1 - \lambda_t\, dt$. The default rate is not a constant and can vary according to the following diffusion process:

$$d\lambda_t = \mu(\lambda_t, t)dt + v(\lambda_t, t)dw_t \tag{1C}$$

where

μ = the drift term
v = the volatility of the default rate
dw = a standard Weiner process

and the value of Q_T is dependent on the random process λ. Therefore, default events ($Q_T = 1$) cannot be predicted with precision, and default comes as a surprise to the investor. This allows Flesaker *et al* to write the conditional probability that no default occurs between times t and T given that no default has occurred at time t as:

$$\text{Probability}\,[Q_T = 0; Q_t = 0] \;=\; \exp\left\{-\int_t^T \lambda_s ds\right\} \tag{2C}$$

The random default rate is related to the random interest rate by the correlation factor ρ. The correlation coefficient captures the relationship between interest rates and default events because these two processes may be dependent on the same macroeconomic factors such as the business cycle.

---

[21] Robert A. Jarrow and Stuart M. Turnbull, "Pricing Derivatives on Financial Securities Subject to Credit Risk," *Journal of Finance* (March 1995), pp. 53-85.
[22] Flesaker, Hughston, Schreiber, and Sprung, "Taking all the Credit."

Flesaker *et al* break down a risky corporate coupon bond into a series of zero-coupon bonds where each zero-coupon bond relates to either a coupon payment or final maturity payment of the original risky coupon bond. These zero-coupon bonds are denoted $B(t,T)$. If a bond defaults ($Q_T = 1$), then a constant recovery rate R is assumed to be realized. Given that up to time t no default has occurred, the expected value of $B(t, T)$ is:

$$B(t, T) = E\left[((1 - Q_T) + RQ_T) \times \exp\left\{-\int_t^T r_s ds\right\}\right] \quad \text{(3C)}$$

If $Q_T = 0$, equation (3C) reduces to a standard formula for the risk neutral price of a default-free zero-coupon bond with a payoff of 1 at time T:

$$B(t,T) = E\left[\exp\left\{-\int r_s ds\right\}\right] \quad \text{(4C)}$$

However, if a default event has occurred ($Q_T = 1$) then the value of $B(t,T)$ is:

$$B(t, T) = R \times E\left[\exp\left\{-\int r_s ds\right\}\right] \quad \text{(5C)}$$

Flesaker *et al* indicate that equations (2C) and (3C) may be combined to yield:

$$B(t, T) = RP(t, T) + (1 - R)E_t\left[\exp\left\{-\int_t^T (r_s + \lambda_s)ds\right\}\right] \quad \text{(6C)}$$

where

R = the remaining fraction of bond payments that are recoverable

$P(t,T)$ = the risk neutral price for a default free zero coupon bond with a payout of 1 at time T:

$$P(t, T) = E_t \left[\exp \left\{ -\int r_s ds \right\} \right] \tag{7C}$$

In their model, Flesaker *et al* specify the following process for short-term interest rates:

$$dr = \beta(\alpha - r)dt + \sigma dz \tag{8C}$$

where

α = a time varying target level
β = the rate of mean reversion
σ = a measure of local volatility
dz = a second standard Weiner process and $dwdz = \rho dt$

In equation (6C), the annualized default rate, λ, may be thought of as the credit spread over the referenced risk-free rate. For example, if we expect no recovery upon default ($R = 0$), then equation (6C) reduces to:

$$B(t, T) = E \left[\exp \left\{ -\int_t^T (r + \lambda)ds \right\} \right] \tag{9C}$$

In this case, all of the credit risk is priced through λ, the spread over the short-term interest rate. If partial recoveries after default are considered, then the credit spread should be reduced and the risky short rate would approximate $r + (1 - R)\lambda$.

To value the credit spread option, the risky coupon bond is broken down into several zero-coupon bonds whose prices are determined by $B(t, T)$ and $P(t, T)$. Each risky zero-coupon bond represents either a coupon payment or final maturity payment of the original risky bond. The yield to maturity of each zero-coupon bond is then calculated and the credit spread may be then expressed as a function of the various zero-coupon bond prices, $B(t, T)$ and $P(t, T)$.

The payoff at maturity to a credit spread option is Max (credit spread $- K$, 0). Once the credit spread has been determined as discussed above, risk neutral pricing is used to determine the value of the credit spread call option:

$$C = E_t \left[\max(\text{spread} - K, 0) \times \exp\left\{ -\int_0^t r_s \, ds \right\} \right] \tag{10C}$$

Chapter 6

Credit Risk Management

INTRODUCTION

U p to now, the discussion of credit derivatives and credit risk has been analyzed from the standpoint of a single instrument. Whether that instrument was a credit option, credit swap or a special purpose vehicle, its value was examined separate from the remainder of an investment manager's portfolio. In this chapter, we review credit risk management from a portfolio standpoint.

The purpose of this chapter is not to discuss new credit derivative structures, but rather, to examine how credit risk is properly measured and monitored within an investment portfolio. The application of credit derivatives cannot begin until a portfolio manager has fully assessed her level of credit risk. Only then can the portfolio manager choose that credit derivative which is most consistent with her existing credit profile.

Several credit risk management models have been developed over the past few years to measure and control the risk inherent in credit sensitive assets. For instance, Credit Suisse Financial Products has developed a model called CreditRisk+ that draws from Credit Suisse's methodology for setting loan loss provisions. KPMG has developed a Loan Analysis System that addresses the critical valuation problems associated with the optionality of loan instruments. KMV Corp. has developed an estimated default frequency that is based on option pricing theory as opposed to historical default probabilities.[1] Finally, J.P. Morgan & Co. has developed CreditMetrics, a methodology for measuring the credit value at risk over a specific investment horizon.

This chapter begins with a discussion on the nature of credit risk. We then examine two general paradigms for measuring and

---

[1] For a more detailed discussion of these risk models see Barclays Capital, "Modeling Credit Risk," *Derivatives Strategy* (January 1998), p. 4.

controlling credit risk. Lastly, we provide a simple demonstration of the CreditMetrics methodology.[2]

THE NATURE OF CREDIT RISK

Credit risk differs from market risk in the nature of the distribution of credit returns. Whereas market risk is generally assumed to have a normal or "bell shaped" distribution of returns, credit risk is defined by skewed returns and a fat downside tail.[3] The different shapes of these returns have important implications for risk measurement.

If market returns approximate a normal distribution, then only two statistical measures are needed to describe the entire distribution: the mean and standard deviation. These two measures are easily computed from the first two moments of the normal distribution. From the mean and standard deviation, one can compute confidence intervals for random values.

Furthermore, the mean and standard deviation are consistent with the efficient frontier theory of modern portfolio management. Under the efficient frontier theory, only the mean return and standard deviation of a portfolio are needed to determine whether the portfolio is "efficient" in the sense of receiving the maximum expected return for a given level of risk. Lastly, the expected return of a portfolio and its standard deviation may be used to determine a risk-adjusted return in the manner of the Sharpe Ratio.[4]

---

[2] CreditMetrics is a registered trademark of J.P. Morgan & Co. Incorporated. For a more detailed discussion of this method, the reader should consult Blythe Masters, *Introduction to CreditMetrics*, J.P Morgan & Co. Incorporated, 1997; and Greg Gupton, Christopher Finger and Mickey Bhatia, *CreditMetrics Technical Document*, J.P. Morgan & Co. Incorporated, 1997. We choose the CreditMetrics methodology because it is readily available at J.P. Morgan's web site (www.jpmorgan.com) and because it has gained a broad following. The two reference documents cited above may be downloaded from the Internet.

[3] Although, even with market returns, the tails of the distribution tend to be "fat." That is large outlier events are observed with greater frequency than would be predicted by a perfect bell shaped distribution of security returns. These large tails are a measure of the kurtosis of the distribution.

[4] The Sharpe Ratio is measured as:
    [Expected Return – Risk Free Rate] ÷ Standard Deviation
The Sharpe Ratio is used as a measure of risk-adjusted return. It measures the return on an asset after subtracting the risk-free rate (every risky asset must earn some amount above the risk-free rate or no one would purchase it) and dividing it by a unit of risk measure—its standard deviation. The Sharpe Ratio is often used to compare two assets for their risk/return tradeoff. In other words, one asset may have a higher absolute return but only at the cost of taking on an excessive quantity of risk.

Exhibit 1: The Distribution of Market and Credit Returns

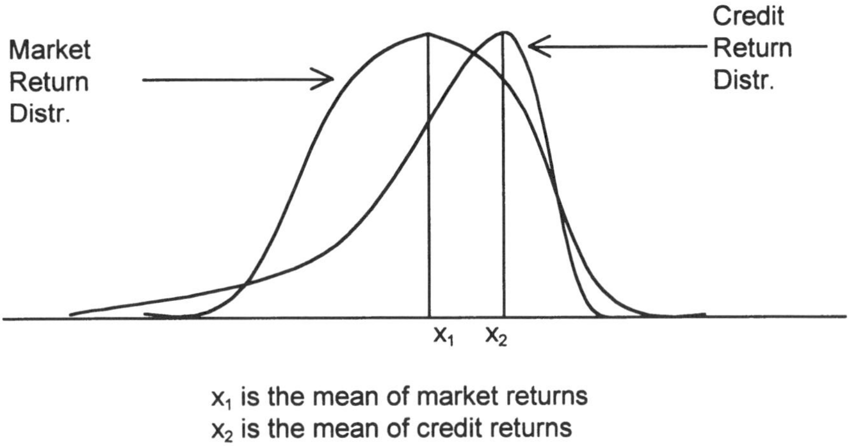

x₁ is the mean of market returns
x₂ is the mean of credit returns

The returns to credit risk tend to be skewed because there is a relatively small likelihood of earning substantial price appreciation for a fixed income asset, but there is a very large likelihood of earning a small profit through interest earnings. As a result, the distribution tends to be skewed around a positive value but with a very small positive tail reflecting limited upside potential. Conversely, fixed income assets are at risk to downgrades and defaults, and these credit events can have a dramatic negative impact on the value of a fixed income asset. Although these events may have a remote probability of occurring, their ability to produce large losses contributes to the skewed distribution of credit returns, producing large downside tails.

Exhibit 1 demonstrates the normal or "bell-shaped" curve typically associated with most market returns as well as the skewed curve with a large downside tail that distinguishes the returns to credit exposure. A credit risky portfolio may be thought of as one that has a long fat tail. This indicates that there is a greater likelihood that actual credit losses will exceed expected credit losses. Put another way, there is a higher probability of extreme outcomes from credit returns than from market returns.

Another implication of the skewed credit distribution is that the mean and standard deviation are no longer sufficient to fully describe the distribution of credit returns. Higher moments of order must be calculated to describe the skewness and fat "tailness" of the credit distribution.[5] Consequently, credit returns adjusted for risk as measured by the standard deviation may not be a true measure of whether a proper return is earned on the credit portfolio.

Credit risk management requires monitoring and controlling both expected credit losses as well as unexpected credit losses. Expected credit losses are generally accounted for through reserving policies such as a reserve for bad debts or loan loss reserve. These losses are measured by the mean of the skewed credit distribution in Exhibit 1. Unexpected credit losses are those losses that occur in the long fat tail of the credit distribution. In the case of a bank, it is the role of equity capital to absorb these losses. In the case of a portfolio manager, diversification principles apply to ensure that unexpected credit losses do not occur all at the same time.

Unfortunately, credit risk is difficult to get one's arms around because of several interdependent variables. As discussed previously, credit events can occur with credit migrations, with changes in credit spreads, and with credit losses in the event of default. Not only are there correlations among the variables which affect each type of credit event, there may be correlations across these three types of credit events. Such interactions make modeling credit risk computationally difficult.

As a practical matter, credit risk management systems typically assume the different types of credit events have a zero correlation. That is, credit migrations are independent of changes in the credit spread, which in turn are independent from the factors that determine the amount of loss in the event of default. Credit risk models then attempt to specify independent probability distributions for each type of credit risk event. We will discuss credit risk modeling in more detail below. For the time being the reader should note that credit risk management is still an art as much as a science.

A GENERAL DISCUSSION OF CREDIT RISK MODELS

Banks and other financial institutions are logical sites for developing credit risk models. Although there is considerable diversity among

---

[5] The first and second moments of a distribution are necessary to determine its mean and standard deviation (e.g., for a normal or bell shaped distribution). However, the third moment of the distribution is required to measure skewness and the fourth moment of the distribution is required to measure the kurtosis or fat tails of the distribution.

U.S. banks in the application of credit risk management, two general categories of risk models are used: "top down" and "bottom up."[6]

Top-Down Model

Top-down models attempt to measure the total risk of a business unit, line of business or credit portfolio. By their very nature, they measure the sum of the credit, market, and residual operating risks. They do not break out the individual risk factors, but instead attempt to use peer group analysis to estimate capital requirements.

This approach relies on the ability to observe the capital ratios of market competitors as well as the historical volatility associated with a product line or portfolio of credit dependent assets. By analyzing the capital ratios of market comparable companies, the credit risk manager can determine the appropriate amount of capital required to achieve a desired credit rating.

Alternatively, the credit risk manager can study the historical cash flows associated with a portfolio or business unit. From the volatility of these cash flows, the credit risk manager can attempt to develop a credit distribution of returns such as those discussed above, keeping in mind the potential for fat downside tails.

Top-down models may not be the best choice for banks and other financial institutions because they are affected by both credit and market risk. These models have more applicability for the allocation of capital in nonfinancial companies. As a result, top-down models are best suited for reviewing the performance of broad lines of credit business such as credit card operations or middle market bank loans.

Bottom-Up Models

More commonly, financial institutions use *bottom-up models* that separate credit risk from market risk and operating risk. Bottom-up models differ from top-down models in that they explicitly consider variations in credit quality when monitoring credit risk. Bottom-up

---

[6] For a full discussion on U.S. banking risk models, see Federal Reserve System Task Force on Internal Credit Risk Models, *Credit Risk Models at Major U.S. Banking Institutions: Current State of the Art and the Implications for Assessments of Capital Adequacy*, May 1998. The Federal Reserve System Task Force refers to these models as "aggregative models" or "structural models."

models attempt to quantify credit risk at the level of each credit facility, be it a junk bond or a high yield loan.

Bottom-up models may be further divided into two subcategories: default-mode or mark-to-market models.[7]

Default-Mode Models

The *default mode* (DM) credit risk model is the most common approach among banks currently. Very simply, this credit model assumes a credit asset such as a loan can assume only one of two values: default or no default. Under this approach, if the loan does not default, there is no credit loss, and the loan is valued at book value. If the loan defaults, then the size of the credit loss is measured as the present value of the difference between the loan's book value (determined by the borrower's contractual obligations) and the loan's actual net cash flows over the workout period.

The DM model of credit risk is a binary model because only two states of the world matter: default or no default. Therefore, the binary options discussed in Chapter 2 and the credit default swaps discussed in Chapter 3 are natural hedging tools under this credit risk methodology.

The rational for the DM model of credit risk management is that the secondary markets are not sufficiently developed to support a full mark-to-market approach to credit risk. Thus, banks view loans as "buy and hold" assets. Either the loan pays off or the bank suffers a loss because the opportunities to achieve a transparent market price are limited.

However, as discussed in Chapter 1, the bank loan market is becoming less segmented as more non-bank participants enter the fray. Consequently, even though the DM model of credit risk management is more prevalent, it can be expected that more financial institutions will move towards a mark-to-market methodology as the secondary credit market develops.

Mark-to-Market Models

The *mark-to-market* (MTM) methodology recognizes that the value of a credit portfolio can decline without a default event occurring. Fur-

---

[7] See the Federal Reserve System Task Force at p. 18.

thermore, the MTM methodology recognizes that credit risk is not one-sided. It allows credit-sensitive assets to increase in value due to favorable credit events such as credit upgrades or narrower credit spreads. In contrast, the DM model of credit risk does not recognize any increase in value due to upward credit migrations or favorable spreads.

While the DM model of credit risk may be more prevalent among banks, the MTM methodology is preferred among fund managers. Because fund managers must calculate and report net asset values on a regular basis (for mutual funds, on a daily basis), the DM methodology is not sufficient. Banks, however, have longer planning horizons (usually one year), and do not need to report the value of their loan portfolios with the same regularity as fund managers. For them, the DM methodology is more convenient.[8]

The MTM methodology may be considered a more general approach of the DM methodology. Instead of only two states of the world, the MTM methodology is a multi-state approach. It allows for credit upgrades and downgrades as well as defaults. A credit loss under the MTM approach would be defined as a reduction in value of the portfolio due to a deterioration in credit ratings, an increase in credit spreads, or a default.

As an example, consider a loan issued by a BBB rated company. If the company is downgraded to BB, the market value of the loan will surely decline. The MTM methodology measures this decline. However, under the DM methodology, no credit event has occurred because the company has not defaulted on the loan. Similarly, if the company were upgraded to an A rating, the MTM methodology would recognize the positive increase in value, but the DM paradigm would maintain the loan at its original book value.

Consider a self-amortizing bank loan. Under the MTM methodology, the current value of a loan may be measured as:

$$V(k) = C/[1 + r_1 + cr_1] + C/[1 + r_2 + cr_2] + \ldots + C/[1 + r_n + cr_n] \quad (1)$$

where

$$V(k) = \text{the value of the loan issued by company } k$$

---

[8] Most banks, however, use the MTM methodology for their trading accounts. Nonetheless, our discussion in this chapter is managing portfolio credit risk, not trading account credit risk.

C = the constant amortized loan payment
r_i = the zero-coupon risk-free discount rate for period i
cr_i = the market determined credit spread for issuer k for time period i
n = the number of periods until maturity of the loan

In words, the value of the loan issued by company k is dependent on the current term structure of interest rates (r_i) and the current market credit spread (cr_i) for company k. In one year's time (assume the time to the next coupon) the value of the loan may change due to changes in credit spreads. The credit spreads may change due to macroeconomic factors such as a recession, or microeconomic factors such as credit rating changes.

In one year, the bank will receive its first amortization payment of C. Assume that the credit spread has increased from (cr) to ($cr + x$), where (x) represents a certain basis point increase in the credit spread for company k. If we assume that the zero-coupon risk-free curve remains unchanged, the MTM value of the loan in one year is:

$$V(k) = C + C/[1 + r_1 + (cr + x)_1]$$
$$+ \ldots + C/[1 + r_{n-1} + (cr + x)_{n-1}] \qquad (2)$$

where the terms are all defined as above, and the loan now has ($n-1$) periods until maturity. Note that the MTM methodology explicitly accounts for changes in the credit spread (denoted by the term x). It does not matter whether the change in the credit spread is the result of a macroeconomic or microeconomic event. All that matters is that the MTM model incorporate the changes in the credit spread into measuring the current loan value. Furthermore, the value of x can be negative, indicating a decline in the credit spread for company k.

Note that equations (1) and (2) used in the MTM model are identical to the formulas used to construct credit options on bank loans in Chapter 2. Consequently, MTM models are consistent with the credit derivative technology discussed in earlier chapters. It is not by chance that credit risk management and credit derivative construction recognize the same economic principles. If they did not, there would be no effective way to monitor, measure, and control credit derivatives within a credit risk methodology.

Exhibit 2: General CreditMetrics Approach
Value at Risk Due to Credit

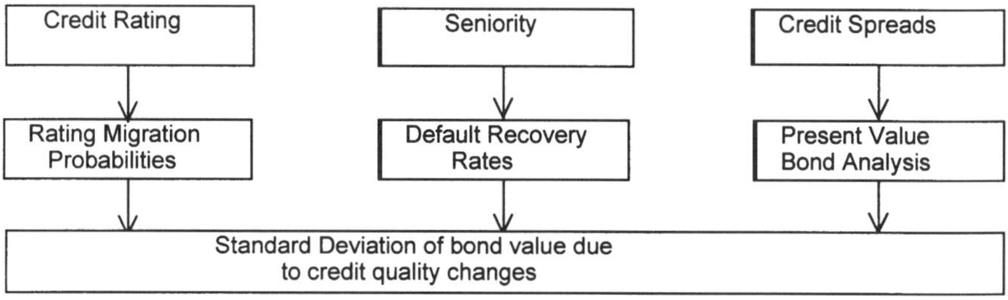

Credit Rating	Seniority	Credit Spreads
↓	↓	↓
Rating Migration Probabilities	Default Recovery Rates	Present Value Bond Analysis

Standard Deviation of bond value due to credit quality changes

Source: Greg M. Gupton, Christopher C. Finger, and Mickey Bhatia, *CreditMetrics — Technical Document*, J.P. Morgan & Co., 1997, p. 23.

AN APPLICATION OF CREDIT RISK MANAGEMENT

Despite the problems discussed above, credit risk may be measured in a systematic manner. J.P. Morgan & Co. Incorporated has developed *CreditMetrics* that uses bond migration matrices and default recovery rates to determine the credit risk in a portfolio. CreditMetrics is a MTM methodology because it explicitly recognizes changes in value, both positive and negative.

The application of CreditMetrics involves three steps. First, the credit risk exposure of each fixed income instrument must be calculated. Second, CreditMetrics determines the probability of credit rating changes based on changes in firm asset value. Lastly, within a portfolio, correlations must be determined between two or more credit risky assets to determine the concentration of credit risk. Exhibit 2 demonstrates the general CreditMetrics methodology.

Step 1: Determining the Credit Risk Exposure of Individual Assets

For ease of demonstration, we will construct a portfolio containing two lower rated bonds. Both bonds have three years remaining to maturity and both are senior secured debt of the respective issuers. Issuer No. 1 has a BBB rating, and its bond has an annual coupon of 8%. Issuer No. 2 has a BB rating, and its bond has an annual coupon of 9%. Both bonds pay a face value of $100 at maturity.

For each issuer/bond we must determine the probability of its credit migration over a time horizon. We will use a period of one year for the migration horizon (the time frame for most credit matrices). Over the 1-year period, three general events can happen to each bond: the issuer's credit rating can remain unchanged, it can be upgraded, or it can be downgraded (including default). Each outcome has a probability associated with it to indicate the likelihood of each type of credit event.

A 1-year horizon is chosen for two reasons. First, much of the academic and research literature is conducted with annual data, and this leads to credit transition matrices with one year horizons. Second, the nature of credit risk is that it typically unfolds over time as opposed to overnight catastrophes that instantly bankrupt a company. In other words, in the normal course of business, a bank or portfolio manager could mitigate its credit risk over a 1-year time period. Most commercial lines of credit, for instance, are extended in terms of years.

Nonetheless, the 1-year time horizon is a convention. Regulators may want to review the capital adequacy of banks under stressful scenarios which might not conveniently fall into 1-year periods. Although the markets for credit derivatives and commercial loans have become deeper and more liquid, they have not been fully exposed to broad credit shocks.

Furthermore, if credit risk activities are taken on a more frequent basis, the 1-year risk horizon will not be realized. Consequently, the credit transition matrix must be adjusted to the portfolio manager's investment horizon. For our purposes, we will use a 1-year horizon.

The probabilities of credit migration are determined historically. Standard and Poor's, Moody's and the other NRSROs all perform credit migration analysis. The outcome of this analysis is a credit transition matrix. Exhibit 3 demonstrates a typical credit transition matrix. For instance, note that for a BB rated issuer, the probability that, after one year, it remains BB rated is about 80%. Conversely, the probability that this same issuer might be upgraded to a BBB rating is almost 8%, while the probability that it might be downgraded to single B is close to 9%.

In practice, transition matrices can be developed for each industry in which an issuer operates. However, for our simple demonstration, we will assume that the transition matrix in Exhibit 3 is suitable for both issuers in our portfolio. Also, it is important to note that CreditMetrics assumes that each obligor and credit risky investment will be labeled with a credit rating. CreditMetrics does not calculate credit ratings. Rather, it accepts them as input parameters.

As a first step, we will measure the expected value and volatility of each bond due to credit risk. To value a high yield bond at each state of credit quality, we need to develop a zero-coupon credit curve for each rating category, and then use this zero-coupon credit curve to discount the bond's cash flows with respect to each level of credit rating. The zero-coupon credit curve is the same set of discount rates as used in equations (1) and (2) for MTM pricing.

A zero-coupon credit curve may be derived by a method known as "bootstrapping." First, an industry term structure is determined using an average yield to maturity (or yield to first call) for a representative sample of industry bonds at a specific credit rating. From this term structure, it is possible to derive a series of equivalent zero-coupon discount rates for each maturity level presented in the original term structure.[9] This procedure is repeated for a sample of industry bonds at each credit rating level until a complete zero-coupon credit curve is developed across the credit rating spectrum.

Exhibit 3: Transition Credit Matrix

Initial	Credit Rating After One Year (%)							
Rating	AAA	AA	A	BBB	BB	B	CCC	Default
AAA	90.81	8.33	0.68	0.06	0.12	0	0	0
AA	0.7	90.65	7.79	0.64	0.06	0.14	0.02	0
A	0.09	2.27	91.05	5.52	0.74	0.26	0.01	0.06
BBB	0.02	0.33	5.95	86.93	5.3	1.17	0.12	0.18
BB	0.03	0.14	0.67	7.73	80.53	8.84	1	1.06
B	0	0.11	0.24	0.43	6.48	83.46	4.07	5.2
CCC	0.22	0	0.22	1.3	2.38	11.24	64.86	19.79

Source: Standard & Poor's *CreditWeek*, April 15, 1996; reprinted in Greg M. Gupton, Christopher C. Finger and Mickey Bhatia, *CreditMetrics — Technical Document*, J.P. Morgan & Co. Incorporated, 1997, p. 25

---

[9] For an excellent demonstration of the bootstrapping method, see John Hull, *Options, Futures and other Derivative Securities* (Upper Saddle River, NJ: Prentice Hall, 1997).

Exhibit 4: Bond Valuations for a Credit Migration
Zero-coupon credit curve discount rates

Rating	Year1	Year 2	Year 3
A	6.25%	6.75%	7.50%
BBB	6.50%	7%	8%

Valuation of BBB rated bond upon migration to A rated

$$\text{Current Value } \$101.48 = \frac{\$8}{1.0625} + \frac{\$8}{(1.0675)^2} + \frac{\$108}{(1.075)^3}$$

Valuation of BB rated bond upon migration to BBB rated

$$\text{Current Value } \$102.84 = \frac{\$9}{1.065} + \frac{\$9}{(1.07)^2} + \frac{\$109}{(1.08)^3}$$

For purposes of our example, we will assume that the same zero-coupon credit curve applies for the two bonds in our sample. However, the use of the same zero-coupon credit curve for both bonds is a significant simplification. Ideally, a credit forward curve should be developed for each industry. In other words, each industry has its own special credit characteristics that must be captured in a unique zero-coupon credit curve. Still, for illustrative purposes, the assumption that the same zero-credit curve applies to both bonds will not hurt our example.

To continue the example, assume that the credit forward curve for an A and a BBB rated issuer is that given in Exhibit 4. We further assume that both issuers migrate upwards one credit rating category (from BBB to A and from BB to BBB). The interest rates presented in Exhibit 4 are the zero-coupon credit discount rates applicable for each time period associated with each bond's cash flows. The value of each high yield bond is then a straightforward present value operation using the zero-coupon credit discount rates.

Exhibit 4 shows that if the BB rated bond were to migrate up one credit rating category, its value would be $102.84. For the BBB rated bond, the migration to an A rating results in a value of $101.48. Even though the zero-coupon credit curve discounts more heavily for BB rated bonds, the migration from BB rated to BBB rated results in a better migration value than moving from BBB rated to A rated. The higher coupons associated with the BB rated bond are more highly valued as it moves up the credit rating curve.

Exhibit 5: Bond Values with Credit Migration

BBB Rated Bond			BB Rated Bond		
Year End Rating	Value ($)	Probability (%)	Year End Rating	Value ($)	Probability (%)
AAA	$104.00	0.02	AAA	$108.00	0.03
AA	$103.00	0.33	AA	$107.00	0.14
A	$101.48	5.95	A	$105.00	0.67
BBB	$100.00	86.93	BBB	$102.84	7.73
BB	$95.00	5.30	BB	$100.00	80.53
B	$87.00	1.17	B	$95.00	8.84
CCC	$75.00	0.12	CCC	$80.00	1.00
Default	$58.00	0.18	Default	$58.00	1.06
Mean	$99.57			$99.17	
Std. Dev.	$2.68			$5.01	

Exhibit 4 demonstrated how to determine the value of a credit risky bond in the event of an upward credit migration. In a similar manner, the value of each high yield bond can be determined for each level of credit migration, upwards as well as downwards. Exhibit 5 presents the indicative values for the two high yield bonds in our portfolio at each level of credit migration as well as the associated probabilities of credit migration taken from Exhibit 3.

The value of each bond in the event of default is simply the recovery rate for a bankrupt issue. Altman and Kishore find that the average recovery rate for a senior secured bond issue is about $58 for every $100 of bond issue.[10] We assume that both bonds have this seniority class, and accordingly, both receive the same expected recovery value in the event of default.

Using the information in Exhibit 5 we can determine the expected value and volatility for each bond due to credit risk. The mean value and standard deviation of each bond are given by the formulae:

$$\text{Mean} = \Sigma^i \text{ probability}(i) \times \text{bond value}(i) \tag{3}$$

Standard Deviation
$$= [\Sigma^i \text{ probability}(i) \times \{\text{Mean} - \text{bond value}(i)\}^2]^{1/2} \tag{4}$$

---

[10] See Edward Altman and Vellore Kishore, "Almost Everything You Wanted to Know about Recoveries on Defaulted Bonds," *Financial Analysts Journal* (November/December 1996), pp. 57-64.

where

Mean = the expected bond value weighted by the probability of each credit state i

probability(i) = the probability that a bond will migrate to credit rating i

bond value(i) = the value of each bond at credit rating level i

Σ^i = the summation over all credit states from i = AAA to i = default

For the BB rated bond, the expected value is $99.17 and its standard deviation is $5.01. For the BBB rated bond, the expected value is $99.57, and its standard deviation is $2.68.[11] It should come as no surprise to the reader that the lower credit quality bond has the higher standard deviation.

The standard deviations calculated in Exhibit 5 represent the credit risk for each individual bond. However, we must be careful when using the standard deviation to measure credit risk because this is a symmetric measure of dispersion. Credit risk, as discussed above, is not symmetrically distributed. The large fat tails associated with a credit distribution indicate that the downside potential is much greater than the upside potential.

For instance, with respect to the BBB rated bond, the highest value possible (associated with a migration to AAA) is $104. This value is only 1.65 standard deviations away from the mean of $99.57. However, the lowest value possible is $58, which is 15.5 standard deviations away from the mean value. Therefore, the standard deviation of credit risk, while an easy statistic to calculate, must be used with great caution.

The next step is to prepare a table of all of the possible combined values of the two bonds at year end. For instance, if the BB rated bond migrates to BBB rated, and if the BBB rated bond migrates to A rated, their combined value in this state will be $204.32. Given that there are eight rating categories (from default to AAA) and two bonds, the num-

---

[11] CreditMetrics adds one additional refinement to the calculation of standard deviation for bonds. Instead of assuming that the recovery value is constant in the event of default, Credit-Metrics measures the variation in recovery values and incorporates this measure into its calculation for the standard deviation of bond value. Variability of recovery rates does not affect the expected value of the bond, but it can increase the standard deviation of bond values.

ber of possible combined values that the 2-bond portfolio may achieve is 8^2, or 64 different values. Using the values presented in Exhibit 5 for the two bonds depending on their state of credit quality, we can develop a complete table of portfolio values. This is given in Exhibit 6.

Step 2: Determining the Probability of Credit Rating Changes

So far, this has been the easy part. The above discussion covered the first general step of CreditMetrics: the determination of the credit exposure of individual assets and the volatility of asset value due to changes in credit quality. The next step, determining the probability of credit rating changes based on asset values, requires some knowledge of both option and probability theory.

In order to measure the expected value of the portfolio and its standard deviation, the probability of each portfolio state must be determined. This requires an assessment of the joint probability of both bonds being associated with each one of the 64 portfolio values. In other words, a joint distribution of bond values must be determined to calculate the likelihood of achieving any one of the 64 values presented in Exhibit 6.

For instance, we must determine the probability of Issuer No. 1 remaining BBB rated given that Issuer No. 2 remains single BB rated. Then we must determine the probability of Issuer No. 1 migrating upwards to an A rating while Issuer No. 2 remains BB rated, and so on. In this manner, we determine the joint probability for each one of the 64 portfolio values presented in Exhibit 6.

Exhibit 6: Combined Values of 2-Bond Portfolio

		Issuer No. 1 (BBB)							
		AAA	AA	A	BBB	BB	B	CCC	Default
Issuer No. 2 (BB)		$104	$103	$101.48	$100	$100	$95	$80	$58
AAA	$108	212	211	209.48	208	208	203	188	166
AA	107	211	210	208.48	207	207	202	187	165
A	105	209	208	206.48	205	205	200	185	163
BBB	102.84	206.84	205.84	204.32	202.84	202.84	197.84	182.84	160.84
BB	100	204	203	201.48	200	200	195	180	158
B	95	199	198	196.48	195	195	190	175	153
CCC	80	184	183	181.48	180	180	175	160	138
Default	58	162	161	159.48	158	158	153	138	116

If it is assumed that both bonds are independent of each other, then the joint probabilities for each credit state are easily determined. In this case, the joint probability is simply the product of the individual probabilities given in Exhibit 5. For example, under the assumption of independence, the joint probability that Issuer No. 1 remains BBB rated and Issuer No. 2 remains BB rated is $0.8693 \times 0.8053 = 0.700$ or 70%.

However, it is unlikely that the credit risks embedded within the two bonds are independent of each other. Even if the two underlying issuers are not from the same or related industry, their respective credit ratings will be affected by macroeconomic factors such as the current business cycle. Therefore, the correlations between the credit migrations for the two bonds must be measured before we can determine portfolio credit risk.

Unfortunately, the correlations between the credit migrations of the two bonds cannot be observed. While credit risk correlations are unobservable, firm values are. Therefore, CreditMetrics uses a technique to link firm value to credit ratings. Since firm values are observable in the market place, credit correlations may be estimated using firm value as a proxy.

To begin with, firm value can be expressed in terms of option pricing models. The shareholders of a company may be viewed as owning a call option on the firm's assets where the strike price of the call option is equal to the face value of the outstanding debt. In this manner, the shareholders may exercise their option by paying off the firm's bondholders and then selling the firm's assets for their fair market value. The gain to the shareholders is the difference between the strike price (equal to the firm's aggregate debt) and the cash flows from the sale of the firm's assets. This idea was first expressed by Black and Scholes in their seminal option pricing paper published in 1973.[12]

In 1974, Merton extended the Black and Scholes theory by considering the credit risk component of the firm's outstanding debt as a put option on the value of the firm's assets.[13] Under this theory,

---

[12] See Fischer Black and Myron Scholes, "The Pricing of Options and Corporate Liabilities," *Journal of Political Economy* (1973), pp. 637-654.

[13] See Robert C. Merton, "On the Pricing of Corporate Debt: The Risk Structure of Interest Rates," *Journal of Finance* (May 1974), pp. 449-470.

the value of a firm's debt may be measured as a risk-free debt obligation less a put option written on the value of the underlying assets of the firm. Debtholders in a company have effectively sold a put option to the company's equityholders. If the value of the firm's assets declines sufficiently such that they can no longer satisfy the firm's liabilities, then the equityholders of the company have the option to put the assets back to the firm and walk away, i.e., default on the company's outstanding bond obligations.

This option theoretic model of firm value can be extended to credit migration. In addition to the default threshold, there are credit rating thresholds. As the value of the company's assets decline, the put option held by the shareholders becomes more valuable. The value of the put option changes according to changes in credit rating. Eventually, if the value of the company's assets declines sufficiently, the company will be unable to meet its debt obligations, and it will default.

CreditMetrics assumes that there is a series of levels for firm asset value that determine the firm's credit rating. For instance, for Issuer No. 1, assume that from an asset value of $400 million up to $800 million, the company retains its triple B rating. However, from an asset value of $800 million up to $950 million, the firm receives a credit rating of single A, from $950 million up to $1 billion, the firm receives a double A rating, and from $1 billion and above, the firm receives a AAA rating. Similarly, declining firm values will fall within certain credit rating ranges. Eventually, the value of the firm can decline to such a low value that default becomes a reality. Exhibit 7 demonstrates how credit rating thresholds are tied to a distribution of firm value.

Exhibit 7: Credit Rating Thresholds as a Function of Firm Value

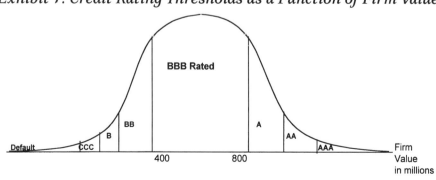

The importance of this step is that it provides a direct link between firm value and credit rating. Correlations between credit ratings across firms are not directly observable in the marketplace. However, correlations between firm values are observable. Consequently, the knowledge of firm value correlations combined with the link to credit rating thresholds allows CreditMetrics to develop a joint probability distribution of likely credit migrations for both bonds in our portfolio.

Using the credit migration probabilities from Exhibit 3, we can apply probabilities to asset levels. For instance, in Exhibit 3, the probability that Issuer No. 1 remains triple B rated is 0.8693. Therefore, we can conclude that:

Probability [Issuer No. 1 rating remains BBB]
  = Probability [\$400 million ≤ asset value < \$800 million]
    = 0.8693   (5)

There is an 86.93% probability that Issuer No. 1's asset value will remain between \$400 million and \$800 million over the next year. From this discussion it is possible to assign probabilities to each level of asset value for each issuer. CreditMetrics assumes that for each issuer there are asset levels which correspond to credit ratings such that it is possible to map firm asset values in one year's time to credit ratings in one year's time.

If the asset values are known which correspond with credit ratings, it is possible to map changes in asset value (asset returns) into changes in credit ratings. If we define R_{BBB} as the minimum return necessary for Issuer No. 1 to retain its BBB rating, and R_A as the minimum return necessary for Issuer No. 1 to achieve a single A credit rating, then the probability of remaining BBB rated may be expressed as:

Probability [BBB] = Probability $[R_{BBB} \leq R < R_A]$ (6)

where R = the return on Issuer No. 1's assets.[14]

Taking this one step further, if we assume that the asset returns to each company are normally distributed with a standard

---

[14] We define the probability of default as:

  Probability [Default] = Probability $[R < R_{CCC}]$

This is slightly different from how CreditMetrics defines default.

deviation σ and a mean return μ,[15] then the probability that Issuer No. 1 remains BBB rated may be defined as:

$$\text{Probability [BBB]} = \text{Probability } [R_{BBB} \leq R < R_A]$$
$$= \Phi[(R_{BBB} - \mu_1)/\sigma_1] - \Phi[(R_{BB} - \mu_1)/\sigma_1] \qquad (7)$$

where $R_A > R_{BBB} > R_{BB}$ and

μ_1 = the expected return on the assets of Issuer No. 1

σ_1 = the standard deviation of the return on the assets of Issuer No. 1

Φ = the symbol for the cumulative distribution of the standard normal distribution

In words, equation (7) says that the probability that Issuer No. 1 retains its BBB rating is equivalent to the probability that its level of assets remains between \$400 million and \$800 million. This is also equivalent to the probability that the change in asset value, R, falls between R_{BBB} and R_A.

To measure the probability of remaining BBB rated, we must take the area under the standard normal distribution up to the limit of Issuer No. 1's BBB rating. This area is measured by the value $\Phi[(R_{BBB} - \mu_1)/\sigma_1]$. From this amount we must subtract the area under the standard normal curve which corresponds to the probability of Issuer No. 1 being rated BB or below. This amount is measured by $\Phi[(R_{BB} - \mu_1)/\sigma_1]$. The difference is the area under the normal curve in Exhibit 7 between firm values of \$400 million and \$800 million.

For example, assume that the firm value of Issuer No. 1 is currently \$600 million. Consequently, it has a BBB rating because firm value is between \$400 million and \$800 million. However, if, in one year's time, the change in value of firm assets is at least \$200 million, then Issuer No. 1 will be upgraded to a single A rating because \$600 million plus \$200 million equals \$800 million, the credit threshold for a single A rating. This implies that the R_A must equal at least 33% (\$200 million/\$600 million).

The probabilities associated with each credit rating threshold may be calibrated to the probabilities presented in the transition

---

[15] Asset returns, unlike credit returns, are assumed to be normally distributed.

matrix in Exhibit 3. For instance, we know from this matrix that the probability that Issuer No. 1 remains BBB rated is 86.93%. Therefore, we may set the following probability:

Probability [Issuer No. 1 remains BBB]
$$= \Phi[(R_{BBB} - \mu_1)/\sigma_1] - ([(R_{BB} - \mu_1)/\sigma_1] = 0.8693 \qquad (8)$$

Similarly, we can derive expressions for the probability of each credit threshold in terms of a normal distribution of asset returns. This allows CreditMetrics to describe the credit evolution of each issuer according to its asset return distribution.

Once the distribution of credit levels has been determined for each issuer, the next step is to derive the joint evolution of credit ratings for the two issuers. If it is assumed that the two asset returns are normally distributed and related to each other by a correlation factor, ρ, then their joint distribution can be described by a bivariate normal distribution. This distribution can then be used to determine the probability of each of the 64 states of portfolio values presented in Exhibit 6.

For example, using the bivariate normal distribution, the probability that Issuer No. 1 remains BBB rated while Issuer No. 2 remains BB rated may be expressed as:

$$\text{Probability}[R_{BBB} \le R_1 < R_A, R_{BB} \le R_2 < R_{BBB}]$$
$$= \int_1 \int_2 f(R_1, R_2; \Sigma)(dR_2)dR_1 \qquad (9)$$

where

$\int_1$	= the integral over the area of the distribution curve where the asset returns to Issuer No. 1 remain between R_{BBB} and R_A
$\int_2$	= the integral over the area of the distribution curve where the asset returns to Issuer No. 2 remain between R_{BB} and R_{BBB}
$f(R_1, R_2; \Sigma)$	= the probability density function for the bivariate normal distribution
Σ	= the covariance matrix between the two asset returns, which depends on the correlation coefficient, ρ

This integration is used to determine each of the 64 probabilities for joint ratings moves of the two issuers.

Step 3: Determining Issuer Correlations

The last step is to measure the relationship between debt issuers. CreditMetrics determines the correlation coefficient between two issuers based on their equity returns. As discussed above, equity returns are readily observable while credit movements are less so. Practically, it would be an overwhelming job to construct a correlation matrix to measure all of the correlations across thousands of debt issuers. To overcome this problem, CreditMetrics uses a two step procedure to measure the correlation coefficient between two issuers.

First, CreditMetrics constructs industry indices in various countries and determines the correlations across these industries. As a result, CreditMetrics can determine, for instance, the correlation between the U.S. banking industry and the U.K insurance industry. Second, CreditMetrics maps individual issuers by their industry participation. For instance, one use company may have 80% of its business in banking and 20% in insurance.

In this manner, CreditMetrics determines each company's participation in industry and country exposure. For example, the same company may further divide its 80% banking exposure into 60% U.S. banking exposure, 10% U.K banking exposure, and 10% Germany banking exposure, while its 20% insurance exposure is all domestic U.S. exposure. Identifying companies by their industry and country exposures allows CreditMetrics to simplify its correlation calculations.

When all of the probability and option theory is said and done, CreditMetrics can produce a transition matrix of joint credit moves similar to the one presented in Exhibit 8. The purpose of producing a probability matrix of joint credit movements is so that an expected value for the 2-bond portfolio may be calculated. If we multiply the matrix of joint probabilities in Exhibit 8 times the matrix of combined portfolio values in Exhibit 6, we get Exhibit 9. This matrix presents the expected value of the 2-bond portfolio for each joint credit migration cell.

Exhibit 8: Joint Rating Probabilities for Issuers No. 1 and No. 2 (in percent)

Issuer No. 2 (BB) Ratings		AAA	AA	A	BBB	BB	B	CCC	Default	Total
		0.02	0.33	5.95	86.93	5.3	1.17	0.12	0.18	
AAA	0.03	0	0	0	0.03	0	0	0	0	0.03
AA	0.14	0	0	0	0.1	0.01	0	0	0	0.11
A	0.67	0	0.01	0.05	0.2	0.08	0	0	0	0.34
BBB	7.73	0	0.1	0.12	6.3	0.43	0.05	0.03	0.04	7.07
BB	80.53	0.03	0.2	4.3	71	4.1	0.6	0.2	0.1	80.53
B	8.84	0	0.17	0.6	7.4	0.6	0.14	0.07	0.06	9.04
CCC	1	0	0.1	0.2	0.9	0.08	0.06	0.04	0.04	1.42
Default	1.06	0	0.05	0.2	1	0.09	0.05	0.03	0.04	1.46
	Total	0.03	0.63	5.47	86.93	5.39	0.9	0.37	0.28	100

Exhibit 9: Expected Value of Each Migration Cell for the Two Bond Portfolio

Issuer No. 2 (BB)	AAA	AA	A	BBB	BB	B	CCC	Default	Total
AAA	$0.00	$0.00	$0.00	$0.06	$0.00	$0.00	$0.00	$0.00	$0.06
AA	$0.00	$0.00	$0.00	$0.21	$0.02	$0.00	$0.00	$0.00	$0.23
A	$0.00	$0.02	$0.10	$0.41	$0.16	$0.00	$0.00	$0.00	$0.69
BBB	$0.00	$0.21	$0.25	$12.78	$0.87	$0.10	$0.05	$0.06	$14.32
BB	$0.06	$0.41	$8.66	$142.00	$8.20	$1.17	$0.36	$0.16	$161.02
B	$0.00	$0.34	$1.18	$14.43	$1.17	$0.27	$0.12	$0.09	$17.60
CCC	$0.00	$0.18	$0.36	$1.62	$0.14	$0.11	$0.06	$0.06	$2.53
Default	$0.00	$0.08	$0.32	$1.58	$0.14	$0.08	$0.04	$0.05	$2.29
Total	$0.06	$1.23	$10.87	$173.09	$10.71	$1.72	$0.64	$0.42	$198.74

Mean	$198.74
Std. Dev	$6.52

The sum of all the cells in Exhibit 9 provides the expected value for the 2-bond portfolio. This value is $198.74. Notice that this is equal to the sum of the expected values of the two bonds given in Exhibit 5: $99.57 + $99.17 = $198.74.

Diversification, therefore, does not increase the expected value of the portfolio. In fact, the expected value of the portfolio is just the sum of the individual expected bond values. What does change, however, is the risk of the portfolio.

In Exhibit 9, the standard deviation of the portfolio due to credit risk is $6.52. Compare this amount to the standard deviations for the individual bonds due to credit risk of $2.68 and $5.01. If the BBB rated bond and the BB rated bond were perfectly correlated with respect to credit risk, the standard deviation of the portfolio would be the sum of their respective standard deviations, or $7.69. However, since the two bonds are less than perfectly correlated, there is some diversification benefits.

The benefits to diversification can be measured by the difference between $7.69 and $6.52. This amount, $1.17, is the reduction in credit risk due to portfolio diversification. The less correlated the two high yield bonds are, the smaller will be the portfolio standard deviation due to credit risk.

EXPANDING CREDIT RISK MANAGEMENT BEYOND A TWO-ASSET PORTFOLIO

As discussed above, the credit risk management of even a simple 2-bond portfolio requires an understanding of option pricing and probability theory. Extending this risk management to a large portfolio of credit risky assets becomes even more complicated.

One problem with the risk methodology discussed above is that it only provides a standard deviation of portfolio credit risk. Our previous discussion of fat tailed credit distributions indicates that this may not be a sufficient measure of the credit risk in a portfolio of assets. How, then, can we examine a portfolio to determine the size of its "tail"?

The answer is simulation. To provide a better analysis of credit risk, Monte Carlo simulation may be used to generate a distribution of credit returns. Monte Carlo simulation is a sampling technique that generates portfolio "scenarios" to reflect possible future outcomes of portfolio value. The simulation generally proceeds in three steps.

First, asset return levels that correspond to credit thresholds are determined as discussed above. Then computer simulation is used to generate scenarios of asset returns by sampling from a normal distribution that reflects the returns to the underlying issuer. These return scenarios are then mapped to credit ratings. The outcome of each simulation run is just the credit rating at the end of the established time horizon (typically one year) for each obligor in the portfolio.

Depending on the size of the portfolio, thousands of these scenarios may be generated. For instance, for a 20-bond portfolio, it would not be unusual to generate 20,000 simulated scenarios. Generally, the more assets in your portfolio, the more simulations you must run to generate a reasonable distribution of credit returns that reflects the interactions of the potentially correlated assets.

The second step is to take the simulated credit ratings for each issuer and credit sensitive asset and translate them into a portfolio value. This requires the same methodology as discussed above where changes in credit ratings lead to changes in asset values.[16] By mapping credit ratings into bond values a portfolio value may be determined for each scenario.

The last step is to summarize the many simulated runs of credit movements into a distribution of portfolio values. This can be done by plotting the simulated portfolio values versus their relative frequency. This distribution of portfolio values should resemble the skewed distribution presented in Exhibit 1 for credit returns.

The key advantage to simulation over an analytical calculation is the observation of the distribution of credit returns. Because of the skewness and fat "tailness" of credit returns, the mean and standard deviation are not sufficient statistics to calculate confidence intervals. Confidence intervals assume a normal distribution. Therefore, the usual value-at-risk statistics calculated for market risk will be inapplicable for credit risk.

However, if an investor has a distribution of credit returns (albeit simulated), she can observe directly that portfolio value below which a certain percentage of the simulated values are observed. For example, assume that 5% of the simulated portfolio values are observed below $10 million. Then the portfolio manager

---

[16] For this step, CreditMetrics distinguishes between non-default scenarios and default scenarios. In a default scenario, there is considerable variability with respect to recovery rates. Therefore, if a default scenario is simulated for any bond, a second simulation is conducted to determine its recovery rate based on the input parameters of average recovery rate and standard deviation.

can say that, over the chosen time horizon, the value of the portfolio due to credit risk should not decline below $10 million more than 5% of the time. The ability to observe the distribution of portfolio values allows the portfolio manager to pick any percentage threshold level below which portfolio values are observed.

As mentioned several times already, credit returns tend to be skewed while market returns tend to be normally distributed. Because of the different dynamics that generate the distributions of credit and market returns, credit risk statistics and market risk statistics cannot be combined. In other words, the value-at-risk numbers generated from market risk models cannot be added to the credit risk calculations.

Additionally, market risk and credit can be related. For instance, volatility in market interest rates can increase the risk of credit downgrades for credit sensitive assets. Consequently, the interrelation between market risk and credit risk also prohibits the summing of their statistics. If the correlation of the portfolio market risk and credit risk is positively correlated, summing their respective risk statistics would overstate the total portfolio risk, while if the correlation is negative, summing would understate the portfolio risk.

The solution then is to review the portfolio market exposure separate from its credit exposure. Although these risks may overlap (and in fact, can be the same thing if credit risk is perfectly correlated with market risk), the key point is that the portfolio manager can asses the amount credit risk embedded within her portfolio. From this point it is her decision to hedge or increase her credit exposure.

CONCLUSION

Credit risk is much different from market risk in that there is greater exposure to the downside and less exposure to the upside. The non-normal nature of credit risk necessitates a separate measurement from market risk to determine its impact on a portfolio. While analytical methods can be applied to measure credit risk, these methods fail to fully capture the large downside tail associated with credit risky assets. Consequently, Monte Carlo simulation is often used to build a distribution of credit return scenarios. From a simulated distribution of credit returns, the portfolio manager can determine threshold portfolio values below which a chosen percentage of portfolio values are expected to be observed.

Two general types of credit risk management may be applied: default mode and mark-to-market models. Default mode risk management models only recognize changes in value of credit risky assets upon the occurrence of default, while mark-to-market models, in contrast, allow for changes in value of credit risky assets outside of actual default. Although the default mode model is consistent with the traditional method of managing credit risk in loan portfolios, the mark-to-market methodology is more consistent with current value-at-risk models. Consequently, mark-to-market models — such as CreditMetrics — have gained considerable acceptance in the investment community.

Chapter 7

Documentation and Regulation of Credit Derivatives

INTRODUCTION

C redit derivatives are privately negotiated agreements traded over the counter. The lack of an exchange-traded product means that there is very little regulation from either the Securities and Exchange Commission (SEC) or the Commodity Futures Trading Commission (CFTC). Instead, credit derivatives are regulated by two other sources.

First, credit derivatives are regulated through the content of individually negotiated contracts. The International Swaps and Derivatives Association (ISDA) has recognized the need to provide a common format for credit derivative documentation. In early 1998, ISDA released a standard contract form to document credit derivatives. The first part of this chapter reviews this form and explains how it works.

Second, although the SEC and the CFTC have not issued regulations concerning credit derivatives, the banking authorities have. Specifically, the Federal Reserve Board, the Office of the Comptroller of the Currency, and the Federal Deposit Insurance Corporation have issued regulations regarding credit derivatives. This chapter flows nicely from Chapter 6 because much of the credit derivatives regulation adopted by the banking authorities revolves around appropriate risk management techniques.

CREDIT DERIVATIVES DOCUMENTATION

Although the first credit derivatives began to appear on the financial market scene in 1993, it was not until 1998 that the ISDA developed a standard contract to capture these trades. Establishing an industry standard by which to document a derivatives transaction is an important step in the development of any derivative market. It indicates that a critical mass of trading has come together such that all participants in the market recognize the need for a common reference point.

Additionally, standardized documentation can be an effective substitute for government regulation.[1] As we will see below, ISDA documentation is quite flexible and can accommodate the unique needs of the parties to a credit derivative transaction. In one sense, ISDA acts like a self regulatory organization in that it produces fair and objective documentation to ensure that all participants in the credit derivative market are on the same playing field. This is in contrast to government regulation which, while usually drafted with good intentions, cannot possibly accommodate all of the special needs of participants in the derivatives market.

This section begins with a brief review of the purpose of ISDA. We then review the significant provisions of the ISDA credit derivative contract and provide some sense of how they work with respect to underlying credit derivative transactions. Lastly, we consider some of the benefits to using a standard contract form.

What is ISDA?

ISDA is the recognized global trade association representing participants in the swaps and derivatives markets. These markets include interest rate derivatives, commodities, equity swaps, swaptions, and credit derivatives. ISDA was established in 1985 by a consortium of large broker-dealers and money center banks that were active in the interest rate swap market. Since then ISDA has grown to about 330 members worldwide that constitute the major market for privately negotiated derivatives.

ISDA's board of directors is drawn and elected annually from its primary members. The board of directors sets ISDA's strategy and policies, essentially collecting the current industry issues from

---

[1] See Gerald Gay and Joanne Medero, "The Economics of Derivatives Documentation: Private Contracting as a Substitute for Government Regulation," *The Journal of Derivatives* (Summer 1996), pp. 78-89.

participants in the over-the-counter derivatives market. These issues can include developing documentation for new over-the-counter instruments such as credit derivatives.

The primary purpose of ISDA is to encourage the prudent and efficient development of privately negotiated derivatives by (1) promoting practices conducive to the efficient conduct of business, including the development and maintenance of derivatives documentation, (2) promoting sound risk management practices, (3) developing high standards of commercial conduct, (4) advancing international public understanding of the business, (5) educating members on regulatory, legal, documentation, tax, accounting, and operational issues affecting derivatives transactions, and (6) creating a forum for the analysis and discussion of derivative transactions.

Perhaps the most important endeavor of ISDA has been the development of the *ISDA Master Agreement*. This is the authoritative contract used by industry participants because it established international standards governing privately negotiated derivative trades. The Master Agreement reduces legal uncertainty by providing uniform contractual terms for all derivative participants. It also provides for a reduction in counterparty credit risk by allowing for the netting of contractual obligations. The original Master Agreement was introduced in 1987 and revised in 1992.

ISDA Documentation for Credit Swaps
In 1998, ISDA released its contract form for credit derivatives.[2] The documentation is primarily designed for credit swap transactions, either total return credit swaps or credit default swaps. However, the contract form is sufficiently flexible that it also can be used as a framework for documenting a credit put option or a credit spread option. We discuss the key provisions of the ISDA credit swap contract in the order that they appear in the contract. Capitalized terms used in this chapter are defined terms consistent with the ISDA documentation.

Trade Date
The date the parties enter into the credit derivative transaction.

---

[2] See International Swaps and Derivatives Association, *Confirmation of OTC Credit Swap Transaction, Single Reference Entity, Non-Sovereign*, 1998.

Effective Date

The date when contractual payments under the credit derivative trade begin to accrue.

Termination Date

The parties to a credit swap specify at the outset when the credit swap will terminate. If no credit event has occurred by the maturity of the credit swap, then the swap terminates at the Scheduled Termination Date — a date specified by the parties in the contract.

However, the Termination Date under the contract is the earlier of the Scheduled Termination Date or a date upon which a Credit Event Notice and a Notice of Publicly Available Information have been given. Therefore, notice of a Credit Event terminates a credit swap.

Buyer

This simply identifies which party is purchasing either the credit protection or the total return on a Reference Obligation. This is usually the investor.

Seller

This is the seller of the credit protection or the total return on the Reference Obligation. This is usually the dealer.

Reference Obligation

This is the underlying asset upon which the credit derivative is based. Under the credit swap terms, the Reference Obligation can be a single asset such as a corporate bond or several assets including bonds, loans, leases, and other obligations.

Reference Entity

This is the referenced issuer who issues the Reference Obligation.

Reference Price

The parties can specify a Reference Price for the Reference Obligation. This Reference Price is essentially a strike price. It is a decline in value below this Reference Price that will determine the size of the payment upon the occurrence of a Credit Event. The Reference Price is typically specified in percentage terms.

Calculation Agent

The party designated to determine the required payments under the credit derivative transaction. This can be (and usually is) one of the parties to the credit swap agreement. However, the contract can specify an objective third party.

Fixed Payments

The ISDA format allows the Fixed Rate Payer to pay either a single bullet amount or a periodic amount. In the first case, the swap is similar to that presented in Exhibit 1 of Chapter 3. This is the simplest type of credit default swap where the Dealer promises to pay a cash amount to the Investor if there is a credit event. In return, the Dealer receives a floating payment from the Investor, usually equal to LIBOR plus a spread.

In the second case, the Dealer promises to pay on a periodic basis a known payment to the Investor in return for the total return on the referenced asset. This is the example of Exhibit 3 in Chapter 3 where the Investor agrees to give up the uncertain cash flows of the referenced asset in return for a certain payment from the Dealer.

Floating Payments

The Floating Payments are the counterparts to the Fixed Payments we just discussed. These payments are usually the Investor's side of the transaction. As mentioned above, these payments could be LIBOR plus a spread, or the total return on an asset.

It is important to note that the terms "Floating Payment" and "Fixed Payment" are perfectly general. For instance, if we consider the total return swap in Exhibit 5 of Chapter 3, both the Dealer and the Investor agree to pay a "floating" amount. In the Dealer's case, it is the total return on a referenced asset, and in the Investor's case it is LIBOR plus a spread.

Therefore, the terms "Floating Payment" and "Fixed Payment" are just conventions. These terms can be defined in any creative way in which the parties will agree to be bound. Furthermore, under standard ISDA terms, the floating-rate payer is usually called the "Seller" and the fixed-rate payer is usually called the "Buyer." Once again, this is just a convention because the seller of the credit protection is typically the Dealer who often is the fixed-rate payer.

Conditions to Payment

In order for a payment to be collected upon the occurrence of a Credit Event, three conditions must be satisfied:

1. The affected party must deliver a Credit Event Notice.
2. The affected party must deliver a Notice of Publicly Available Information.
3. The Calculation Agent must determine that Materiality exists.

A Credit Event Notice is an irrevocable notice given by one party to the credit swap to its counterparty that a Credit Event has occurred. ISDA allows for the notice to be given in writing or orally, including by telephone, but the parties may negotiate their preferred type of notice.

A Notice of Publicly Available Information is a notice that confirms the occurrence of a Credit Event. This notice must reference a source of Publicly Available Information which can include any internationally recognized published or electronically displayed news source such as the *Wall Street Journal*, Reuters electronic terminals, or Bloomberg terminals. Additionally, the parties to the credit swap can specify a minimum number of Publicly Available Information sources that must confirm the occurrence of a Credit Event.

Materiality

This term is negotiated by the parties. For instance, if the underlying asset is a junk bond, materiality can be defined in terms of a price decline. The parties to the swap can state what dollar or percentage decline in value of the referenced bond is sufficient to qualify as a material Credit Event. Usually, Materiality is stated as a 1% to 5% price decline from the Initial Price (referred to as the Price Decline Requirement). The Initial Price may equal the Reference (Strike) Price, or the Reference Price may be set at a different value.

Conversely, instead of a price decline, materiality can be defined in terms of increasing credit spreads. Recall from our discussion of credit options in Chapter 2 that an increase in credit spreads for a referenced issuer means a decline in value for a referenced asset. Therefore, materiality can be defined in terms of a minimum credit spread increase (the Spread Widening Requirement) that must occur before a Credit Event is recognized.

Materiality, however, is determined by the Calculation Agent. The Calculation Agent is usually a point of negotiation in ISDA agreements. Almost always, the Dealer who is selling the credit derivative wishes to remain the Calculation Agent. However, this raises a potential conflict of interest because the Dealer/Calculation Agent might not want to recognize a Credit Event to prevent its payment obligation to the Investor.

Fortunately, ISDA provides for a Dispute Resolution in the contract. In the event that a party to the credit swap does not agree with a determination made by the Calculation Agent, the disputing party has the right to require that the determination be made by a disinterested third party that is a dealer of credit derivative instruments. The Calculation Agent gets to pick the disinterested third party, but only after consultation with the disputing party.

The determination made by the third party is binding on the credit derivative participants unless there is manifest error. The costs, if any, from using the third party shall be borne by the disputing party if the third party substantially agrees with the Calculation Agent, and shall be borne by the non-disputing party if the third party does not substantially agree with the Calculation Agent. Bottom line, if the Investor believes that the Dealer/Calculation Agent has not properly recognized a Credit Event, it can challenge the Dealer, but it must be prepared to pay any costs associated with the challenge should its dispute prove unjustified.

Furthermore, upon the occurrence of a Credit Event, the Calculation Agent must determine the current market value of the Referenced Obligation to determine if there has been a material decline in value. This is accomplished by obtaining third party quotes form other dealers and taking the average of the bids, offers, or mid-market quotes. This is just one more check and balance to ensure that the Calculation Agent performs its determinations in an objective fashion.

Credit Events

This is the most important section of the document. In this section, the parties agree as to what constitutes a Credit Event for a credit default payment. ISDA provides a list of eight Credit Events: Bankruptcy, Credit Event upon Merger, Cross Acceleration, Cross Default,

Downgrade, Failure to Pay, Repudiation, and Restructuring. The parties to a credit swap may include all of these events, or select only those that they believe are most relevant.

Bankruptcy means that a referenced issuer: (1) is dissolved; (2) becomes insolvent or unable to pay its debts as they become due; (3) makes a general assignment, arrangement or composition for the benefit of creditors; (4) institutes, or has instituted against it, a proceeding seeking a judgement of insolvency or bankruptcy, or any relief under any bankruptcy or insolvency law; (5) has a petition presented for its winding-up or liquidation; (6) has a resolution passed for its winding-up, official management, or liquidation; (7) seeks or becomes subject to the appointment of an administrator, provisional liquidator, conservator, receiver, trustee, custodian or other similar official for all or substantially all of its assets; (8) has a secured party take possession of all or substantially all of its assets, or has a distress, execution, attachment, sequestration or such other legal process levied, enforced or sued on against all or substantially all of its assets; (9) causes or is subject to any event with respect to it which, under the applicable laws of any jurisdiction, has an analogous effect to any of the events specified in items 1-8; or (10) takes any action in furtherance of, or indicating its consent to, approval of, or acquiescence in, any of the foregoing acts.

In sum, bankruptcy includes any official (court directed) or private action which results in an issuer relinquishing control of its assets, operations, or management. The referenced issuer may initiate these proceedings itself, or it may be forced to act by outside parties. Bankruptcy also occurs if the issuer cannot pay its outstanding debts as they become due. Consequently, poor operating performance and lack of short-term financing can force a bankruptcy.

Credit Event Upon Merger means that the referenced issuer has consolidated, amalgamated or merged with another entity, or has transferred all or substantially all of its assets to another entity, and the creditworthiness of the resulting, surviving or transferee entity is materially weaker than that of the referenced issuer before the consolidation. For instance, if the combined entity has a lower credit rating after a merger than the Reference Entity before the merger, a credit event has occurred, subject to a determination of materiality.

Cross Acceleration means the occurrence of a default, event of default, or some other similar condition (other than a failure to make any required payment) with respect to another outstanding obligation of the Reference Entity, which has resulted in the other obligation becoming due and payable before it would otherwise become due and payable. In other words, if the referenced issuer defaults on any other bond, loan, lease, or obligation, for purposes of the credit swap, this counts for a Credit Event as if the issuer had defaulted on the Reference Obligation.

Cross Default is defined similarly to Cross Acceleration except that the other outstanding obligations are *capable* of being declared due and payable before such time as they would otherwise become due and payable. The distinction between Cross Acceleration and Cross Default is a fine one. For practical purposes a Cross Acceleration is an actual default event on another outstanding obligation, while a Cross Default is an event which provides the obligation holder with the ability to declare a default.

Downgrade means a reduction in credit rating of the Reference Entity, or if the Reference Obligation is no longer rated by any rating agency. The parties to the agreement can specify below what level of credit rating a Credit Event will occur. Generally, the Specified Rating is set equal to the Reference Entity's current credit rating so that any downgrade results in a Credit Event. The parties can also specify the applicable Rating Agencies, although any nationally recognized statistical rating organization usually qualifies.

Failure to Pay means that, after giving effect to any applicable grace period, the Reference Entity fails to make, when due, any payments equal to or exceeding any required payment of any outstanding obligation. Failure to Pay is a more narrow case of Cross Acceleration and Cross Default. Under the latter two conditions, the failure to perform under any loan or bond covenant constitutes a Credit Event. However, under Failure to Pay, the lack of a cash payment constitutes a Credit Event.

Repudiation means that the Reference Entity refutes, disclaims, repudiates, rejects or challenges the validity of, in whole or part, any of its outstanding obligations. Basically, if the Reference Entity refuses to pay on any of its obligations, the Investor may declare a Credit Event on the Reference Obligation.

Lastly, *Restructuring* means a waiver, deferral, restructuring, rescheduling, standstill, moratorium, exchange of obligations, or other adjustment with respect to any obligation of the Reference Entity such that the holders of those obligations are materially worse off from either an economic, credit, or risk perspective. In other words, if the Reference Entity works out a deal with its creditors on any outstanding obligation where the revised terms of that obligation are materially less favorable to the creditors, then the Investor may declare a Credit Event on the Reference Obligation.

In total, these eight events attempt to capture every type of situation that could cause the credit quality of the Reference Entity to deteriorate, or cause the value of the Reference Obligation to decline. As demonstrated above, Credit Events need not be limited only to the underlying asset in the credit swap; they may be tied to any outstanding obligation of the Reference Entity.

Settlement

The ISDA document allows for either cash or physical settlement. Cash settlement is the typical procedure. This is just the exchange of cash flows either on a scheduled payment date or upon the occurrence of a Credit Event. These exchanges of cash flows are demonstrated in Exhibits 1 through 8 in Chapter 3. However, there does not have to be a bilateral exchange of cash flows in a credit swap.

Consider a credit default swap of the type presented in Exhibit 1 in Chapter 3. In our discussion of this credit swap, the Investor pays a periodic amount to the Dealer in return for a cash payment in the event of default. The cash payment was equal the difference between a specified price (the Reference Price) and the market value of the asset after the credit event. However, the Dealer and the Investor can agree that the Dealer will pay the full Reference Price in return for delivery of the Reference Obligation.

Although this is not the typical settlement procedure, the Dealer may choose this alternative if it believes that it will be able to recover more value on a defaulted asset than what is priced in the market. For instance, recall from our discussion in Chapter 2 on credit put options that defaulted senior secured bonds trade, on average, 58 cents on the dollar. A dealer may believe that the recovery value of the Reference Obligation is potentially worth more than what the market may price it at in the event of default, and therefore, may be willing to pay for the Reference Price for its delivery.

The Benefits of Standard Documentation

The above discussion reviewed the key provisions of the ISDA credit derivative documentation. The important point is that the ISDA form provides a roadmap for credit derivative users. All of the material terms that need to be defined or negotiated are laid out for the parties in a logical order. A summary of this roadmap is presented in Exhibit 1.

Prior to the development of the ISDA form for credit derivatives, participants in the markets developed their own in-house documents, which were different from dealer to dealer. This lack of uniformity in legal terms and definitions made negotiations difficult and time consuming, especially for novice investors with little experience in this new market. As a result each transaction was often documented separately even between the same counterparties. The standard ISDA contract has greatly reduced the time committed to the negotiation process and consequently, has significantly reduced legal expenses.

This roadmap also helps transparency. All of the material economic and legal terms must be defined in the agreement. Therefore, an uninitiated investor in the credit derivatives market will be prompted to consider all of the key issues associated with a credit derivatives transaction. In effect, even if the parties to the agreement are an experienced dealer and a novice investor, the ISDA documentation will put them on equal footing.

Most importantly, liquidity is enhanced. Standard terms consistently applied across credit derivative transactions provide a common reference point, a "contractual benchmark," for all participants. If all participants use the same document, then the sale, assignment and transfer of credit derivatives is more easily facilitated. Without a standard form, the market can become fragmented, as investors search not only for the most favorable pricing, but also for the most favorable contract form. A standard contract form for credit derivatives is analogous to standardized futures contracts traded on a futures exchange; it provides a common denominator upon which all parties can transact.

Exhibit 1: ISDA Credit Derivatives Docmentation

Step 1
Define basic terms   Trade Date
                            Effective Date
                            Scheduled Termination Date
                            Reference Entity
                            Reference Obligation
                            Reference Price or Initial Spread
                            Calculation Agent
                            "Seller" and "Buyer"

Step 2
Define Fixed Payment   Periodic — set a schedule of Fixed Payment Dates
                            Bullet — Upon the occurrence of a Credit Event

Step 3
Define Floating Payment   LIBOR + spread — periodic insurance payment to
                               protect against default
                            Asset total return — exchange uncertain cash flows for
                               certain payments from Fixed Payment payer

Step 4
Notice of Credit Event   Establish the manner in which notice may be given
                            Establish the sources of Publicly Available Information
                            Establish the number of Public Sources
                            Establish who determines Materiality

Step 5
Define Credit Events   Bankruptcy
                            Credit Event upon Merger
                            Cross Acceleration
                            Cross Default
                            Downgrade
                              -define Rating Agencies
                              -establish Specified Rating
                            Failure to Pay
                            Repudiation
                            Restructuring

Step 6
Define Materiality   Specify the Price Decline Requirement or
                            Specify the Spread Widening Requirement

Step 7
Define Settlement Terms   Cash Settlement: Periodic or Bullet Payment vs.
                               Floating Payment
                            Physical Settlement: Delivery of Referenced Obligation
                               in return for payment of Reference Price

REGULATION OF CREDIT DERIVATIVES

The regulation of credit derivatives has been driven primarily by the banking regulatory authorities.[3] This is not surprising because the primary business of banks is extending credit. Consequently, these institutions have been the leaders in analyzing credit risk and developing credit derivatives. Furthermore, as our discussion of Credit-Metrics in Chapter 6 indicated, banks have also been at the forefront of designing systems to control credit risk.

The regulation of credit risk and credit derivatives in the banking sector has been developed over the past ten years. The initial development was the Basle Accord in 1988 promulgated by the Bank for International Settlements (BIS) that established international risk-based capital standards for banks. Since then these standards have evolved to include credit derivatives contained in a bank's trading portfolio.

We begin this section with a review of the initial Basle Accord. We then discuss the recent amendments to this Accord which affect a bank's trading book and the credit derivatives it may contain. Lastly, we review the specific application of risk-based capital guidelines to credit derivatives.

The Basle Accord

In December 1987, the Basle Committee on Banking Regulations and Supervisory Practices issued a consultative paper containing a

---

[3] There are three national banking authorities in United States: the Federal Deposit Insurance Corporation (FDIC), the Office of the Comptroller of the Currency (OCC), and the Federal Reserve System (FRS). The nation's banks can be divided into three types according to which governmental body charters them and whether or not they are members of the Federal Reserve System. Banks chartered through the Department of the Treasury are national banks (they have the word "national" in their name) and are regulated by the OCC. Banks chartered through individual states are divided into those banks which have chosen to be members of the FRS (these are known as "state member banks") and those that choose not to join the FRS ("state non-member banks"). State member banks are regulated by the FRS and state non-member banks are regulated by the FDIC. The FRS also regulates bank holding companies; companies set up with several subsidiaries, one of which is either a national or state bank. Also, because the FDIC insures all bank deposits (up to $100,000) it is the back-up regulator to the FRS and the OCC. Together, these three authorities audit and supervise all national and state chartered banking corporations in the United States. Collectively, we refer to these three agencies as the "banking authorities" or the "banking agencies." Although these three agencies generally agree on banking policy, we will see that there are some differences as to how they regulate credit derivatives.

proposal for allocating capital based on credit risk. The objective of this paper was to achieve a greater convergence in the measurement and assessment of capital adequacy internationally and to strengthen the capital positions at major international banks. This paper was issued to the "Group of Ten" countries for comment (actually there are 12 countries in all: Belgium, Canada, France, Germany, Italy, Japan, Luxembourg, the Netherlands, Sweden, Switzerland, the United Kingdom, and the United States).

On July 11, 1988, this paper was endorsed by the central bank governors of the Group of Ten countries, and became known as the "Basle Accord." Although the Accord was directed at large international institutions, it was adopted by the U.S. banking authorities for domestic banks as well.[4] Capital adequacy is one of the critical factors that the U.S. banking authorities must review when examining the safety and soundness of individual banks. Therefore, the risk-based capital standards were adopted to ensure uniform capital standards for all U.S. banks.

The risk-based capital framework consists of (1) a definition of capital for risk-based capital calculations, (2) a system for calculating risk-weighted assets by assigning assets and off-balance sheet items to one of four broad risk weight categories, and (3) a schedule for achieving a minimum supervisory ratio of capital to risk-weighted assets. A bank's risk-based capital ratio is calculated by dividing its qualifying total capital base by its risk-weighted assets. This ratio must equal or exceed 8%.

Qualifying capital is broken down into two categories: Tier 1 capital and Tier 2 capital. Tier 1 capital (core capital) consists of common stockholder's equity, noncumulative perpetual preferred stock, and the minority interests in the equity capital accounts of consolidated subsidiaries. Tier 2 capital (supplementary capital) includes allowances for loan and lease losses, cumulative perpetual preferred stock, hybrid securities including convertible debt securities, and subordinated debt. Tier 1 capital must be at least 4% of a bank's risk-weighted assets.

Under the risk-based capital standards, a bank's balance sheet assets and credit equivalent amounts of off-balance sheet items are

---

[4] See Federal Deposit Insurance Corporation, "Capital Maintenance; Final Statement Policy on Risk-Based Capital," 12 *CFR* 325, March 21, 1989.

assigned to one of four risk categories according to the issuer/obligor of the asset, or the guarantor of such asset. The aggregate dollar amount in each category is then multiplied by the risk weight assigned to that category. The resulting weighted values for each risk category are then summed to determine the bank's total risk-weighted assets.

Category 1 assets are assessed a zero percent risk weight. Essentially, assets in this category are considered to be free of credit risk, and therefore, no risk-based capital need be assigned to them. This category includes cash, balances due from Federal Reserve Banks and banks of OECD countries, gold bullion, and any securities, loans, leases or other claims unconditionally guaranteed by any OECD central government.[5] Category 1 risk assets also includes any securities, loans, leases or other claims issued by a U.S. agency whose principal and interest payments are guaranteed by the U.S. Government.[6]

Category 2 assets receive a 20% risk weight. These include short-term claims on U.S. banks and foreign banks (including demand deposits), cash items in the process of collection, portions of any claims which are collateralized by a segregated deposit account of the lending bank, and long-term claims on U.S. depository institutions and OECD banks. This category also includes claims on U.S. government-sponsored agencies such as Fannie Mae or Freddie Mac. Lastly, claims on international organizations such as the World Bank fall into this category.

Category 3 assets receive a 50% risk weight. These include mortgages fully secured by first liens on one to four family residential properties, private label mortgage backed securities, revenue bonds (local or national government bonds that are repaid from the revenue generated by the public works project), and any other claims, loans or leases of a state or political subdivision within the United States or other OECD country.

---

[5] OECD stands for Organization for Economic Cooperation and Development. Countries that belong to the OECD are generally considered to be politically and fiscally sound such that their debt obligations contain no credit risk.

[6] For risk-based capital purposes, a U.S. Government agency is defined as any instrumentality of the U.S. Government whose debt obligations are fully and explicitly guaranteed as to the timely payment of principal and interest. These agencies include the Government National Mortgage Association, the Veterans Administration, the Federal Housing Administration, the Farmers Home Administration, the Export-Import Bank, the Overseas Private Investment Corporation, the Commodity Credit Corporation, and the Small Business Administration.

Lastly, category 4 assets receive a full 100% risk weight. These are the usual risky assets of most balance sheets: shareholder equity in corporations, claims on non-OECD banks and governments, customer loans, corporate bonds, claims on foreign and domestic private sector obligors, and real estate loans not secured by a first lien.

Derivatives Under the Basle Accord

Generally, derivatives are incorporated into the risk-based capital calculations in a two-step procedure. First, a credit equivalent amount for each item is determined by applying credit conversion factors. These factors, ranging from 0 to 100%, are intended to reflect the risk characteristics of the activity in terms of a balance sheet equivalent. Second, the credit-equivalent amount is categorized in the same manner as on-balance sheet items, e.g., by credit risk category.

For derivative contracts, credit equivalent amounts are calculated by taking the sum of:

1. the current exposure of the derivative contract, measured by its mark-to-market value, plus
2. an add-on value as an estimate of future credit exposure of the contract.

If the mark-to-market value of a derivative is positive, this amount equals the contract's current exposure. However, if the mark-to-market value is zero or negative then the current exposure is zero. The add-on factor is estimated by multiplying the notional principal value of the derivatives contract by a credit conversion factor. These conversion factors are listed in Exhibit 2.

Exhibit 2: Credit Conversion Table for Off-Balance Sheet Items

Remaining Maturity	Interest Rate	Exchange Rate and Gold	Equity	Commodity Excluding Precious Metals	Precious Metals Excluding Gold
< 1 year	0%	1.00%	6.00%	10.00%	7.00%
1-5 years	0.50%	5.00%	8.00%	12.00%	7.00%
> 5 years	1.50%	7.50%	10.00%	15.00%	8.00%

For instance, suppose a bank enters into a 2-year, $10 million notional interest rate swap to protect against an increase in short-term interest rates. After 6 months, the swap has a positive mark to market value of $100,000. From Exhibit 2, the credit conversion factor is 0.005 (remaining maturity is between 1 and 5 years and the conversion category is Interest Rate). Therefore, the credit equivalent amount for this interest rate swap is:[7]

$$\$100,000 + (0.005) \times (\$10,000,000) = \$150,000.$$

Once the credit equivalent amount has been determined for a derivative contract, that amount is assigned to the risk category appropriate for the counterparty. For instance if the swap was transacted with another OECD bank, it would fall into risk category 2, the credit category for the seller of the interest rate protection. From our discussion above, we know that this risk category carries a risk weight of 20%. Therefore, the risk-based capital that needs to be allocated to this swap is:

$$(0.20) \times (\$150,000) \times (0.08) = \$2,400$$

Credit Derivatives under the Federal Reserve System

From Exhibit 2 it is unclear which category credit derivatives fall into. To clarify the treatment for credit derivatives, the Federal Reserve Board issued a supervisory letter in 1996 that stated that for purposes of risk-based capital calculations credit derivatives should be treated as off-balance sheet direct credit substitutes.[8] Consequently, the full notional amount of the contract should be converted at 100% to determine the credit equivalent amount to be included in the risk-based capital calculations.

---

[7] The risk-based capital standards do allow for bilateral netting arrangements. *Netting* refers to the offsetting of positive and negative mark-to-market values in determination of the current exposure to be used in the calculation of a credit equivalent amount. Any legally enforceable form of bilateral netting of derivative contracts is recognized. In particular, ISDA format contracts of the types discussed in this chapter are recognized for netting purposes.

[8] See Federal Reserve System, "Supervisory Guidance for Credit Derivatives," SR 96-17, August 12, 1996. We note that this guidance only applies to banks that are members of the Federal Reserve System. State non-member banks, for instance, are not bound by this supervisory letter.

If a bank sells credit protection through a credit derivative transaction it must assign its credit exposure to the risk category appropriate for the issuer of the underlying asset. Let's take the same example as above except, instead of an interest rate swap, the bank sells credit protection through a credit default swap. The notional amount of the swap is $10 million, the mark-to-market value is $100,000, the time remaining on the swap is 1.5 years, and the underlying asset is a bond issued by an OECD bank (risk category 2). Under Federal Reserve System rules, the credit equivalent amount of the default swap is:

$$\$100,000 + \$10,000,000 = \$10,100,000$$

and the risk-based capital charge for the credit default swap is:

$$(0.20) \times (\$10,100,000) \times (0.08) = \$161,600$$

The much higher capital charge is due to the guarantee-like nature of a credit default swap. With a credit default swap, it is as if the underlying OECD bond is on the balance sheet of the guarantor bank. The large difference in capital requirements between an interest rate swap and a credit default swap raises the issue of regulatory arbitrage. If there were a way to reclassify a credit default swap as an interest rate swap, the guarantor bank could save $159,200 in regulatory capital charges.

Although there does not seem to be any way to justify a reclassification, a guarantor bank that provides credit protection through a credit derivative may mitigate the credit risk associated with the transaction by entering into a second, offsetting credit derivative transaction with another counterparty. Banks that have entered into such back-to-back trades may treat the first credit derivative trade as guaranteed by the second trade for risk-based capital purposes.

The risk-based capital requirements, however, are beneficial to a purchaser of credit protection. If a bank buys credit protection for a credit risky asset, it may assign to that asset the risk category of credit protection seller. In effect, the bank transforms the risk category of a credit risky asset to that of the credit protection seller. This allows the bank to manage its risk-based capital more efficiently.

Exhibit 3: Reduction of Risk Based Capital
Risk-Based Capital for Customer Loan

Asset	Notional Amount	Risk Category	Risk-Based Capital %	Required Capital
Loan	$10,000,000	100%	8%	$800,000

Risk-Based Capital for Customer Loan and Credit Put Option when Option Seller is an OECD Bank

Asset	Notional Amount	Risk Category	Risk-Based Capital %	Required Capital
Loan	$10,000,000	20%	8%	$160,000
Put Option	$10,000,000	20%	8%	$160,000
			Total	$320,000

Consider a bank that owns a $10 million customer loan on its balance sheet. As an asset class, customer loans rank in risk category 4; a 100% risk capital allocation is required. The bank is worried about the value of the loan deteriorating and buys an at-the-money credit put option on the customer loan to protect against downgrades or defaults. The put option is sold by a large U.S. bank (risk category 2). Even if the credit protection buying bank must allocate risk-based capital to the purchase of the credit put option, combined the put option and the customer loan result in a lower risk-based capital charge than that required for the customer loan itself.

Exhibit 3 demonstrates this arbitrage. The fact that the put option was sold by a higher credit quality issuer than the obligor on the customer loan allows the credit protection buying bank to lower its risk-based capital requirement by $480,000. If we assume that the bank has an average cost of capital of 10%, this represents a savings of $48,000 in capital charges on an annual basis.

THE MARKET RISK AMENDMENT

In 1997, the BIS recognized that banks are exposed to *market risk* as well as credit risk. While the Basle Accord addressed the capital requirements to meet a bank's credit risk, the Market Risk Amendment (MRA) established new capital standards to account for a bank's market risk.[9] The MRA became mandatory for all U.S. banks on January 1, 1998.

The MRA established a set of quantitative and qualitative requirements for trading risk management. The quantitative capital requirements distinguish between general market risk and *specific risk* and are used to determine the appropriate level of risk capital. The qualitative standards are imposed to ensure that proper procedures are used to measure and manage market risk.

Under the MRA, market risk is defined as the risk of loss from adverse movements in the values of assets and liabilities, including off-balance sheet positions. The factors that affect market risk can be changing interest rates, commodity prices, foreign exchange rates, and equity prices. A key change in the MRA is that it distinguishes the risks of the *banking book* from the *trading book*. While the banking book contains the usual credit sensitive assets such as customer loans and mortgages, the trading book generally contains market sensitive assets such as stock, bond, commodity, and foreign exchange positions.

Market risk exposures are generally more transparent than the banking book assets because there typically is a liquid market for actively traded assets. Furthermore, trading book positions are usually marked to market on a daily basis while banking book assets are not adjusted as frequently. (Recall our discussion from Chapter 6 that many banks use a default mode of valuation for their balance sheet assets.) Therefore, under the MRA, a bank's trading book positions are subject to a new set of risk-based capital standards that account for market risk. Additionally, a bank's trading book positions are no longer included in the credit risk-based capital standards that apply to banking book assets, and are not subject to the 8% capital requirements established by the Basle Accord.

Most derivative contracts, including credit derivatives, are contained on a bank's trading book. These derivatives are now gov-

---

[9] The Federal Deposit Insurance Corporation, the Federal Reserve Board and the Department of the Treasury — Office of the Comptroller of the Currency all adopted the MRA as a joint final rule in September 1996. See "Risk Based Capital Standards: Market Risk," *OCC Bulletin* 96-49, September 6, 1996. Furthermore, for all federally chartered banks that have implemented the MRA, FRS supervisory letter *SR* 96-17 is superseded to the extent that credit derivatives are contained in the trading book of the bank. To the extent that credit derivatives are maintained on the banking book, federally chartered banks must still apply *SR* 96-17.

erned by the MRA for capital charges. However, to the extent any derivatives (including credit derivatives) remain on a bank's banking book, the capital charges are determined by Basle Accord as discussed above.

Quantitative Market Risk Requirements

The quantitative market risk requirements can be broken down into three categories: (1) market risk, (2) specific risk, and (3) counterparty risk. These three risks measure the exposures to macroeconomic factors that affect the broad economy, microeconomic factors that influence the value of individual securities, and transactional factors that arise from trading in the over-the-counter market. The quantitative market risk requirements were promulgated to calculate the amount of risk-based capital necessary to support these three risk categories.

Market Risk

Market risk is measured by a bank's own internal *value-at-risk* (VAR) model. VAR models use historical data to perform statistical analysis about the magnitude and likelihood of market risk losses. In Chapter 6 we demonstrated how credit risk distributions typically exhibit large downside "tails." Value-at-risk models attempt to measure the amount and likelihood of losses that exist in the downside tail of a distribution. In a sense value-at-risk is a "one tail" test because it is only concerned with the likelihood of losses; value-at-risk models do not examine positive returns.

Value-at-risk models produce an estimate of the maximum dollar amount a bank could lose over a specified period of time. This estimate is usually given within a range of statistical confidence, e.g., 99% or 95%. For instance, suppose that a bank had a monthly value-at-risk value of $50 million at a 95% level of confidence. Translated, this means that, over the course of any given month, the bank could expect to lose more than $50 million only 5% of the time.

Under the MRA standards, the value-at-risk estimates for a bank's trading book must be calculated on a 10-day, 99% confidence level. In other words, the MRA requires banks to determine the estimated dollar amount of lost value over a 10-day trading period that could be exceeded only 1% of the time. Another way to say this is that the value-at-risk estimate is a loss amount over a 10-day period that the bank could expect not to exceed 99% of the time.

The MRA amendment requires banks to calculate value-at-risk measures for four categories of market risk: interest rates, equity prices, foreign exchange rates, and commodity prices. In deriving the overall VAR calculation, a bank may take into account historical correlations within the four risk categories (e.g., across equity prices), but not across the risk categories themselves. In other words, the MRA assumes that the risks associated with interest rates, equity prices, foreign exchange rates and commodity prices are independent of one another. As a result, the overall VAR value is the sum of the VAR amounts for each risk category.

Once the VAR measures for the four risk categories have been summed, the risk-based capital charge for market risk equals the greater of (1) the prior day's overall VAR amount, or (2) the average of the preceding 60 day's overall VAR measure multiplied by a factor of 3. In practice, the previous day's VAR estimate should rarely exceed the 60 day average times a scaling factor of 3.[10] The total risk-based capital requirement for a bank is then the amount of capital required for credit risk as determined by the Basle Accord plus the amount of capital required to cover a bank's market risk.

The multiplication factor of 3 was implemented to ensure that the daily VAR estimate could be translated into a capital charge that would provide a sufficient cushion against cumulative losses arising from adverse market conditions over a prolonged period of time. The 10-day, 99% confidence level standard means that a bank should expect to have trading losses that exceed its required capital in one 10-day period out of 100; roughly about once every 4 years. Having banks deplete their capital, on average, once every 4 years, is too frequent an occurrence to maintain banking stability. Therefore, the VAR estimate is multiplied by 3 to provide a safety cushion.

The multiplication factor was also added to account for potential weaknesses in the VAR modeling process. For example, VAR models use historical data to estimate future losses. Should

---

[10] See Darryll Hendricks and Beverly Hirtle, "Bank Capital Requirements for Market Risk: The Internal Models Approach," *FRBNY Economic Policy Review* (December 1997), pp. 1-10.

volatilties or correlations suddenly change, the VAR calculations might underestimate the potential losses.

Additionally, most VAR models assume that the distributions of market variables are normally distributed. However, empirical evidence suggests that market variables have, in fact, "fat tails."[11] That is, outlier events are observed with much greater frequency than a normal distribution would predict.

Lastly, VAR estimates are derived during "normal" financial market activity. Shocks to the financial system are not factored in. Such stress tests may not be adequately captured in the VAR modeling process.

Specific Risk

Specific risk is defined as the risk of an adverse movement in the price of an individual security resulting from factors related to that security's issuer. These factors could be a ratings downgrade, a poor earnings report, management turnover, etc. Therefore, specific risk applies to debt and stock positions in a bank's trading book. One might consider market risk and specific risk as being the counterparts to systematic risk and unsystematic risk in a capital asset pricing model framework.[12]

The Basle Committee on Banking Supervision was concerned that a bank's VAR models would not be able to model event or default risk.[13] Therefore, specific risk capital charges are added on to the market risk capital charges in an attempt to capture event driven changes in value like those mentioned above. If a bank cannot measure specific risk through its VAR model then it must apply the table of standard specific risk-based capital charges presented in Exhibit 4. If a bank can track specific risk through its VAR process, then the risk-based capital charge is equal to the VAR estimate times a factor of 4. However, such internally generated specific risk

---

[11] See, for example, John Hull and Alan White, "Value at Risk When Daily Changes in Market Variables are not Normally Distributed," *The Journal of Derivatives* (Spring 1988), pp. 9-19; and Darrell Duffie and Jun Pan, "An Overview of Value at Risk," *The Journal of Derivatives* (Spring 1997), pp. 7-49.

[12] See Hendricks and Hirtle, "Bank Capital Requirements for Market Risk: The Internal Models Approach."

[13] See The Basle Committee on Banking Supervision, "Overview of the Amendment to the Capital Accord to Incorporate Market Risks," January 1996.

charges must equal at least 50% of the standard specific risk charges presented in Exhibit 4.

Under the MRA, a bank must multiply the net market value of each net long or short bond or equity position by the specific risk factors listed in Exhibit 4. Notice that the capital charges for specific risk in the trading book are much less than the risk-based capital charges for assets included in the banking book. This allows banks to conduct regulatory arbitrage by choosing the asset book (banking or trading) which provides the least amount of risk-based capital charges.

For instance, the specific risk-based capital charge for investment grade corporate bonds kept on the trading book ranges from 0.25% (6 months or less until maturity) to 1.6% (for bonds with over two years until maturity). However, on the banking book, all corporate bonds (investment grade and junk) must incur an 8% risk-based capital charge.

Let's take the example of a 2-year investment grade bond with a value of $1 million. On the banking book, this asset falls into risk category 4 (100%) and its credit risk-based capital charge is:

$$\$1,000,000 \times 100\% \times 8\% = \$80,000$$

Exhibit 4: Specific Risk Based Capital Charges

Category of Asset	Remaining Maturity	Risk Factor
Government	N/A	0.00%
Qualifying	less than 6 months	0.25%
	over 6 months but less than 2 years	1.00%
	over 2 years	1.60%
Equity	N/A	4% or 8%
Other	N/A	8%

Government included all debt instruments of the U.S. or OECD countries.

Qualifying includes debt instruments of U.S. or OECD sponsored agencies, U.S. and OECD banks, investment grade corporate debt, and revenue bonds issued by states and political subdivisions of the U.S. or OECD countries.

Equity includes common and preferred stock positions, convertible bonds, non-voting stock, and commitments to buy or sell equity positions. An 8% risk weighting factor applies unless the equity position is held in a portfolio that is both liquid and well-diversified. Then a risk weighting factor of 4% applies.

Other includes everything else including mortgages, customer loans, non-investment grade bonds, and other fixed income positions.

However, on the trading book, this bond is subject to market risk-and specific risk-based capital charges. The specific risk-based capital charge for this bond on the trading book is:

$1,000,000 × 1% = $10,000

The market risk-based capital charge is determined by a bank's internal VAR model. It has been estimated that the capital charges based on VAR models will add approximately 1.5% to 7.5% in risk-based capital charges.[14] Taking the midpoint of this range (4.5%), the market risk based capital charge for this bond is:

$1,000,000 × 4.5% = $45,000

The sum of the market risk-based capital charge and the specific risk-based capital charge equals $55,000 which is $25,000 less than the credit risk-based capital charge that would be required if this bond were on the banking book. The fact that there are two different sets of risk-based regulations depending on the type of asset book that is being considered allows banks to "cherry pick." In other words, banks now have the choice to move assets between the banking book and the trading book in an attempt to seek the least burdensome required capital charges. Bank regulators have recognized the issue of regulatory arbitrage, although no solution has been proposed.[15]

Counterparty Risk

In June 1997, the Federal Reserve System (FRS) released another supervisory letter to address the matching of credit derivative trades and the nature of counterparty risk.[16] With respect to credit derivatives, the FRS has identified three risk elements of credit derivatives against which banking organizations must hold risk-based capital, based upon three types of derivative positions.

---

[14] See Hendricks and Hirtle, "Bank Capital Requirements for Market Risk: The Internal Models Approach."

[15] See Federal Reserve System Task Force on Internal Credit Risk Models, "Credit Risk Models at Major U.S. Banking Institutions: Current State of the Art and the Implications for Assessments of Capital Adequacy," May 1998.

[16] See Federal Reserve System, "Application of Market Risk Capital Requirements to Credit Derivatives," *SR* 97-18, June 13, 1997.

Exhibit 5: Counterparty Credit Risk in Credit Derivaitves

Type of Position	Type of Risk		
	Counterparty Risk	Market Risk	Specific Risk
Open Position	Yes	Yes	Yes
Offsetting Position	Yes	some	some
Matched Position	Yes	No	No

These three positions are (1) matched positions, (2) offsetting positions, and (3) open positions. *Matched positions* are long and short positions in identical credit derivative instruments held over identical maturities and referencing identical assets. *Offsetting positions* include long and short credit derivative positions in reference assets of the same obligor with the same level of seniority in bankruptcy, but have either different maturities or are different credit derivative structures (i.e., long a credit put option and short a credit default swap). *Open positions* are those which do not qualify for either an offsetting or matched position.

Exhibit 5 presents the three types of risks associated with each credit derivative position. In the case of matched risk, only counterparty risk is present; matched positions eliminate both market risk and specific risk. Offsetting positions retain some market and specific risk exposure to the extent of the mismatched maturities or credit derivative instruments. For these two types of positions, the risk-based capital charges are reduced accordingly.

However, it is clear from Exhibit 5 that all three types of credit derivative positions are exposed to counterparty credit risk. In Chapter 5 we briefly touched on the subject of counterparty risk. Recall that credit derivatives are privately negotiated transactions. Therefore, they depend on each party to the transaction to perform its respective obligations. Counterparty risk is the risk that one party to a credit derivative trade will not uphold its end of the bargain.

For instance, suppose Bank A purchases a credit put option on the debt of Company B from Bank C. If Company B is downgraded, Bank A will depend on the performance of Bank C to pay out on the put option. If Bank C does not fulfill its contractual obligations, Bank A will suffer a credit loss.

Therefore, the FRS requires member banks to add an additional component to its market risk-based capital charges to account for counterparty risk. Counterparty risk is calculated by adding the mark-to-market value of the credit derivative plus an add-on factor to account for future credit exposure. This is very similar to how derivative contracts on the banking book are handled under the Basle Accord, and an 8% risk-based capital charge applies to the credit equivalent amount of counterparty credit risk.

The add-on factor is based on the credit quality of the underlying asset or issuer. If the underlying asset is either investment grade or well secured by high quality collateral, the equity add-on factor applies. If the underlying asset is below investment grade, unrated or unsecured, then the commodity add-on factor applies. The equity and commodity add-on factors are the same that applied for derivatives under the Basle Accord, and are listed in Exhibit 2.

For example, assume that a bank purchases a credit put option to protect the potential decline in value of a $1 million junk bond contained in its portfolio. The junk bond has two years until maturity. For counterparty risk purposes, the junk bond qualifies for the commodity add-on conversion factor from Exhibit 2 (12% conversion factor). The put option has two years remaining to maturity, has a current mark-to-market value of $50,000, and was sold by an OECD bank (risk category 2). The amount for counterparty risk is:

$$\$50,000 + (12\%) \times (\$1,000,000) = \$170,000$$

where $50,000 is the mark-to-market value of the credit put option and $120,000 is the amount of future credit exposure. From this calculation it seems that the market risk-based capital requirements for counterparty risk are non-trivial. However, the credit put option was issued by an OECD and this reduces the risk category of the counterparty risk to category 2 (20%). Therefore, the credit equivalent amount of the counterparty risk is:

$$\$170,000 \times 20\% = \$34,000$$

Lastly, it is upon this amount that an 8% risk-based capital charge is levied:

$$\$34,000 \times 8\% = \$2,720$$

$2,720 is the amount of risk-based capital that must be allocated for counterparty credit risk. Based on an initial amount of $170,000 of counterparty risk, this represents a capital requirement of only 1.6%.

Backtesting of Market Risk Models

One of the interesting parts of the MRA is that it allows each bank to *choose its own risk model* to determine the capital requirements for market risk. The U.S. banking agencies do not propose how the banks measure value-at-risk. Instead, they establish the parameters by which value-at-risk amounts must be determined, e.g., at a 99% confidence interval for a 10-day market move.

In order to provide some control over the models used by the banks, the U.S. banking agencies can require a bank to adjust its multiplication factor (initially set at 3) for market risk. This adjustment is made based on an assessment of the quality and historical accuracy of the bank's risk management system. In other words, the banking agencies require each bank to *backtest* its VAR model to determine its accuracy.[17]

Backtesting is the process by which a mathematical model is audited to compare the values generated by the model to observable values in the marketplace. It provides feedback as to the accuracy of the mathematical model values compared to actual outcomes. With respect to market risk, backtesting involves comparing the VAR estimate generated by a bank's value-at-risk model against the bank's actual daily profit and losses.

Under the MRA guidelines, the VAR estimates must be measured at a 99% confidence level. Therefore, when backtesting a bank's VAR model, we should expect to see trading losses which exceed the VAR estimate only 1 time out of 100 trading days. If the actual trading losses exceed the amount predicted by a bank's VAR model a sufficient number of times, the bank will be subject to a multiplication factor greater than 3.

---

[17] See "Risk Based Capital Standards; Market Risk; Internal Models Backtesting," *OCC Bulletin* 96-21 (March 7, 1996).

Exhibit 6: Adjusting the Multiplication Factor for Market Risk

Number of Exceptions	Multiplcation Factor	Cumulative Probability
0 to 4	3.00	10.78%
5	3.40	4.12%
6	3.50	1.37%
7	3.65	0.40%
8	3.75	0.11%
9	3.85	0.03%
10 or more	4.00	0.01%

To adjust the multiplication factor, the backtesting procedures for the MRA use a statistical test based on the number of times in a year that actual trading losses exceed the VAR estimate. Each instance where the actual trading losses exceed the VAR estimate is termed an exception. If a bank's VAR model is accurate, few exceptions should be observed.

The higher multiplication factor is based on a statistical test that calculates the probability that an accurate VAR model would produce a certain number of exceptions over one trading year.[18] Banks with 5 or more exceptions in one year of backtesting are subject to a higher multiplication factor, up to a factor of 4. Exhibit 6 presents the multiplication factors based on the number of exceptions produced by backtesting.

The cumulative probability numbers in Exhibit 6 indicate the probability that an accurate model would generate more than the number of exceptions reported in the first column. The cumulative probability figures are generated using a binomial distribution and a sample size of 250 trading days. As an example, the probability of observing 10 or more exceptions from an accurate VAR model is only 0.01%.[19]

---

[18] The backtest requirement is calibrated to a 1-day trading loss standard, while the VAR estimates used to determine the required amount of market risk-based capital are calibrated to a 10-day standard. This discrepancy is justified based on the necessity of having sufficient data by which to conduct a backtest. In a 250-day trading year, there are only 25 10-day periods. This is not a large enough sample size to generate robust statistical probabilities. Therefore, the supervisory backtest is calibrated to a 1-day standard with 250 observation points to improve the power of the statistical probabilities.

[19] In theory, the cumulative probabilities generated by a binomial test should be independent of the design of each bank's VAR model. Therefore, the same test for exceptions should be applicable across all banks. See Hendricks and Hirtle, "Bank Capital Requirements for Market Risk: The Internal Models Approach."

Backtesting must be performed quarterly. If backtesting results in more than four exceptions, the bank must increase its multiplication factor for the next operating quarter. Backtesting results that generate 10 or more exceptions indicate a deficient VAR model because the probability of so many exceptions is remote. Under the qualitative market risk guidelines, a bank is directed to improve its risk measurement and management.

Qualitative Market Risk Requirements

The qualitative market risk requirements are designed to ensure that a bank has a sound risk management framework surrounding its market risk capital calculations. Specifically, these standards ensure the integrity of a bank's VAR model.

First, a bank must have a risk control unit that is independent from its trading units. Simply put, those individuals who measure and monitor a bank's market risk should not be the same individuals who generate the market risk. Second, this unit must report directly to the senior management of the bank. Banks typically have risk management reports reviewed by an executive committee of the board of directors. Third, the risk management unit must be responsible for designing and implementing the bank's VAR models, and for reviewing the output from these models on a daily basis. Typically, risk management departments review the VAR estimates within the context of a bank's established trading limits. Lastly, a bank should conduct a periodic review of its risk management models. This review may be conducted by a bank's internal auditing department, with the results of the audit reported to senior management as well as the bank's outside auditors.

The qualitative market risk requirements take on greater importance in light of the backtesting of the VAR models. If a bank's backtesting indicates a significant number of exceptions, the qualitative requirements must be applied to ensure greater integrity of the model. For instance, an independent review of the VAR model by a bank's inside or outside auditors might be warranted to detect possible modeling flaws. Additionally, the bank may wish to review its risk unit to ensure that it has sufficient resources devoted to the modeling, measuring, and monitoring of market risk. Finally, there is nothing like an exception report (especially one made to bank regulators) to grab senior management's attention. In sum, the qualitative market risk requirements ensure that a bank's risk modeling is an organic, instead of static, process.

CONCLUSION

The credit derivatives market has come of age with the development of a standard ISDA contract to document these transactions. In addition to providing a common reference point, a standard form permits derivatives dealers to reduce their transaction costs, increase transparency, and enhance liquidity. Furthermore, all participants in the credit markets know the parameters by which they must negotiate these tailored investments. This saves time and reduces legal costs. Lastly, a standard contractual form provides an effective substitute for unnecessary government intervention.

The U.S. banking authorities have taken proactive steps in regulating credit derivatives by ensuring that banks maintain sufficient risk-based capital. A recent development has been the distinction between the trading book and the banking book, and the development of separate risk-based capital requirements. These regulatory requirements are summarized in Exhibit 7.

The trading books at large national banks have become significant contributors to operating performance. Additionally, these trading books require large amounts of operating capital to trade effectively. The recognition that the banking book and the trading book are affected by separate risks and require separate capital treatment is an important step in bank regulation.

Exhibit 7: Flowchart of Risk-Based Capital Charges

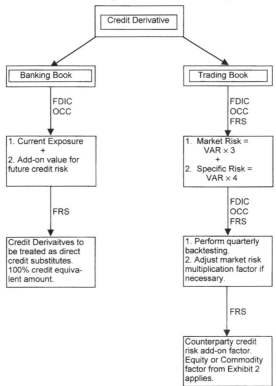

FDIC is the Federal Deposit Insurance Corporation.
OCC is the Office of the Comptroller of the Currency.
FRS is the Federal Reserve System.

Chapter 8

Accounting and Tax Implications of Credit Derivatives

INTRODUCTION

R ecently both the Financial Accounting Standard Board
(FASB) and Congress have implemented new accounting
and tax guidelines for derivative transactions. In June 1998
FASB released its long awaited Statement of Financial Accounting
Standards No. 133: *Accounting for Derivative Instruments and
Hedging Activities* (FAS 133), and in August 1997 Congress passed
The Taxpayer Relief Act of 1997. These regulations have a direct
impact on the accounting and tax treatment of derivatives.

 We begin this chapter with a detailed discussion of FAS 133,
and an examination of how different types of credit derivatives are
accounted for under this new release. Next we consider the application of The Taxpayer Relief Act to credit derivatives, as well as
other pertinent tax code provisions.

ACCOUNTING FOR DERIVATIVE INSTRUMENTS AND HEDGING ACTIVITIES

Accounting for derivatives is an issue that has perplexed accoun-
tants and industry participants for years. As the size of the derivatives market has grown each year the demand for consistent
accounting treatment has grown with it. Over the past several years,
the Financial Accounting Standards Board has wrangled with the
accounting for derivatives in various releases. In an attempt to deal

with the disclosure of the off-balance sheet nature of many derivatives, FASB released Statement No. 105 *Disclosure of Information about Financial Instruments with Off-Balance Sheet Risk and Financial Instruments with Concentrations of Credit Risk* in March 1990, and Statement No. 119, *Disclosure about Derivative Financial Instruments and Fair Value of Financial Instruments* in October 1994.

Still, this was enough.[1] The issues surrounding the accounting treatment of derivatives continued to swirl until FASB released the exposure draft *Accounting for Derivative and Similar Financial Instruments and For Hedging Activities* ("Exposure Draft"), on June 20, 1996. After a year of deliberations, the FASB released a follow-up report to the Exposure Draft on July 17, 1997. It was another year of deliberation and comment before the FASB released its final rule in June 1998. FAS 133 applies to all entities and industries and is effective for all fiscal reporting years beginning after June 15, 1999.[2]

As a threshold question, we should ask whether or not FAS 133 applies to credit derivatives. The answer is short and cute: yes and no. As we will see, FASB has carved out some exceptions to FAS 133 that apply to credit derivative transactions.

We begin this section with a discussion of four fundamental conclusions regarding derivatives reached by the FASB. We then describe the basic accounting concepts now required for the recording of derivative instruments. Lastly, we examine some of the special circumstances by which credit derivatives are excluded from FAS 133.

Fundamental Conclusions Regarding Derivative Instruments

In a nutshell, FAS 133 requires that an entity recognize all derivative instruments as either assets or liabilities in the statement of

---

[1] In fact, the Securities and Exchange Commission entered the fray and issued its own rules for derivatives disclosure in the financial statements of public companies. See Mark Anson, "Accounting for Derivatives: New Disclosure Regulations Proposed by the Securities and Exchange Commission," *Derivatives Quarterly* (Summer 1996), pp. 15-25.

[2] FAS 133 supersedes FAS 105 and FAS 119 as well as FAS 80, *Accounting for Futures Contracts*. Additionally, FAS 133 amends parts of FAS 52, *Foreign Currency Translation*.

financial position and measure the value of those derivatives at fair value.[3] Central to the notion of fair value accounting are four conclusions regarding the financial impact of derivatives.

1. *Derivatives are assets and liabilities and should be reported in the financial statements.* Derivatives are assets or liabilities because they are rights or obligations that may be settled in cash. Prior to the issuance of FAS 133, many derivatives were excluded from the balance sheets of reporting entities because, unlike traditional financial assets such as stocks and bonds, derivatives often reflect only a mutual exchange of promises documented in standard contract formats[4] without any initial exchange of tangible consideration.

2. *Fair value is the only relevant measure for derivatives.* The financial press is well-documented regarding the huge losses associated with derivatives trading.[5] The leveraged nature of derivatives can make their value more volatile than the underlying economic variable from which they derive their value, and the value of a derivative instrument can change

---

[3] FAS 133 defines a derivative instrument as a financial instrument or other contract that meets three criteria:
- It has one or more underlyings and one or more notional amounts, or payment provisions or both. Those terms determine the amount of the settlement or settlements, and, in some cases, whether or not a settlement is required.
- It requires no initial net investment or an initial net investment that is smaller than would be required for other types of contracts that would be expected to have a similar response to changes in market factors.
- Its terms require or permit net settlement, it can readily be settled net by a means outside the contract, or it provides for delivery of an asset that puts the recipient in a position not substantially different from net settlement.

[4] The standard contract form for most derivative transactions is the International Swaps and Derivatives Association (ISDA) 1992 Master Agreement.

[5] See "Top Managers at Barings Face Fresh Criticism," *The Financial Times Limited* (July 20, 1996), p. 4; "Orange County Seeks Protective Order Vacating Depositions," *Derivatives Litigation Reporter* (April 22, 1996), p. 12; Procter & Gamble Reaches Accord with Bankers Trust," *Los Angeles Times*, part D (May 10, 1996), p. 2; "Lack of Care Costs Funds; Wisconsin Audit Cites 'Excessive Risk' in Derivatives Losses," *Pensions & Investments* (July 24, 1995), p. 32; "Pier 1 Shareholders Fault Board for $20MM Derivative Losses; Board Blames Refco," *Derivatives Litigation Report* (May 27, 1996), p. 3; "Daiwa Debacle Shows Flaws in High-Voltage Finance," *Asahi News Service* (September 29, 1995); "How Copper Lost its Luster for Sumitomo," *New York Times* (June 15, 1996), p. 31.

quickly. Consequently, fair value accounting of derivatives is more relevant to financial statement users than cost when assessing the liquidity or solvency of an entity because it reflects the current cash equivalent of the entity's derivative positions.

3. *Only items that are assets or liabilities should be reported in the financial statements.* While this decision might seem obvious from the discussion above, this statement is meant to address changes in value of derivative instruments. That is, gains and losses from derivative instruments are not to be considered separate assets and liabilities because they do not have the essential characteristics of assets and liabilities as described above. Under the new rules for hedge accounting, gains and losses on derivative instruments are either recognized in current income or deferred to shareholders' equity.

4. *Hedge accounting should be limited to those transactions that meet reasonable criteria.* Because hedge accounting is elective and relies on management's intent, it should not apply in all circumstances where management asserts that a relationship exists between a derivative instrument and a balance sheet item. The primary purpose of hedging is to link items or transactions whose changes in fair value are expected to offset each other. Consequently, an existing asset or liability must exist on the balance sheet, or a forecasted transaction must be reasonably probable before a derivative instrument can qualify as a hedge.

Accounting for Credit Derivatives under FAS 133

Under FAS 133, derivatives fall into one of four categories: (1) derivatives that have no hedging designation; (2) derivatives that qualify for a fair value hedge; (3) derivatives that qualify for a cash flow hedge; and, (4) derivatives that qualify for a foreign currency hedge. We discuss cash flow hedges and foreign currency hedges only briefly because they are not applicable to credit derivatives, while devoting most of our time to examining the first two categories.[6]

---

[6] For a more extensive discussion on cash flow hedges, see Mark Anson, "Accounting for Derivatives Part II: New Rules from FASB, *Derivatives Quarterly* (Winter 1997), pp. 7-25.

Derivatives that have No Hedging Designation

This is the easiest type of derivative to account for under FAS 133. The gain or loss on a derivative transaction not designated as a hedging instrument must be reported in current earnings.

Consider the total return credit swap of Exhibit 5 in Chapter 3. The purpose of this swap from the investor's point of view is to receive the economic exposure to a credit risky asset that it does not have on its balance sheet. This type of transaction has no hedging component to the investor. Instead, its purpose is to acquire credit risk, not hedge it.[7]

Notice that at the time that this swap is entered into by the parties, the fair value of the swap is zero. In other words, at time $t = 0$ the swap is a fair bargain to both parties because the present value of swap payments promised to be paid by one party is exactly equal to the present value of swap payments promised by its counterparty. Therefore, the net present value of the swap to both parties is zero. Similarly, at maturity, the value of a swap is also zero. However, during its life, a swap can have either positive or negative value.

Furthermore, at the outset of a swap, there is no exchange of cash flows. Rather, the parties to a swap obligate themselves to make future payments. As a result, no accounting entry is required at the time a swap is initiated because there is no asset value to record and there is no cash inflow or outflow to recognize.

However, at the end of one period, the swap payments will be netted and one party will receive a net payment from its counterparty. Under the usual accounting procedures, the net inflow is recorded as income by one party, and the net outflow is recorded as a charge to earnings by the counterparty.

FAS 133 comes into play at the end of the first period when swap payments are netted. At this point the swap most likely has a positive value to one party and a negative value to the counterparty. The reason is that market variables such as interest rates can, and do, change over time. In fact, even the simple amortization of swap payments over time can result in positive and negative swap values.

---

[7] However, from the dealer's point of view, if it already owns the credit risky asset on its balance sheet, the payment of total return to the investor in return for an annual payment may be considered a fair value hedge of the underlying credit risk asset.

The result is that, after one period, the swap will have a positive present value to one party and a negative present value to its counterparty.[8] Under FAS 133, any change in swap value must be recorded in current income as either a gain or loss.

Let's see how this works. Exhibit 1 presents a 2-year total return credit swap on a high-yield bond. The bond has a face value of $1,000, matures in two years, carries a coupon rate of 9%, and has a current market value of $990. An investor enters into a 2-year swap with a notional value of $1,000 with a dealer whereby the investor will receive the total return on the high-yield bond and the dealer will receive LIBOR + 200 basis points.

Exhibit 1: Determine the Value of a Total Return Credit Swap

Treasury zero-coupon curve
1 year   6%
2 year   7%
1 year forward rate   8%

$T = 0$

Present value of total return payments to investor
$$\$95/1.06 + \$95/(1.07)^2 = \$172$$

Present value of floating payments to dealer
$$\$85/1.06 + \$105/(1.07)^2 = \$172$$

Net present value of the swap to the investor and the dealer
$$\$172 - \$172 = \$0$$

$T = 1$

Present value of total return payment to investor
$$\$95/1.08 = \$87.96$$

Present value of floating payment to dealer
$$\$105/1.08 = \$97.22$$

Net present value of swap to dealer
$$\$97.22 - \$87.96 = \$9.26$$

Net present value of swap to investor
$$\$87.96 - \$97.22 = (\$9.26)$$

---

[8] It is possible that a swap will remain with a net present value of zero to both parties, but this situation will occur only by coincidence if changes in market variables exactly offset the amortization of the swap payments.

In Exhibit 1 we present the zero-coupon Treasury yield curve which we will use to discount the cash flows under the credit swap.[9] The 1-year rate is 6% and the 2-year zero-coupon rate is 7%. Using the bootstrapping technique discussed in the appendix to Chapter 4, we can derive the 1-year forward rate in one year's time as 8%. One year LIBOR is 6.5%.

With the high-yield bond, the investor expects the bond price to "roll up" the maturity curve by $10 over the next two years (from $990 to $1,000). Let's assume that the bond will, in fact, increase in value by $5 in each of the next two years. Combined with the 9% coupon, the investor expects to receive each year a total return of $95. Using the zero-coupon discount rates, we can see that the present value of the total return payments to the investor is $172.

At the end of one year, the investor promises to pay to the dealer LIBOR + 2%, or 8.5%, on a notional amount of $1,000 (a payment of $85). However, what does the investor expect to pay at the end of year two? The only way to predict this is to forecast what 1-year LIBOR will be one year from now. From our zero-coupon yield curve, we know that the forecasted 1-year Treasury rate one year from now is 8%, an increase of 200 basis points over the current 1-year Treasury rate of 6%. We assume that LIBOR will also jump by 200 basis points next year to a rate of 8.5%.[10] Therefore, the investor expects to pay a floating rate of 10.5% at the end of year two (a payment of $105).

From Exhibit 1, the present value of the floating payments promised by the investor also equal $172. Therefore, at the start of the swap, the net present value to both parties is zero. Now assume that at the end of the first year of the credit swap both the 1-year Treasury rate and LIBOR increase by the projected 200 basis points. In Exhibit 1, the present value of the swap to the investor is now a negative $9.26 and it is a positive $9.26 to the dealer.

[9] The discount rate used to determine the present value of the swap cash flows should represent the riskiness of those cash flows. Generally, the market convention is to assume that an appropriate discount rate is one that corresponds to the risk level of the floating-rate payment underlying a swap. This is a common assumption that allows the floating rate to be used as the discount rate. For simplicity, in our example, we assume that both counterparties are of high investment grade quality and apply the zero-coupon Treasury curve as the discount rate.
[10] If LIBOR did not change in sync with Treasury rates, financial engineers would figure a way to arbitrage this discrepancy.

Exhibit 2: Application of FAS 133 to a Total Return Credit Swap

Time $t = 0$
No accounting entries necessary

Time $t = 1$

Investor	Debit	Credit
Cash	$10	
Earnings		$10
To record swap income		
Earnings	$9.26	
Swap Liability		$9.26
To record loss on swap value		

Time $t = 2$

Investor	Debit	Credit
Earnings	$10	
Cash		$10
To record swap expense		
Swap Liability	$9.26	
Earnings		$9.26
To record change in swap value		

Under FAS 133, at the end of the first period, the investor must record a net inflow of swap payments of $10 ($95 − $85), and a loss of swap value of $9.26. The $9.26 represents the present value of the investor's net outflow next period ([$95 − $105]/1.08). These accounting entries are given in Exhibit 2. As these entries indicate, the investor's current income of $10 from the swap payment is offset by the present value of next period's outflow. The dealer's entries are the exact opposite of that for the investor.

At the end of period 2, the swap matures. At the maturity of a swap, its present value becomes zero again because there are no further cash flows to be paid. Therefore, the investor will record a positive change in swap value from a negative $9.26 to zero. Additionally, the investor must now pay a net outflow to the dealer equal to $10 ($95 − $105). These entries are also presented in Exhibit 2.

Fair Value Hedges

An entity may designate a derivative instrument as hedging the exposure to changes in the fair value of an asset or a liability or an identifiable portion of the hedged item that is attributable to a particular risk. Assets and liabilities that exhibit fair value exposures are dependent on the changes of underlying market variables.

Specifically, an asset or liability is eligible for fair value hedging:

> If the hedged item is a financial asset or liability, a recognized loan servicing right, or a nonfinancial firm commitment with financial components, the designated risk being hedged is (1) the risk of changes in the overall fair value of the entire hedged item, (2) the risk of changes in its fair value attributable to changes in market interest rates, (3) the risk of changes in its fair value attributable to changes in the related foreign currency exchange rates, or (4) *the risk of changes in its fair value attributable to the obligor's creditworthiness* (emphasis added).[11]

Consequently, FAS 133 specifically identifies credit risk as a reasonable risk to qualify for fair value hedge accounting. Under FAS 133 the gain or loss on a derivative instrument designated as a fair value hedge must be recognized in current earnings. Additionally, the change in value of the item being hedged must also be recorded in current earnings.

In a perfect world the gain or loss on the derivative instrument would exactly offset the loss or gain on the asset being hedged, and there would be no impact on earnings. However, hedges are rarely perfect and usually result in some basis risk. In other words, the derivative instrument may not precisely match the economic movement of the underlying hedged item. Under FAS 133, any difference that does arise would be the result of *hedge ineffectiveness*, and must be recognized in current earnings. As a result, any hedge ineffectiveness will directly affect earnings because there will be no offsetting adjustment in value of the underlying hedged item. A couple of examples will help to illustrate this point.

---

[11] See Financial Accounting Standards Board, Statement of Financial Accounting Standards No. 133, *Accounting for Derivative Instruments and Hedging Activities* (June 1998), para. 21. If the risk being hedged is not the overall change in fair value, then two or more of the other risks (interest rate, foreign exchange, or credit risk) must be identified to qualify for fair value hedge accounting. As a practical matter, credit derivatives should qualify as a hedge against a change in overall value of a financial asset or liability.

Exhibit 3: Fair Value Hedge Accounting for a Costless Credit Put Option

Transaction	Cash		Put Option		Junk Bond		Earnings	
	Dr	Cr	Dr	Cr	Dr	Cr	Dr	Cr
Time $t = 0$								
No accounting entry								
Time $t = 1$								
Change in option value			$20					$20
Change in junk bond value						$20	$20	
Sale of junk bond	$80							$80
Current market value of bond						$80	$80	
Settlement or sale of option	$20			$20				
Total	$100		$20	$20		$100	$100	$100

Consider an investor who buys a credit put option as a fair value hedge to protect against the decline in value of a junk bond. The bond has a current market price equal to its face value of $100, the option is struck at-the-money, the maturity of the option is one year, and the investor sells the junk bond at the end of one year.

For illustrative purposes, we assume that there is no cost to the put option. This assumption may be a bit unrealistic, but it will simplify our demonstration of FAS 133. We will relax this assumption in a moment.

At the end of one year, the bond has declined in value by $20 and the intrinsic value of the credit put option is $20. Notice that the change in value of the credit put option exactly offsets the change in value of the junk bond. At the end of one year the investor settles the option and sells the bond. The impact on the entity's income statement is zero. Exhibit 3 demonstrates the accounting entries for this fair value hedge.

We can see from Exhibit 3 that there is no impact on earnings. This is because $100 is debited to earnings as an expense from the decline in value of the junk bond ($20) and the cost of goods sold for the sale of the junk bond ($80). Similarly, $100 of income is credited to earnings from the increase in value of the put option ($20) and the revenue from the sale of the junk bond ($80). If we look at the totals for all of the accounting entries across the bottom of Exhibit 3, we see that all of the debits and credits cancel each other out, so there are no accounting "loose ends." More importantly, in the Earnings column, the debits and credits also cancel out so that there is no net effect on the income statement of the investor.

Exhibit 4: Fair Value Hedge Accounting for a Costly Credit Put Option

Transaction	Cash Dr	Cash Cr	Put Option Dr	Put Option Cr	Junk Bond Dr	Junk Bond Cr	Earnings Dr	Earnings Cr
Time $t = 0$								
Purchase the credit put option		$5	$5					
Time $t = 1$								
Change in option value			$15					$15
Change in junk bond value						$20	$20	
Sale of junk bond	$80							$80
Current market value of bond						$80	$80	
Settlement or sale of option	$20			$20				
Total	$100	$5	$20	$20		$100	$100	$95

Now consider the case where the investor must make an upfront payment for the credit put option of $5. In one year the bond has decline in value by $20 and the current value of the put option is $20. Now we have an example of hedge ineffectiveness. Although the value of the put option equals the decline in value of the junk bond, the investor initially had to pay $5 for the option. Therefore, the net gain on the option is only $15 and consequently, only this amount effectively hedged the decline in value of the junk bond. The remaining amount of $5 must be charged to income as an expense of hedge ineffectiveness. This is demonstrated in Exhibit 4.

Looking at the total across the bottom of Exhibit 4 we see once again that the debits and credits cancel each other out. However, within the Earnings column, the debits and credits do not cancel each other out. What remains is a net debit of $5, the expense for purchasing the credit protection. Under FAS 133 guidelines, this is the amount of hedge ineffectiveness and must be charged against current income. More intuitively, the amount of $5 simply represents the cost of credit protection. This is an expense that must be charged against earnings.

Financial Guarantees do not Qualify as Fair Value Hedges

Financial guarantee contracts are not subject to FAS 133 if they provide for payments to be made only to reimburse the credit protection buyer for a loss incurred because the issuer fails to make a payment when it is due. FASB believes that a default is an identifiable event which can be insured by a financial guarantee. This is different from a contract to reimburse a credit protection buyer in response to a change in an underlying asset's value or a change in an issuer's change in creditworthiness.

Therefore, a credit default swap like that presented in Exhibit 1 in Chapter 3 is exempt from the requirements of FAS 133 because the credit protection seller makes a payment if and only if a default occurs. FAS 133 interprets this type of credit swap as a financial guarantee. If the asset deteriorates in value, the credit protection seller has no obligation. Therefore, a credit default swap does not protect against a decline in an issuer's creditworthiness. Instead, the credit protection seller's obligation is to ensure that the credit protection buyer is made whole in the event of default.

This type of credit derivative is another form of off-balance sheet activity. Banks have been using this type of credit insurance in the form of standby letters of credit for years. It is simply a commitment by the bank to pay the credit protection buyer in the event that a referenced issuer fails to repay a loan, junk bond or emerging market debt. In the event of default, the bank advances funds to the credit protection buyer to cover the amount of her loss.

This type of activity is considered off-balance sheet because, although there is a referenced asset and issuer, the bank does not record any asset or liability on its balance sheet. Instead, the bank will record fee income (debit cash, credit fee income) from the credit protection buyer, and the credit protection buyer will record a cash expense for credit protection (credit cash, debit swap expense). In sum, only the income statements of the parties are affected, their respective balance sheets remain unchanged.[12]

---

[12] Footnotes to corporate financial statements often contain disclosures relating to contingent losses. Under FAS 5, *Accounting for Contingencies*, firms are required to accrue a loss (recognize a liability) if both of the following conditions are met:

   1. It is probable that assets have been impaired or a liability incurred; and
   2. The amount of the loss can be reasonably estimated.

FAS 5 defines "probable events" as those "more likely than not" to occur, suggesting that a probability of more than 50% is required before recognition is mandated. Footnote disclosure is required when it is reasonably possible that a loss has occurred or when it is probable that a loss has occurred but the amount cannot be reasonably estimated. Therefore, if an issuer referenced in a credit default swap is likely to default, disclosure may be required. However, if the prospects for default are remote, no footnote or balance sheet disclosure is required.

Cash Flow Hedges

An entity may designate a derivative contract as hedging the exposure to variability in future expected cash flows that is attributable to a particular risk. Cash flow hedges are usually associated with a forecasted transaction such as the sale of inventory at a future date. The classic example of a cash flow hedge is the farmer who sells futures contracts today to lock in the price of his grain sales at harvest time. Consequently, cash flow hedges are not applicable to credit derivatives; we include a short discussion of them for completeness.

For cash flow hedges, the effective portion of the gain or loss on a derivative contract is recorded as a component of *comprehensive income* (outside of current earnings) and reclassified into earnings in the same period or periods during which the hedged forecasted transaction affects earnings. In other words, gains and losses on a cash flow hedge are not immediately reported in earnings. Rather, the gains and losses are accumulated on the balance sheet until the forecasted transaction occurs, and then are charged to earnings. Any ineffective portion of the cash flow hedge (that portion of the hedge gain/loss that does not precisely match the loss/gain of the forecasted transaction) is reported in earnings in the period in which it occurs.

Foreign Currency Hedges

Foreign currency hedges are classified as either a foreign currency fair value hedge or a foreign currency cash flow hedge. The rules for these transactions function just as discussed above for fair value hedges and cash flow hedges. Foreign currency hedges that hedge the fair value of an asset denominated in a foreign currency must record the gain or loss on the derivative instrument in current income. Conversely, the gain or loss on a hedge of a forecasted foreign currency denominated transaction must be reported in comprehensive income, while the ineffective portion of a foreign currency cash flow hedge must be reported in current income.

Embedded Derivatives Under FAS 133

A financial contract that does not in its entirety meet the definition of a derivative instrument may contain an embedded derivative—

some explicit or implicit term that affects some or all of the cash flows or value of the financial contract. The best example of this situation is a credit linked note. The effect of embedding a derivative instrument in a cash instrument (the "host instrument") is that some or all of the cash flows promised under the note will be modified by the embedded credit derivative. Under FAS 133, embedded derivatives must be separated from the host instrument and accounted for as a derivative if the following criteria are met:

- The economic characteristics and risks of the embedded derivative instrument are not clearly and closely related to the economic characteristics and risks of the host instrument.
- The hybrid instrument (the host instrument plus the embedded derivative) is not currently measured at fair value with changes in fair value reported in earnings as they occur.
- A similar stand-alone instrument with the same terms as the embedded derivative would be subject to the provisions of FAS 133.

Since the second and third criteria are straightforward to determine, it is the first issue that receives the most scrutiny. According to FAS 133, the creditworthiness of the debtor and the interest rate on a debt instrument are considered to be clearly and closely related. Therefore, for debt instruments that have the interest rate reset in the event of (1) the violation of a credit risk related covenant, (2) a change in the debtor's credit rating, or (3) a change in the debtor's creditworthiness indicated by an increased credit spread over a reference interest rate, the embedded instrument would *not* be separated from the host instrument.

Consider the example of the International Finance Corporation of Thailand bond presented in Chapter 2. With this bond, the interest rate was increased if the credit rating deteriorated. This was demonstrated in Exhibit 10 in Chapter 2. Under FAS 133, because these embedded credit call options were clearly and closely related to the underlying issuer's creditworthiness, they would not be separated from the IFCT bond and would not have separate accounting.

Furthermore, under FAS 133, call and put options that can accelerate the repayment of principal on a debt instrument are considered to be clearly and closely related to the debt instrument unless both (1) the debt involves a substantial premium or discount (most common with zero-coupon bonds), and (2) the put or call option is only contingently exercisable. In the IFCT bond example, the exercise of the embedded put was contingent on the issuer falling below investment grade. However, the bond was originally issued at 99.925, there was no substantial premium or discount. Consequently, the credit put option would not be accounted for separately.

If we examine the more general case of credit linked notes such as that presented in Exhibit 3 of Chapter 4, the conclusion would be different. In this example, the credit forward, credit call option, and credit put option referenced the creditworthiness of an issuer different from the issuer of the credit linked note. Therefore, the three embedded derivative instruments are not clearly and closely related to the risks of the host note, and they must be separated from the credit linked note and accounted for separately. Under FAS 133, these credit derivatives would be accounted for as derivative instruments that have no hedging designation. (See Exhibit 2.)

Potential Volatility in Earnings and Equity

One of the concerns voiced about FAS 133 is that accounting for changes in fair value of derivatives and hedged items will increase the volatility of earnings. It may be argued that changes in fair values of derivative instruments do not provide any revenue to an entity, and therefore, should not be included in the income statement. The new derivative reporting requirements may increase the volatility of reported earnings even though there have been no cash flows associated with the derivative instrument.

Yet derivative contracts are typically leveraged investment views on interest rates, credit quality, credit spreads, indexes or some other underlying economic variable. These instruments can result in substantial benefits and liabilities to an entity that will eventually translate into real cash inflows or outflows. Therefore, it could be argued that it was the prior guidance on accounting for derivatives that obscured an entity's earnings volatility. The prevailing view is that FAS 133 does not create volatility, but rather, reveals it.[13] In fact, it can be argued that FAS 133 now requires the reporting of earnings volatility which always existed but, under prior accounting statements, was never reported.

TAX TREATMENT OF CREDIT DERIVATIVES

The Taxpayer Relief Act of 1997 (the "Act") contained provisions designed to crack down on certain derivative transactions used by large institutions and wealthy individuals to reap economic gains from appreciated asset positions while not recognizing any tax liability. The result is that the tax advantages of many derivative transactions have been eliminated or diminished. However, curiously, the Act carved out certain exemptions that, while not specifically intended to grant relief to credit derivative trades, nevertheless apply to these transactions.

We begin this section with a brief overview of the Act, and then discuss why it does not apply to credit derivatives. We then look at other Internal Revenue Code provisions to see which do apply to credit derivatives. Lastly, we provide a few examples on how credit derivatives are taxed.

The Taxpayer Relief Act of 1997

The Taxpayer Relief Act of 1997 (the "Act") was signed into law in August 1997. The Act made several major changes to the tax code which impacted the way mutual funds operate, the way people invest in IRAs, and the way derivative transactions are taxed. One of those changes pertains to constructive sales and impacts derivative strategies commonly used by investors and brokerage firms to lock in "paper profits."

The United States Congress had become concerned in recent years with respect to numerous financial transactions developed by Wall Street brokerage houses which allowed institutional clients and wealthy taxpayers to reduce, defer, or eliminate their risk of loss from

---

[13] See G. Robert Smith, Gary Waters, and Arlette C. Wilson, "Improved Accounting for Derivatives and Hedging Activities," *Derivatives Quarterly* (Fall 1998), pp. 15-20.

an underlying investment without recognizing any taxable disposition. Yet, like most sales of property, these transactions provided the taxpayer with cash, payments, or other property in return for the interest in the underlying investment that the taxpayer had given up. Therefore, the taxpayer was compensated for giving up the economic rights to the underlying investment, but did not recognize a taxable gain.

The Act introduced a new Section 1259 of the Internal Revenue Code (IRC) to address derivative transactions. Section 1259 requires a taxpayer to recognize the gain (but not the loss) upon entering into a *constructive sale* of any *appreciated financial position* in stock, a partnership interest, or certain debt instruments as if that position were sold, assigned or otherwise terminated at its fair market value on the date of the constructive sale.[14] To consider the impact of this rule on credit derivatives, we need to review some of the Act's defined terms.

Constructive Sales

Section 1259(c) treats a taxpayer as having made a constructive sale of an appreciated financial position if the taxpayer:

(1) Enters into a short sale of the same or substantially identical property.[15]

(2) Enters into an offsetting notional principal contract with respect to the same or substantially identical property.

(3) Or enters into a futures or forward contract to deliver the same or substantially identical property.

A constructive sale may also occur if the taxpayer enters into one or more transactions that have "substantially the same affect" as

---

[14] In addition to the requirement that capital gain be recognized upon the constructive sale of an appreciated financial position, two other transaction events apply: (i) an adjustment is made to the amount of any gain or loss subsequently taken into account with respect to the position; and (ii) the taxpayer's holding period with respect to the position begins anew at the time the constructive sale agreement is entered into. For a full discussion on the implications of the Taxpayer Relief Act of 1997, see Mark Anson, "The Impact of the Taxpayer Relief Act of 1997 on Derivative Transactions," *The Journal of Derivatives* (Summer 1998), pp. 62-72.

[15] The Act does not define the term "substantially identical." However, the same phrase is used in IRC Section 1091 with respect to wash sales of "substantially identical stock or securities." Under this code section, securities are considered "substantially identical" if they are not substantially different in any material feature or in several material features considered together.

the three transactions described above. Under this rule, more than one appreciated financial position or more than one offsetting transaction can be aggregated to determine whether a constructive sale has occurred.

The tax code generally defines "offsetting notional principal contracts" as swaps.[16] Therefore, a credit default swap of the type in Exhibit 3 of Chapter 3 would qualify. In this exhibit, the investor promises to pay the dealer the total return on the underlying asset in return for periodic payments. In effect, the investor has sold the economic rights to the asset to the dealer, and has received a payment in return. This is a constructive sale under the Act.

Appreciated Financial Position

The constructive sales rules are defined in terms of "appreciated financial positions." Section 1259(b) defines an appreciated financial position (AFP) as any position with respect to any stock, partnership interest, or debt instrument where there would be a gain if the position were sold, assigned, or otherwise terminated at its fair market value. A "position" for purposes of an AFP is defined as an investment in the underlying security, a futures or forward contract, a short sale, or an option.

Although Section 1259(b) does not include the term "swap" within the definition of a "position," it is likely that such contracts would be considered a "position" because of their economic equivalence to forward or futures contracts. In any event, the constructive sales rules apply to either an initial investment in a derivative contract or an investment in an underlying security.

However, Section 1259(b) carves out an exception to appreciated financial positions for "straight debt." A fixed income obligation qualifies as straight debt if:

(1) the debt unconditionally entitles the holder to receive a specified principal amount;
(2) the interest payments with respect to such debt meet the requirements of IRC Section 860G(a)(1)(B)(i) (that interest payments or other similar amounts accruing on the debt are

---

[16] See IRC, Section 1.446-3.

payable at a fixed rate or payable at a specified variable rate); and

(3) the debt is not convertible, either directly or indirectly, into stock of the issuer or any related entity.

Therefore, a short credit derivative position combined with a debt instrument satisfying the above criteria will not result in a constructive sale. This means that a credit derivative on a bank loan, emerging market debt, or a junk bond (as long as the junk bond is not convertible into equity) is not covered by Section 1259 even if the investor receives an economic benefit from the transaction. It is unclear why this exception was carved out for debt investments. While it may generally be true that debt instruments do not share to the same extent the appreciation of equity investments and therefore, may have only small gain to realize (see our discussion on the distribution of credit returns in Chapter 6), we note that there is no *de minimis* exception to Section 1259. That is, any amount of gain, no matter how small, can be recognized under the constructive sales rules.

Continuing with our example of the credit default swap in Exhibit 3 of Chapter 3, the investor swaps the total return on the underlying credit risky asset in return for periodic payments from the dealer. In effect, the investor sells a credit risky asset and receives periodic income from the sale from the dealer. However, if the underlying asset qualifies as straight debt, a constructive sale will not be recognized. Instead, the exchange of payments from the credit swap is taxed under more conventional tax rules.

Taxation of Credit Swap Contracts

Swaps fall under the notional principal contract guidelines of IRC Regulation 1.446-3. A notional principal contract is defined as "a financial instrument that provides for the payment of amounts by one party to another at specified intervals calculated by reference to a specified index upon a notional principal amount in exchange for specified consideration or a promise to pay similar amounts." A specified index can be a fixed rate, price, securities index, interest rate index, or amount. In short, notional principal contracts include interest rate swaps, currency swaps, basis swaps, equity swaps, and commodity swaps. Although Section 1.446-3 does not specifically identify credit swaps, the general consensus is that these credit derivative instruments fall under this tax provision.[17]

Total Return Credit Swap

Consider a 2-year total return credit swap that the parties enter into on April 1, 1998. The investor promises to pay the total return on a junk bond (interest plus capital appreciation) to the dealer in return for LIBOR + 200. Assume that LIBOR is currently 6%, that the coupon on the junk bond is 8.5%, that payments are to be made April 1 1999, and that the notional value of the swap is $1 million.

Under Rule 1.466-3, the swap participants must recognize the ratable portion of swap income in the tax year to which that portion applies. Assume both the dealer and the investor have calendar tax years. Therefore, at December 31, 1998, they must calculate the ratable income or expense associated with the credit swap. For the dealer, its payment April 1, 1999 is certain (8% × $1,000,000). Therefore, its ratable swap payment as of December 31 is:

$$8\% \times \$1,000,000 \times (277/365) = \$60,712$$

However, the exact amount that the investor must pay to the dealer next April cannot be determined with certainty. Instead, the investor must determine the amount that would be payable as of December 31 even though its payment obligation is not until April 1. Assume that from April 1, 1998 until December 31, 1998 the bond has appreciated in value by $10,000. On December 31 the ratable portion of the investor's payment is:

$$[8.5\% \times \$1,000,000 + \$10,000] \times (277/365) = \$72,096$$

---

[17] See David S. Miller, "An Overview of the Taxation of Credit Derivatives," Chapter 3 in Frank J. Fabozzi (ed.), *The Use of Derivatives in Tax Planning* (New Hope, PA: Frank J. Fabozzi, Inc., 1998); and David Z. Nirenberg and Steven L. Kopp, "Credit Derivatives: Tax Treatment of Total Return Swaps, Default Swaps, and Credit-Linked Notes," *The Journal of Taxation*, August 1997. One reason why IRC Section 1.446-3 does not specifically include credit derivatives is that this tax section was drafted in 1993, at the time the credit derivatives market was just beginning. Nonetheless, the definition of a notional principal contract under IRC Section 1.446-3 is very broad and a total return swap such as those contemplated in Chapter 3 falls within its intended applications.

The difference between $60,712 and $72,096 is $11,384. Accordingly, for 1998, the dealer has net income of $11,384 and the investor has a net deduction of $11,384.[18]

On April 1, 1999 the dealer makes its full payment of $80,000. Now, however, assume that the junk bond has declined in value by $5,000. Therefore, the investor's payment obligation on April 1 is:

$$8.5\% \times \$1,000,000 - \$5,000 = \$80,000$$

On April 1, 1999, the payments between the dealer and the investor cancel out; there is no net payment made by either party. However, the investor recorded a swap expense and the dealer recorded swap income of $11,384 for the 1998 tax year. For purposes of determining their net income or net deduction from this credit swap for the tax year ended 1999, the investor and the dealer must adjust their 1999 income by $11,384. This is the difference in the prorated capital appreciation of the junk bond between December 31, 1998 (+$10,000 × 277/365) and April 1, 1999 (−$5,000 × 277/365).

Another way to consider this is to look at the investor's ratable swap payment on December 31, 1998 as if the junk bond had declined in value by $5,000 by this time. Then the investor's ratable payment obligation would have been 8.5% × $1,000,000 × (277/365) − $5,000 × (277/365) = $60,712. Subtracting this amount for the dealer's ratable payment of $60,712 equals $0. Therefore, if the junk bond had declined in value by $5,000 by December 31, 1998, neither the investor nor the dealer would have recorded swap income or expense. Exhibit 5 presents these calculations.

To round out the example, assume that on April 1, 1999 1-year LIBOR is 6.5%. Also for simplicity, assume that there is no change in the junk bond's value at the end of 1999. Consequently the dealer's and investor's ratable swap payments as December 31, 1999 are the same:

$$8.5\% \times \$1,000,000 \times (277/365) = \$64,507$$

---

[18] See IRC Section 1.446-3, Example 3.

Exhibit 5: Tax Treatment of a Total Return Credit Swap

December 31, 1998
Investor Ratable Payment
$[8.5\% \times \$1,000,000 + \$10,000] \times (277/365)$ = $72,096

Dealer Ratable Payment
$8\% \times 1,000,000 \times (277/365)$ = $60,712
Recognized Swap Expense to Investor   ($11,384)
Recognized Swap Income to Dealer $11,384

April 1, 1999
Investor Swap Payment
    $8.5\% \times \$1,000,000 - \$5,000$ = $80,000
Dealer Swap Payment
    $8\% \times \$1,000,000$ = $80,000

December 31, 1999
Investor Ratable Amount
    $8.5\% \times \$1,000,000$ = $64,507
Dealer Ratable Amount
    $8.5\% \times \$1,000,000$ = $64,507
Recognized Swap Income/Expense   = $0
Adjustment to Investor's income for prior deduction = $11,384
Adjustment to Dealer's income for prior income   =   ($11,384)

Consequently, there is no tax expense or income to the dealer or the investor based on 1999 ratable payments. However, the dealer's taxable income must be decreased by $11,384 to reduce the excess swap income from 1998, and the investor's taxable income must be increased by $11,384 to reverse its prior year tax deduction. If the junk bond had retained its $10,000 capital appreciation between December 31 and April 1, there would be no need for subsequent tax corrections.

Notice that the investor gains a small advantage in this recognition of swap income. In the first year the investor records a tax deduction, then reverses this entry in the second year with the recognition of swap income in the same amount. However, over the course of one year, the investor earns the time value of money on its tax shield.

If we assume that the investor is in the 35% tax bracket and has a cost of capital of 12%, then the value of the tax shield is:

$$[0.35 \times \$11,384] - [(0.35 \times \$11,384) \div (1.12)] = \$426.90$$

The amount $[0.35 \times \$11,384]$ is the current value of the tax deduction to the investor in the first year from recording a ratable swap expense. The amount $[(0.35 \times \$11,384) \div (1.12)]$ is the present value of the tax liability next year from the reversing entry. The difference between the two is the net tax advantage to the investor.

Compared to the transaction size of $1 million, the tax shield is only 0.04269%, or about 4 basis points. This does not seem like much of an advantage. However, even though the relative size of the tax advantage is small, if an entity is active in the swap market, the cumulative size of these tax advantages can be significant.

Credit Default Swap

If we consider a credit default swap of the type in Exhibit 1 of Chapter 3, we must consider whether such a transaction still meets the requirements of a notional principal contract under IRC Section 1.446-3. The prevailing view is that it still qualifies as a notional principal contract under Section 1.446-3 because it is a financial instrument in which payments by one party are made at specified intervals based on a specified index applied to a specified notional amount. [19]

Under this analysis, the periodic payments made by the investor are considered income to the credit protection seller and an expense to the investor. However, the characterization of the payment by the credit protection dealer in the event of default is less clear. If the credit default payment is considered to be a non-periodic payment (a payment other than periodic or termination), then it is likely to be recorded as income to the investor and an expense to the credit protection seller. In contrast, if the credit default payment is considered to be a termination payment, then the investor must record a capital gain and the credit protection seller must record a capital loss. [20]

This uncertainty can be resolved if one argues that the credit default payment is not a termination payment, but instead, a payment required under the terms of the credit default swap. Even

---

[19] See Nirenberg and Kopp, "Credit Derivatives: Tax Treatment of Total Return Swaps, Default Swaps, and Credit-Linked Notes."
[20] See IRC, Section 1.446-3(h), Example 1.

though credit default swaps usually terminate after the payment of a credit default amount, the economic and contractual purposes of the payment are to protect against credit risk, not terminate the swap.

This issue may be clarified by IRC Section 1.446-4, *Hedging Transactions*. If the credit default swap is held as a hedge against the decline in value of a reference security held by the investor, then Section 1.446-4 should apply. Under this code section, periodic and non-periodic payments made pursuant to the terms of the swap may be classified as income and expense under IRC Section 1.446-3.[21]

Just to complicate matters, we provide one last twist. If a credit default swap were treated as a credit put option for tax purposes, the investor would be treated as the holder of the option and the credit protection seller would be treated as the seller of the option. Under this view, the periodic payments made by the investor would not be immediately deducted from, or included in, income. Instead, the premium paid or received must be capitalized and recorded for tax purposes when the option is sold, exercised, or has expired.[22] The gain or loss on the expiration, termination or sale of the credit default swap would then be capital gain/loss to the investor and credit protection seller.

Credit Linked Notes

The tax treatment for a credit linked note depends on whether the note is classified as a contingent payment debt instrument (CPDI). Generally, a CPDI is any debt instrument that provides for one or more contingent payments.[23] However, if the occurrence of credit events during the term of a credit linked note are remote, the classification as a CPDI is less likely. In general, it is a facts and circumstances test to determine whether a credit linked note qualifies as a CPDI.[24]

If a credit linked note is not a CPDI, then the interest paid on the note will be ordinary income to the investor and an expense to the issuer. If there is a credit event and less than the full amount is paid at maturity, the issuer will record cancellation of indebtedness

[21] See IRC, Section 1.446-4(e)(5).
[22] See Nirenberg and Kopp, "Credit Derivatives: Tax Treatment of Total Return Swaps, Default Swaps, and Credit-Linked Notes."
[23] See IRC, Section 1.1275-4.
[24] See Miller, "An Overview of the Taxation of Credit Derivatives."

income, which is considered ordinary income. For the investor, the situation is less clear. Capital gains and losses generally apply upon the sale or disposition of property. If the note is completely worthless, then a capital loss is incurred. If the note has some value less than par, and if the investor is a corporation, then the loss might be charged against ordinary income as a bad debt expense. However, if the investor is an individual, then the loss is generally considered a short-term capital loss.[25]

If a credit linked note is treated as a CPDI then, under Section 1.1275-4(b), the investor and the issuer must go through a series of complicated steps to determine the appropriate tax treatment. First, the issuer must determine the "comparable yield" on the note. This is essentially the yield it would have offered on the note had the note been issued as straight debt.[26]

Second, the note's projected payment schedule must be determined including non-contingent amounts and contingent/embedded payments. The contingent payments are adjusted (and the non-contingent payments, if necessary) in the projected schedule such that the appropriate yield that is produced is equal to the comparable yield. In other words, the projected schedule represents a series of hypothetical payments which, when discounted at the comparable yield, should result in the current price for the note.

Third, the amount of interest for each tax period is determined. This amount is equal to the product of the comparable yield (adjusted for the length of the accrual period) times the issue price of the note. Interest income is included in ordinary income.

Fourth, the amount of income must be adjusted for any differences between the projected and actual contingent payments. If the contingent payment amount received is more than the amount calculated in the projected schedule, the difference is a positive adjustment on the date of the payment. Conversely, if a contingent payment is less than a projected amount, the difference is a negative adjustment.

A net positive adjustment of contingent payments for a tax period is treated as additional interest income. A net negative adjust-

---

[25] See Nirenberg and Kopp, "Credit Derivatives: Tax Treatment of Total Return Swaps, Default Swaps, and Credit-Linked Notes."

[26] See IRC, Section 1.1275-4(b)(4).

ment first reduces the amount of accrued interest earned on the note. If the net negative adjustment exceeds the interest income for the tax period, the excess is treated as ordinary loss by the investor and ordinary income by the issuer.[27]

The amount of any loss for a tax period is limited to the difference between the total amount of interest earned on the note in the prior years and the total amount of net negative adjustments from prior years. Any remaining net negative adjustment may be carried forward for future tax years or until the note is sold or matures. Any outstanding net negative adjustment at the time of sale or maturity is used to reduce the amount realized upon sale or maturity.[28]

Taxation of Credit Options and Credit Forwards

Most options and futures contracts fall under Section 1256 of the tax code. This provision requires the recognition of gain or loss at year end for contracts that are marked-to-market. Section 1256, however, only applies to exchange traded futures and options.[29] Options and futures that are transacted off an exchange (over-the-counter) are not covered by Section 1256 even if they are marked-to-market on a daily basis.

As we have indicated before, credit derivatives are all over-the-counter products. Consequently, the mark-to-market rules of Section 1256 do not apply. Instead, the more general capital gains tax rules apply to credit options and credit forwards. These rules are guided by three factors: (1) the length of time that the credit derivative is held; (2) whether the taxpayer is a corporation or an individual; and (3) and whether there is a capital gain or capital loss.

---

[27] See IRC, Section 1.1275-4(b)(6).

[28] See IRC, Section 1.1275-4(b)(6)(iii)(C).

[29] Section 1256 provides for the following:
1. Each Section 1256 contract held by the taxpayer at the close of the taxable year shall be treated as sold for its fair market value (as determined by the mark-to-market value) on the last business day of the taxable year.
2. A proper adjustment shall be made in the amount of any gain or loss subsequently realized for the gain or loss into account by reason of paragraph (1).
3. Any gain or loss with respect to Section 1256 contracts shall be treated as:
   a. 40% of the gain or loss shall be treated as short-term capital gain
   b. 60% of the gain or loss shall be treated as long-term gain or loss

Holding Period

With respect to the length of time that the credit derivative is held, the IRS Restructuring and Reform Act of 1998 eliminated the 18-month holding period required to achieve the lower 20% long-term capital gains rate. Now, for individual taxpayers, the long-term capital gains rate is 20% for assets held *more than one year.*[30] Note that a credit derivative held for exactly 12 months is subject to the higher short-term capital gains tax rate. Therefore, when purchasing a credit option or forward, the buyer should ensure that the term of the option or forward is one year plus one day from the date of purchase to capture the lower long-term capital gains tax rate.

If the credit option or forward is held for one year or less, then it is subject to the short-term capital gains rate. For individuals and corporations, this rate is equal to the entity's marginal tax rate. In other words, short-term capital gains are taxed like ordinary income. This has important implications based on whether individual or corporate tax rates apply.

Corporate Tax Rates versus Individual Tax Rates

Depending on the type of entity, the capital gains and losses will be recognized differently. If the entity that purchases the credit derivative is a mutual fund or a hedge fund set up as a limited partnership, then the capital gains/losses will pass through to the individual shareholders (mutual fund) or limited partners (hedge fund). In this case, the gain or loss on the credit derivative will be taxed at individual taxpayer rates. On the other hand, if the entity that purchases the credit derivative is a bank or an insurance company, then corporate tax rates apply.

For individuals, net short-term capital gains are treated as ordinary income. Currently, the highest marginal tax rate on ordinary income for individuals is 39.6%. Notice that this rate is almost twice that of the long-term capital gains rate of 20%. Therefore, the holding period of a credit derivative for individuals can have significant tax consequences.

For corporations, long-term and short-term capital gains are taxed at the ordinary corporate income tax rates. There is no beneficial long-term capital gains rate for corporations; the 20% long-term

---

[30] See IRC, Section 1(h).

tax rate applies only to individual taxpayers. Therefore, banks, insurance companies, and other corporate entities are free from the holding period concerns that apply to individual taxpayers.

The tradeoff is that capital gains are taxed at the corporation's marginal tax rate. Corporations are subject to graduated rates ranging from 15% to 38%.[31] However, corporations may apply an alternative tax that limits the tax on corporate capital gains to 35% in tax years in which the marginal corporate tax rate exceeds 35%.[32] Therefore, net capital gains (short or long term) are taxed at a rate no higher than 35% for corporations.

Capital Gains versus Capital Losses

In the preceding discussion, we assumed that there were net capital gains to be taxed, and demonstrated how individual capital gains are taxed differently from corporate capital gains. Capital losses are also treated differently depending on the entity.

For individual taxpayers, short-term capital losses are first used to offset short-term capital gains and long-term capital losses are used to offset long-term capital gains. Any excess short-term capital loss is then used to offset any long-term capital gain and vice versa. Any remaining capital loss, either short or long term, may be used by an individual to offset up to $3,000 of ordinary income (income from primary occupation, interest income, dividend income, etc.). Any remaining capital loss in excess of $3,000 may be carried forward indefinitely by an individual taxpayer.[33]

A corporation offsets short- and long-term capital gains and losses in the same fashion as an individual taxpayer. However, for a corporate entity, capital losses for a tax year may only be used to offset capital gains in that year; no amount may be applied against income from operations.

If the corporation has a net capital loss, it has the choice of carrying the capital loss *back* or *forward* to offset prior or future recognized capital gains. For corporations, capital losses may be carried

---

[31] See IRC, Section 11.

[32] See IRC, Section 1201.

[33] See Federal Tax Guide Reports, *Introduction to Treatment of Capital Losses* (Chicago: Commerce Clearing House, 1998) para. 5590.; and IRC, Section 1211.

back three years, and may be carried forward five years.[34] If the capital loss is not used up by this amount of time, then it is lost to the corporate taxpayer. This may require some tax planning for a corporation because it should only recognize a capital loss if it has sufficient prior capital gains (or expected future capital gains) to absorb the capital loss. Otherwise the tax shield of a capital loss will be wasted.

CONCLUSION

Both the accounting profession and the U.S. Congress have developed rules in an attempt to tame the proliferation of derivative instruments in the financial marketplace. Despite these concerted actions, there are still loopholes where certain derivative instruments, such as credit derivatives, do not fit in. For instance, while certain embedded credit derivatives must be identified apart from their host contract and accounted for separately, others are left "embedded" — their value and impact hidden within another financial instrument.

On the tax side, the most interesting development has been the exclusion of "straight debt" instruments from the definition of *appreciated financial positions* under the Taxpayer Relief Act of 1997. While there does not seem to be any specific reason for this exclusion, it effectively exempts credit derivatives from the provisions of the Act. Therefore, for tax purposes, credit derivatives are taxed separately from the underlying fixed income assets that they may hedge.

---

[34] See IRC, Section 1212.

Index

Books published by Frank J. Fabozzi Associates

Bond Portfolio Managemnt
Fixed Income Securities
Managing Fixed Income Portfolios
Valuation of Fixed Income Securities and Derivatives: Third Edition
Selected Topics In Bond Portfolio Management
Advanced Fixed Income Analytics
Treasury Securities and Derivatives
Managing MBS Portfolios
Corporate Bonds: Structures and Analysis
Collateralized Mortgage Obligations: Structures & Analysis: Second Edition
Handbook of Structured Financial Products
Asset-Backed Securities
The Handbook of Commercial Mortgage-Backed Securities: Second Edition
Trends In Commercial Mortgage-Backed Securities
Handbook of Nonagency Mortgage-Backed Securities
Basics of Mortgage-Backed Securities
Adavances In The Valuation and Management of Mortgage-Backed Securities
Valuation of Interest-Sensitive Financial Instruments
Perspectives on International Fixed Income Investing
Handbook of Emerging Fixed Income and Currency Markets
Handbook of Stable Value Investments
Inflation Protection Bonds
The Handbook of Inflation-Indexed Bonds
Bank Loans: Secondary Markets and Portfolio Management
Handbook of Portfolio Management
Analysis of Financial Statements
Introduction to Quantitative Methods For Investment Managers
Measuring and Controling Interest Rate Risk
Dictionary of Financial Risk Management
Risk Management: Framework, Methods, and Practice
Perspectives on Interest Rate Risk Management for Money Managers and Traders
Essays In Derivatives
Active Equity Portfolio Management
Applied Equity Valuation
Handbook of Equity Style Management: Second Edition
Modeling the Market: New Theories and Techniques
Securities Lending and Repurchase Agreements
Pension Fund Investment Management: Second Edition

For more information, please visit our Web site:

www.frankfabozzi.com